The James Burton Coffman Commentaries
THE HISTORICAL BOOKS, Vol. VII

COMMENTARY ON

First and Second
CHRONICLES

By

James Burton and Thelma B. Coffman

1993

A•C•U PRESS
Abilene Christian University
Abilene, Texas

ISBN 0-89112-087-4
Library of Congress Card Number 93-70445

DEDICATION

This Commentary on Chronicles is lovingly dedicated to our near-neighbor

Kyle Alan Lindner

who has blessed us in many ways. He is a Computer Guru employed by M. D. Anderson Medical Center; and he has found time on many occasions to enable us to survive this Computer Age in which we all live.

Currently he is working on a higher academic degree, as well as discharging his other duties as an employee. A faithful Christian, he also finds the time to aid in the work of the Church.

---*James Burton and Thelma B. Coffman*

PREFACE

We express herewith our profound gratitude and thankfulness to Almighty God through Jesus Christ our Lord for his merciful blessings during the past year for his preservation of our lives and for his enabling us to complete a number of commentaries on the sacred text. We are especially thankful that God has given us the privilege of a thorough study of the Chronicles; because, in this extensive investigation, we have been dramatically corroborated and strengthened in the conviction we have long held of the absolute historicity, accuracy, importance, and utility of First and Second Chronicles.

Second Chronicles, especially, has been falsely maligned and slandered by the radical critics because of the undeniable proof that we find therein that the imaginary, unhistorical, fraudulent ***D Document*** discovered during the reign of Josiah was nothing more than the imagination of evil men who concocted the "document" out of their sick imagination; and that the "book" that was actually discovered was the Book of Moses, the Pentateuch, the Torah, namely, the holy scriptures that have come down to us as the first five books of the OT. After all, the Scriptures thus identify that book no less than five times. The bearing of Second Chronicles on this question makes it one of the most important books in the Old Testament.

---James Burton and Thelma B. Coffman

ABBEVIATIONS

AAOT = Archeology and the Old Testament
AB = Albert Barnes or F. C. Cook
AC = Adam Clarke
A. D. = *Anno Domini*, Year of Our Lord
AMOB = Herbert Lockyer
AnBi= Anchor Bible
ANF = Ante-Nicene Fathers
ASP = Arthur S. Peake's Commentary
ASV = American Standard Version
AV = Authorized Version (King James Bible)

BBC = Broadman Bible Commentary
BC = Before Christ
BWLD = Britannica World Language Dictionary

c. = about
ca. = about
ch. = chapter
chs. = chapters
CFK = C. F. Keil (Keil-Delitzsch OT Commentary)
CRB = Cross-reference Bible

DOUG = George C. M. Douglas
DV = Douay Version of OT

EncBrit = Encyclopaedia Britannica
EOTB = ***Everyone in the Bible*** by Wm. F. Baker

f = verse following
FCC = same as AB
ff = verses following
FHR = Fleming H. Revell Company
FWF = F. W. Farrar in Expositor's Bible

GDH = George DeHoff Commentary

GNB = Good News Bible

HHH = Henry H. Halley
HIST = Historical Books

IB = Interpreter's Bible
ICC = International Critical Commentary
ISBE = International Standard Bible Encyclopedia
JBC = James Burton Coffman
JFB = Jamieson, Fauset and Brown Commentary
JOSA = Flavius Josephus, Antiquities
JRD = J. R. Dummelow Commentary

LBC = Layman's Bible Commentary
Ltd. = English equivalent of incorporated
LXX = The Septuagint Version of the OT

MAPR = Major Prophets
MIPR = Minor Prophets
MH = Matthew Henry Commentary

NBCR = New Bible Commentary Revised
NBD = New Bible Dictionary
NEB = New English Bible
NIV = New International Version
NLBC = New Layman's Bible Commentary
No. = number
NT = New Testament
op. cit. = *opere citato* (work cited above)

p. = page
PBD = Peloubet's Bible Dictionary
pp. - pages
PENT = Pentateuch
PC = Pulpit Commentary
PHC = Preacher's Homiletic Commentary

RSV = Revised Standard Version

TBAA = The Bible and Archaeology
TBC = Teacher's Bible Commentary

vv. = verses
Vol. = volume

WBE = Wycliffe Bible Encyclopedia
WW = Wilson's Word Studies in the OT
WYC = Wycliffe OT Commentary

YACOB = Young's Analytical Concordance of the Bible

Special Abbreviatioins in this Volume

1C = First Chronicles
2C = Second Chronicles
1K = First Kings
2K = Second Kings
1S = First Samuel
2S = Second Samuel

Commentaries by JBC...

NT Vol. 1 = Matthew
NT Vol. 2 = Mark
NT Vol. 3 = Luke
NT Vol. 4 = John
NT Vol. 5 = Acts
NT Vol. 6 = Romans
NT Vol. 7 = 1 & 2 Corinthians
NT Vol. 8 = Galatians - Philippians
NT Vol. 9 = Thessalonians - Philemon
NT Vol. 10 = Hebrews
NT Vol. 11 = James - Jude
NT Vol. 12 = Revelation

PENT Vol. 1 = Genesis
PENT Vol. 2 = Exodus
PENT Vol. 3 = Leviticus/Numbers
PENT Vol. 4 = Deuteronomy

HIST Vol. 1 = Joshua
HIST Vol. 2 = Judges & Ruth
HIST Vol. 3 = I Samuel
HIST Vol. 4 = 2 Samuel
HIST Vol. 5 = 1 Kings
HIST Vol. 6 = 2 Kings

MAPR Vol. 1 = Isaiah
MAPR Vol. 2 = Jeremiah
MAPR Vol. 3 = Ezekiel
MAPR Vol. 4 = Daniel

MIPR Vol. 1 = Joel, Amos, Jonah
MIPR Vol. 2 = Hosea, Obadiah, Micah
MIPR Vol. 3 = Nahum, Habakkuk, Zephaniah, Haggai
MIPR Vol. 4 = Zechariah, Malachi

Ps. 1 = Psalms 1 - 72
Ps. 2 = Psalms 73 - 150

MYS = The Mystery of Redemption

TABLE OF CONTENTS

xxx

I & II Chronicles

INTRODUCTION

The biblical books of Chronicles comprise approximately one sixteenth of the entire Old Testament and cover a time span reaching all the way from Adam to the return of Israel from the Babylonian captivity. Nevertheless we shall limit our comments on these books to a single volume, because about half of Chronicles is parallel (although with a different viewpoint) with other Old Testament passages upon which we have already commented.

Title. The name ***Chronicles*** goes back to Jerome (331-422 AD).[1] "The title assigned in the LXX was ***Things Omitted Concerning the Kings of Judah***."[2] The literal Hebrew title ***Verba Dierum***[3] is translated The ***Events of Days*** or ***Annals***[4] by Cundall. It is evident that Chronicles is as appropriate a name as any that might be suggested. As in the case with both the books of the Samuels and the Kings, Chronicles also was originally a single book; but the translators of the LXX made all three of them into two books each. "This was necessary, because the Greek language required twice as much space as the Hebrew, because the Hebrew language has no vowels."[5]

---

1 PC, Vol. 6a, p. i.

2 ICC, ***Chronicles,*** p. 1.

3 PC, op. cit., p. i.

4 NBCR, p. 369.

5 BBC, Vol. 3, p. 297.

Authorship. There is no valid reason for setting aside the ancient Jewish tradition that Ezra was the author of Chronicles. W. F. Albright affirmed that, "The author of Chronicles is none other than Ezra."[6] Barker spoke of the evidence that supports this view as having "Great force, though not absolutely conclusive."[7] "The assumption that Ezra himself is the author is supported by the Jewish Talmud, Baba Bathra and C. C. Torrey."[8] As Howard approvingly quoted Torrey, "There is not a garment in all Ezra's wardrobe that does not fit the Chronicler exactly."[9]

Date. Chronicles, if written by Ezra, as seems likely, was written at some considerable time after many of the Israelites had returned to Jerusalem; but we must reject the notion of those critics who would find the date of Chronicles at some period within the Greek domination of Israel. Chronicles was most certainly written prior to the Greek period, a fact stressed by Howard.

> There are cogent reasons for dating Chronicles in the Persian period. The relationship of the Aramaic of Ezra with that of the scrolls of the Jewish community of

---

[6] W. F. Albright, ***The Date and Personality of the Chronicler***, in ***Journal of Biblical Literature*** (XI, 1921), pp. 104, 124.

[7] PC, op. cit., p. vi.

[8] BBC, op. cit., p. 297.

[9] NLBC, p. 474.

Elephantine in Egypt, which can be dated in the fourth century B. C., together with the number of Persian words, and the almost total absence of Greek words, definitely point to a period before the overthrow of Persia by Greece.[10]

Speaking of recent discoveries and research, Jacob M. Myers (in Anchor Bible) declares that, "There is ***NOW*** evidence that makes it almost imperative to place the Chronicler in the Persian period."[11]

Unbelieving critics who attempt to date Chronicles in the times of Alexander the Great, are totally frustrated by these facts. They also reject Chronicles as unhistorical. See discussion of this under historicity.

Payne provides what we consider to be dependable dates regarding the books of Chronicles. "Chronicles was composed by Ezra about 450 BC. Since Nehemiah mentions Darius II who began to reign in 423 BC (Neh. 12:22); we may date the incorporation of Chronicles and the close of the OT canon at about 420 BC."[12]

There are two things in Chronicles and in Nehemiah which are seized upon by those who wish to late-date both,[13] namely, (1) the genealogy in 1C 3:19-24, which is falsely interpreted to mean that six generations are listed after Zerubbabel who lived about

---

10 Ibid.

11 AnBi, Vol. 12, p. lxxxvi.

12 WYC, p. 367.

13 BBC, op. cit., p. 299.

537-516 BC, and (2) the list of high priests given in Nehemiah 12:10-23, which includes Jaddua, who was identified by Josephus as high priest in the times of Alexander the Great. Neither of these passages can be received as a valid excuse for late dating Chronicles.

Regarding (1), above, many able scholars deny that the six generations mentioned pertain to Zerubbabel, affirming that. "Zerubbabel's genealogy ends with the grandsons Pelatiah and Jesiah."[14] Furthermore, it is possible that this genealogy, as well as the one mentioned in Nehemiah was added by some later copyist. "The completion of these lists appears to have been after the lifetimes of Ezra and Nehemiah."[15]

In neither reference is there the slightest grounds for late dating Chronicles.

Historicity. In regard to this, we appreciate the simple, emphatic declaration of F. C. Cook. "It (Chronicles) is historical."[16] Of course, unbelieving critics are not free to admit this. "Such men as Adam C. Welch, Robert Pfeiffer, and W. A. L. Elmslie argue that Chronicles cannot reflect authentic history;...a rejection based upon liberalism's prior rejection of the Mosaic authorship of the Pentateuch";[17] a rejection which we have frequently referred to as illogical, fraudulent and absolutely erroneous.

---

14 PC, op. cit., p. iv.

15 NBCR, p. 409.

16 FCC, ***Chronicles***, p. 311.

17 WYC, p. 368

The mythical theories of liberalism which deny the existence of all the forms and ceremonies mentioned in Chronicles as having existed back in the times of Moses stand at the present time, nearing the close of the twentieth century, as naked and unmasked errors. "Recent excavations in ancient Ugarit confirm the authenticity in Canaan of just such elaborate rituals, and in the very century when Moses was leading the children of Israel out of Egypt; and many of the historical statements found in Chronicles have been established by archaeological discoveries."[18]

"In spite of the attacks of Wette and others violently trying to get rid of the evidence in Chronicles for the Mosaic origin of the Sinaitic legislation, the historic truth or credibility of Chronicles is now generally recognized."[19] "There is today no reason to doubt the essential accuracy of the Chronicler and his sources."[20] The bitter hatred of radical critics toward this book which so effectively denies their false allegations regarding the Pentateuch is evident in the writings of Elmslie who called the book, "For the most part dull, incredible...deadwood in the Bible."[21]

We close this section on historicity with these words of C. F. Keil. Following an extensive 45-page introduction to the books of Chronicles in which he discussed all the criticisms and objections, he wrote:

---

18 Ibid.

19 CFK, Vol. 3b, p. 38.

20 NBCR, p. 370.

21 IB, Vol. 3, p. 341.

"These books, in regard to their historical contents, have been composed with care and fidelity, according to the authorities, and are fully deserving of belief."[22]

Sources. Curtis (& Madsen) have compiled the list of the following 'written sources' which are quoted by the author of Chronicles.[23]

1. A Book of the Kings of Israel and Judah, for the reigns of Jotham, Josiah, and Jehoiakim (2C 27:7, 35:27, 36:8).

2. A Book of the Kings of Judah and Israel, for the reigns of Asa, Amaziah, Ahaz, (2C 16:11, 25:26, 28:26, 32:32).

3. A Book of the Kings of Israel, for genealogies (1C 9:1), and for the reigns of Jehoshaphat (2C 20:34) and Manasseh (2C 33:18).

4. A Midrash of the Book of the Kings for the reign of Joash (2C 24:17). See below for discussion of the term ***Midrash***.

5, 6, & 7. The history of Samuel the seer, the history of Nathan the prophet, and the history of Gad the seer, for the reign of David (1C 29:29).

8 & 9. The prophecy of Ahijah the Shilonite, the visions of Iddo the seer, and the prophecy of Nathan (6), for the reign of Solomon (2C 9:29).

10 & 11. The history of Shemaiah and the history of Iddo the seer, for the reign of Rehoboam (2C 12:15).

---

22 CFK, op. cit., p. 45.

23 ICC, op. cit., pp. 21,22.

12. The Midrash of the prophet Iddo for the reign of Abijah (2C 13:22).

13. History of the prophet Jehu, for the reign of Jehoshaphat.

14. A writing of Isaiah the prophet, for the reign of Uzziah (2C 26:22).

15. The vision of Isaiah the prophet in the Book of the Kings of Judah and Israel, for the reign of Hezekiah.

16. A history of the seers for particulars concerning Manasseh (2C 33:19).

17. A genealogical register compiled in the days of Jotham and Jeroboam II (1C 5:17).

18. The later history of David (1C 23:27).

19. The chronicles (lit. the words) of David in which the census taken by Joab was not entered (1C 27:24).

20. A collection of lamentations (2C 35:25).

From the number of sources cited by the author of Chronicles, one must be impressed with such extensive documentation. Furthermore, in instances, where we may check his references to materials in the canonical books, we find the most exact correspondence with the sources quoted; and this provides a very strong grounds of presumption that he was also meticulously accurate in all of his other references as well.

Regarding the So-called Midrash

The use of the term ***midrash*** by critical scholars is generally a code-word for worthless, untruthful tales, invented for the purpose of making or illustrating a point or an idea. Curtis has this: "The Midrash of Kings was a reconstructed history of Israel embellished with marvelous tales of divine interposition, etc., which have been reproduced in Chronicles."[24] The dictionary definition of midrash conceals, rather than reveals what scholars mean by this word.

A MIDRASH IS A STORY DEVELOPED FOR THE PURPOSE OF EDIFICATION.[25]

The meaning here is that, "A midrash is a story (falsehood) developed (invented) for the purpose of teaching. Nothing whatever of such a meaning is to be found in Chronicles. Curtis himself admitted that the Hebrew word actually means ***exposition*** or ***exegesis***.[26]

But this is not all that unbelieving critics have done in their vain efforts to discredit the books of Chronicles. As Oesterley expressed it, "The Chronicler does not appear to have had any sources"[27] other than the canonical books known to us. His thesis is that all the material in Chronicles not taken from the canonical books is therefore fraudulently invented by the Chronicler. How does he dispose of all those 'sources' cited above? Oh well, every one of those sources was allegedly, "Incorporated into that large book of the Kings."[28] Of course, that 'large book' is identified by the

---

[24] ICC, op. cit., p. 23.

[25] Britannica World Language Dictionary.

[26] ICC, op. cit., p. 23.

[27] ASP, p. 315.

[28] Ibid.

unbelieving scholars as the Midrash of the Kings; and by this fraudulent device, they vainly attempt to deny every single one of the Chronicler's sources. What he was really quoting, according to them, was nothing but a massive collection of legendary or mythical tales having no historical value whatever.

The notion advocated by unbelieving enemies of Chronicles that the Chronicler invented the material he used is ridiculous. Francisco wrote: "The Chronicler is faithful in handling his sources, copying them into his text with little change. In places where it was once believed that he had arbitrarily made changes, we now conclude that he was following a text older than the Masoretic text and similar to the fragments discovered in the Dead Sea Scrolls at Qumran."[29]

C. F. Keil stressed the accuracy and dependability of the Chronicler, pointing out that, "In the additions and abridgements of events found in the canonical books, the Chronicler drew his information from other more circumstantial original documents which he had at his command."[30] Also Keil wrote that the very manner of the Chronicler's reference to all those sources, "Indicates that all of those books were in the hands of many of his contemporaries,"[31] hence his continual reference to them. The false critical dictum that the Chronicler only cited all those references to leave a false impression of his scholarship and veracity

---

29 BBC, op. cit., p. 299.

30 CFK, op. cit., p. 14.

31 Ibid., p. 37.

tells us a lot more about the critics than it does about the Chronicler.

The following from Curtis/Madsen is a measure of the hatred and unbelief of the critical community against Chronicles:

> It is possible that the Chronicler cited sources simply to produce the impression that he is writing with authority, and that their titles are mere literary adornments. This is essentially the view of Torrey who wrote: "It is time that scholars were done with these phantom sources."[32]

This allegation, of course, is only the unbelieving critic's method of calling the author of Chronicles an unqualified liar. Believers must reject all such slanders directed against the Bible. There is really no way that an intelligent person can accept such a slander, for the author of Chronicles was a true worshipper of God and a devout believer in the Decalogue. There is no way that he could reasonably be charged with producing a biblical book with hundreds of lies in it.

Purpose. The purpose of Chronicles may be clearly read in the structure and contents of what is written. The work is theological, rather than merely historical; and yet its historical references are most certainly accurate. His principal purpose, as stated by Keil, was, "To draw from the history of the kingship in Israel the proof that faithful adherence to the covenant

---

[32] ICC, op. cit., p. 24.

which the Lord had made with Israel brought happiness and blessing; and that the forsaking of it, on the contrary insured disastrous ruin and a curse."[33]

Another purpose was to demonstrate that the God's true Israel was restricted to those who remained true to the covenant and who accepted the dynasty of David as their legitimate rulers; and that the true people of God were those of the returnees from Babylonian captivity. The Chronicler had little to say of Northern Israel, except in a few instances where their fate touched that of Judah. "He viewed the Northern kingdom as totally apostate from the start (2C 10:19). For him the Northern kingdom was conceived in sin, born in iniquity, and nourished in adultery."[34]

One of the most evident purposes of Chronicles is that of returning Israel to the proper respect and observance of the Law of Moses as given on Sinai; and Chronicles provides absolute, incontrovertible proof of the prior existence and validity of that holy Law. The grand purpose of Chronicles, "Is to raise in the souls of the children of Israel a delight in the splendid worship of the Lord, and to confirm their hearts in fidelity to the Lord and to his Law."[35]

Still another purpose was that of turning the hearts of Israel away from their conception regarding the importance of the political kingdom which, for awhile, they had possessed. The Chronicler stressed the

---

33 CFK, op. cit., p. 15.

34 NBCR, p. 475.

35 CFK, op. cit., p. 20.

superlative importance of worshipping God and seeking to please him.

Francisco cited another evident purpose of Chronicles, namely, that of explaining certain statements in previous canonical writings that were capable of being misunderstood. He did this by giving additional authentic information. "The statement in 1S 22:19 that Elhanan had killed Goliath raised doubts that David had killed him."[36] The Chronicler reveals that, "Elhanan killed Lahmi the brother of Goliath" (1C 20:5). There were several people called Goliath, just as there may be whole families of Smiths or Browns.

Another example of this is seen in comparing 2S 24:1 with 1C 21:1. In the Samuel reference, "It is said that God influenced David to take a census and then became angry with him for doing so. The Chronicler says that it was Satan who tempted David."[37] Both statements are profoundly true. In the ancient Oriental view, God does whatever he allows; and, in that sense, God allowed Satan successfully to tempt David to number the people contrary to God's will. This is no new revelation. Even in the Exodus, it was God who hardened Pharaoh's heart, but it was also the cunning temptation of Satan that prompted Pharaoh to harden his own heart.

Unity of Chronicles. Not even the unbelieving critics have denied the unity of Chronicles. "The unity

---

[36] BBC, op. cit., p. 303.

[37] Ibid.

of style and composition ... is against the patchwork theory of composition."[38] "The unity is unbroken, and we have every reason to believe that we have the work, in almost all respects, exactly as it came from the hand of the author."[39] We have found no significant contrary opinion; and as Howard stated it : "It is scarcely going too far to say that, in style and spirit it is unmistakably one."[40]

Characteristics of Chronicles. (1) The emphasis throughout is religious and theological rather than political. (2) There is a total rejection of the Northern Israel as, in any sense, pertaining to the future of God's people. "The Chronicler viewed the division of the kingdom following the death of Solomon as a deliberate rebellion against the divinely ordered dynasty of David and as a forsaking of the one true place (Jerusalem) where the worship of Israel might be legitimately offered."[41] (3) There is also a rejection of the Samaritan community and of their worship as inadequate. (4) Throughout, there is a remarkable emphasis upon genealogies all the way from Genesis to the grandsons of Zerubbabel. (5) "There is a constant open and direct ascription of all the events in history to divine agency, and (6) a plain reference to every calamity or deliverance as being the consequence of either the good

---

[38] IB, op. cit., p. 347, footnote.

[39] FCC, Chronicles, p. 315.

[40] PC, op. cit., p. xix.

[41] NLBC, p. 475.

or evil deeds of the monarch and/or of the nation."[42] (7) "Special attention throughout Chronicles is given to sacerdotal, ecclesiastical and religious matters."[43] (8) There is a constant appeal for God's people to renounce their lustful longing for the restoration of "the sinful kingdom" and to concentrate their efforts upon fidelity to God and his holy Law. Israel, alas, failed ever to heed this constant appeal which runs like a scarlet thread throughout Chronicles.

Problems in Chronicles. Many able and believing scholars have noted certain problems in Chronicles, especially with regard "to some of the numbers"[44] detailing amounts of money, or numbers of soldiers, etc. "Such numbers appear to have occasionally suffered corruption, though not to any greater extent than that noted in other writings of equal antiquity. "From blemishes of this kind it has not pleased God to keep His Word free; but such blemishes do not affect in the slightest degree the authenticity of Chronicles."[45] Such trivial mysteries (and they do remain mysteries) are of no more importance than a flyspeck on Michelangelo's ***Moses,*** or a wasp-nest on the ***Washington Monument.***

Outline. For any who may desire a more detailed outline of Chronicles, Clyde T. Francisco, writing in

---

42 FCC, op. cit., p. 315.

43 PC, op. cit., p. xiii.

44 FCC, op. cit., p. 325.

45 Ibid.

Broadman Bible Commentary, Vol. 3, provides an excellent outline on pp. 303-305. For our purposes, the brief outline provided by C. F. Keil in the Keil-Delitzsch Old Testament Commentaries, Vol. 3, p. 10 is more than sufficient.

First Chronicles

I. Genealogical registers from primeval times, and of Israel ... Chs. 1-9.

II. History of the Reign of David ... Chs. 10-29.

Second Chronicles

I. The united kingdom from Solomon to the division ... Chs. 1-10.

II. From Rehoboam through the captivity to Cyrus' decree ... Chs. 11-36.

Conclusion. We have given greater attention to our introduction for Chronicles than for many other biblical books, because of the abbreviated treatment which we contemplate for the entire text.

1 Chronicles

I. THE GENEALOGIES (CHAPTERS 1-9)

CHAPTER 1

Verses 1-4, Adam, Seth, Enosh, 2 Kenan, Mahalalel, Jared, 3 Enoch, Mathuselah, Lamech, 4 Noah, Shem, Ham, and Japheth.

Verses 5-7, The sons of Japheth: Gomer, and Magog, and Madai, and Javan, and Tubal, and Meshech, and Tiras. 6 And the sons of Gomer: Ashkenaz, and Diphath, and Togarmah. 7 And the sons of Javan: Elishah, and Tarshish, Kittim, and Rodanim.

Verses 8-16, The sons of Ham: Cush, and Mizraim, Put, and Canaan. 9 And the sons of Cush: Seba, and Havilah, and Sabta, and Ratama, and Sabteca. 10 And Cush begat Nimrod; he began to be a mighty one in the earth. 11 And Mizraim begat Ludim, and Anamim, and Naphtuhim, 12 and Pathrusim, and Casluhim (from whence came the Philistines), and Caphtorim. 13 And Canaan begat Sidon his first-born, and Heth, 14 and the Jebusite, and the Amorite, and the Girgashaite, 15 and the Hivite, and the Arkite, and the Sinite, 16 and the Arvadite, and the Zimarite, and the Hamathite.

Verses 17-23, The sons of Shem: Elam, and Asshur, and Arpachshad, and Lud, and Aram, and Uz, and Hul, and Gether, and Meshech. 18 And Arpachshad begat Shelah, and Shelah begat Eber. 19 And unto Eber were born two sons: the name of the one was Peleg; for in his days the earth was divided; and his brother's name was Joktan. 20 And Joktan begat Almodad, and Sheleph, and Hazarmaveth, and Jerah, 21 and Hadoram, and Uzal, and Diklah, 22 and Ebal, and Abimael, and Sheba, 23 and

Ophir, and Havilah, and Jobab. All these were the sons of Joktan.

Verses 24-27, Shem, Arpachshad, Shelah, 25 Eber, Peleg, Reu, 26 Serug, Nahor, Terah, 27 Abram (the same is Abraham).

Verses 28-31, The sons of Abraham: Isaac, and Ishmael. 29 These are their generations: the first-born of Ishmael, Nebaioth; then Kedar, and Adbael, and Mibsam, 30 Mishma, and Dumah, Massa, Hadad, and Tema, 31 Jetur, Naphish, and Kedemah. These are the sons of Ishmael.

Verses 32-33, And the sons of Keturah, Abraham's concubine: she bare Zimran, and Jokshan, and Medan, and Midian, and Ishbak, and Shuah. And the sons of Jokshan: Sheba, and Dedan. 33 And the sons of Midian: Ephah, and Epher, and Hanoch, and Abida, and Eldaah. All these were the sons of Keturah.

Verses 34, And Abraham begat Isaac. The sons of Isaac: Esau, and Israel.

Verses 35-37, The sons of Esau: Eliphaz, Reuel, and Jeush, and Jalam, and Korah. 36 The sons of Eliphaz: Teman, and Omar, Zephi, and Gatam, Kenaz, and Timna, and Amalek. 37 The sons of Reuel: Nahath, Zerah, Shammah, and Mizzah.

Verses 38-42, And the sons of Seir: Lotan, and Shobal, and Zibeon, and Anath, and Ezer, and Dishan. 39 And the sons of Lotan: Hori, and Homam; and Timna was Lotan's sister. 40 The sons of Shobal: Alian, and Manahath, and Ebal, Shephi, and Onam. And the sons of Zibeon: Ajah, and Anah. 41 The sons of Anah: Dishon. And the sons of Dishon: Hamran, and Eshban, and

Ithran, and Cheran. 42 The sons of Ezer: Bilhan, and Zaavan, Jaakan. The sons of Dishan: Uz, and Aran.

Verses 43-51a, And these are the kings that reigned in the land of Edom, before there reigned any king over the children of Israel: Bela the son of Beor; and the name of his city was Dinhabah. 44 And Belah died, and Jobab the son of Zerah of Bozrah reigned in his stead. 45 And Jobab died, and Husham of the land of the Temanites reigned in his stead. 46 And Husham died, and Hadad the son of Bedad, who smote Midian in the field of Moab reigned in his stead; and the name of his city was Avith. 47 And Hadad died, and Samlah of Masrekah reigned in his stead. 48 And Samlah died, and Shaul of Rehoboth by the River reigned in his stead. 49 And Shaul died, and Baalhanan the son of Achbor reigned in his stead. 50 And Baalhanan died, and Hadad reigned in his stead; and the name of his city was Pai; and his wife's name was Mehetabel, the daughter of Matred. 51 And Hadad died.

Verses 51b-54, And the chiefs of Edom were: chief Temna, chief Aliah, chief Jetheth, 52 chief Oholibamah, chief Elah, chief Pinon, chief Kenaz, chief Teman, chief Mibzar, 54 chief Magdiel, chief Iram. These are the chiefs of Edom.

"All of these genealogies are given in Genesis, as follows: (vv. 1-4) are in Gen. 5:3-22, and 10:1; (vv. 5-23) are in Gen. 10:2-4, 6-8, 13-18a, 22-29; (vv. 24-27) are in Gen. 11:10-26 (cf. 17:5); (vv. 28-34) are in Gen. 25:12-16a, 1-4, 19-26 (cf. 16:15, 21:2f)."[1] See the

---

1 ICC, *Chronicles*, p. 17.

parallel scriptures for our comments.

Peleg ... in his days was the earth divided (v. 10). This is one of the most interesting statements in the Bible, because it corresponds with what is now recognized as a scientifically accepted fact, namely, that, "All of the continents once formed a single land mass. Only yesterday, in earth's time span, the land formed a single supercontinent,"[2] a postulation dramatically supported by the declaration in Genesis that, "The waters under the heaven were gathered unto one place" (1:9). The oceans also were a single body of water with the huge land mass also in a single continent.

Robert Dentan devoted only two pages of comment for all of these first nine chapters, but he surely caught the spirit of the author in these words:

> He refused to tell the story of Israel as though they were a small, isolated, self-contained group. He presents the national history of Israel as the climactic point in the history of the entire human race. ... The prefacing of his book with these genealogies was the author's method of setting in the proper context the story which follows.[3]

xxx

---

[2] Robert S. Dietz and John C. Holden, ***Maps and Drawings***, published by The National Geographic and Atmospheric Administration, Washington D. C.

[3] LBC, Vol. 7, p.130.

CHAPTER 2

Verses 1-2, These are the sons of Israel: Reuben, Simeon, Levi, and Judah, Issachar, and Zebulun, 2 Dan, Joseph, and Benjamin, Naphtali, Gad, and Asher.

Verses 3-4, The sons of Judah: Er, and Onan, and Shelah; which three were born unto him of Shua's daughter the Canaanitess. And Er, Judah's first-born, was wicked in the sight of Jehovah; and he slew him. 4 And Tamar his daughter-in-law bare him Perez and Zerah. All the sons of Judah were five.

Verses 5-8, The sons of Perez: Hezron, and Hamul. 6 And the sons of Zerah: Zimri, and Ethan, and Heman, and Calcol, and Dura; five of them in all. 7 And the sons of Carmi: Achar, the troubler of Israel, who committed a trespass in the devoted thing. 8 And the sons of Ethan: Azariah.

Verses 9-17. The sons also of Hezron, that were born unto him: Jerahmeel, and Ram, and Chelubai. 10 And Ram begat Amminadab, and Amminadab begat Nahshon, prince of the children of Judah; 11 and Nahshon begat Salma, and Salma begat Boaz, 12 and Boaz begat Obed, and Obed begat Jesse; 13 And Jesse begat his first-born Eliab, and Abinadab the second, and Shimea the third, 14 Nethanel the fourth, Raddai the fifth, 15 Ozem the sixth, David the seventh; 16 and their sisters were Zeruiah and Abigail. And the sons of Zeruiah: Abishai, and Jaab, and Asahel, three. 17 And Abigail bare Amasa; and the father of Amasa was Jether the Ishmaelite.

Verses 18-20, And Caleb the son of Hezron begat children of Azubah his wife, and of Jerioth; and these were her sons: Jesher, and Shobab, and Ardon. 19 And Azubah

died, and Caleb took unto him Ephrath, who bare him Hur. 20 And Hur begat Uri, and Uri begat Bezalel.

Verses 21-24, And afterward Hezron went in to the daughter of Machir the father of Gilead, whom he took to wife when he was threescore years old; and she bare him Segub. 22 And Segub begat Jair, who had three and twenty cities in the land of Gilead. 23 And Geshur and Aram took the towns of Jair from them, with Kenath, and the villages thereof, even threescore cities. All these were the sons of Machir the father of Gilead. 24 And after that Caleb was dead in Caleb-ephrathah, then Abijah Hezron's wife bare him Ashur the father of Tekoa.

Verses 25-41, And the sons of Jerahmeel the first-born of Hezron were Ram the first-born, and Bunah, and Oren, and Ozem, Ahijah. 26 And Jerahmeel had another wife whose name was Atarah; she was the mother of Onam. 27 And the sons of Ram the first-born of Jerahmeel were Maaz, and Jamin, and Eker. 28 And the sons of Onam were Shammai, and Jada. And the sons of Shammai: Nadab, and Abishur. 29 And the name of the wife of Abishur was Abihail; and she bare him Ahban and Molid. 30 And the sons of Nadab: Seled, and Appaim; but Seled died without children. 31 And the sons of Appaim: Ishi. And the sons of Ishi: Sheshsan. And the sons of Sheshan: Ahlai. 32 And the sons of Jada the brother of Shammai: Jether, and Jonathan; and Jether died without children. 33 And the sons of Jonathan: Peleth, and Zaza. These were the sons of Jerahmeel. 34 Now Sheshan had no sons but daughters. And Sheshan had a servant, an Egyptian, whose name ws Jarha. 35 And Sheshan gave his daughter to Jarha his servant to wife; and she bare him Attai. 36

And Attai begat Nathan, and Nathan begat Zabad. 37 and Zabad begat Ephlal, and Ephlal begat Obed, 38 and Obed begat Jehu, and Jehu begat Azariah, 39 and Azariah begat Helez, and Helez begat Eleasah, 40 and Eleasah begat Sismai, and Sismai begat Shallum, 41 and Shallum begat Jekamiah, and Jekamiah begat Elishama.

Verses 42-49, And the sons of Caleb the brother of Jerahmeel were Mesha his first-born, who was the father of Ziph; and the sons of Mareshah the father of Hebron. 43 And the sons of Hebron: Korah, and Tappuah, and Rekem, and Shema. 44 And Shema begat Raham, the father of Jorkeam; and Rekem begat Shammai. 45 And the son of Shammai was Maon; and Maon was the father of Beth-zur. 46 And Ephah, Caleb's concubine, bare Haran, and Moza, and Gazez. 47 And the sons of Jahdai: Regem, and Jothan, and Geshan, and Pelet, and Ephah, and Shaaph. 48 Maacah, Caleb's concubine, bare Sheber, and Tirhanah. 49 She bare also Shaaph the father of Madmannah, Sheva the father of Machbena, and the father of Gibea; and the daughter of Caleb was Achsah.

Verses 50-55, These were the sons of Caleb, the son of Hur, the first-born of Ephrathah: Shobal the father of Kiriath-jearim, 51 Salma the father of Bethlehem, Hareph the father of Beth-gader. 52 And Shobal the father of Kiriath-jearim had sons: Haroeh, half of the Menu-both. 53 And the families of Kiriath-jearim: the Ithrites, and the Puthites, and the Shumathites, and the Mishraites; of them came the Zorathites and the Eshtaolites. 54 The sons of Salma: Bethlehem and the Netophathites, Atroth-beth-joab, and half of the Manahathites, the Zorites. 55 And the families of scribes that dwelt at Jabez: the Tirathites, the

Shimeathites, the Sucathites. These are the Kenites that came of Hammath, the father of the house of Rechab.

Although there is a great deal of new material in this chapter (vv. 25-41), other scriptures parallel much of it. "(Vv. 2:1-2) are parallel with Gen. 35:22b-26 and Exodus 1:1-6; (vv. 2:3-4) are in Gen. 38:2-7, 29f, 46:12a, and Nu. 26:18f; (v. 2:5) appears in Gen. 46:12b, Nu. 26:21, Ruth 4:18; (vv. 2:6-8) are related to Josh. 7:1, 1K 5:11; (vv. 2:9-17) parallel with Ruth 4:19-22, 1S 16:8-9, 2S 2:18, 17:35."[1]

Our purpose in this commentary does not require any extensive comment on these genealogies. In the first place, they are not completely understood as to their exact meaning by anyone living millenniums after the generations enumerated. "It is impossible now to unravel these genealogies with any certainty."[2] The duplication of many names, the appearance of many names that cannot be distinguished as applicable whether to persons or places, and other uncertainties greatly complicate the problem of any complete understanding of these chapters. It is also true that textual corruptions in a few places add to the problem.

Nevertheless, the great purpose of the sacred author is fully achieved in these opening nine chapters, which are, in reality, the introduction to the entire Chronicles. The very existence of such extensive records among the Jews is overwhelming evidence that

---

1 ICC, ***Chronicles***, p. 17.

2 NBCR, p. 371.

the NT genealogies (Mt. 1 & Lk. 3) were unanimously received by that whole first century generation as absolutely accurate; nor were those records ever challenged by the enemies of Christianity. The importance of this in the proper identification of the Messiah is indeed significant.

The Caleb of v. 18 was identified by Francisco as "The Caleb of the Exodus";[3] but Payne declared that, "The Caleb of the Exodus came three hundred years later."[4] This is typical of scholarly disagreement on many of such problems in this chapter. The simple truth is that many of such questions cannot be dogmatically answered at the present time.

Jacob M. Meyers, writing in Anchor Bible, stated that, "Such technical details need not detain us."[5]

In the verses which are parallel with other scriptures, see our comments under the parallels.

XXX

---

3 BBC, Vol. 3, p. 310.

4 WYC, p. 371.

5 AnBi, *Chronicles*, p. 12,

CHAPTER 3

Verses 1-9, Now these are the sons of David, that
were born unto him in Hebron: the first-born, Amnon, of
Ahinoam the Jezreelitess; the second, Daniel, of Abigail the
Carmelitess; 2 the third, Absalom, of Maacah the daughter
of Talmai king of Geshur; the fourth, Adonijah the son of
Haggith; 3 the fifth, Shephatiah of Abital; the sixth,
Ithream of Eglah his wife: 4 six were born unto him in
Hebron; and there he reigned seven years and six months.
And in Jerusalem he reigned thirty and three years; 5 and
these were born unto him in Jerusalem: Shimea, and
Shobab, and Nathan, and Solomon, four, of Bathshua the
daughter of Ammiel; 6 and Ibhar, and Elishama, and
Eliphelet, 7 and Nogah, and Nepheg, and Japhia, 8 and
Elishama, and Eliada, and Eliphelet, nine. 9 All these
were the sons of David, besides the sons of concubines; and
Tamar was their sister.

Verses 10-24, And Solomon's son was Rehoboam,
Abijah his son, Asa his son, Jehoshaphat his son, 11
Joram his son, Ahaziah his son, Joash his son, 12
Amaziah his son, Azariah his son, Jotham his son, 13
Ahaz his son, Hezekiah his son, Manasseh his son, 14
Amon his son, Josiah his son. 15 And the sons of Josiah:
the first-born Johanan, the second Jehoiakim, the third
Zedekiah, the fourth Shallum. 16 And the sons of
Jehoiakim: Jeconiah his son, Zedekiah his son. 17 And the
sons of Jeconiah, the captive: Shealtiel his son, 18 and
Malchiram, and Pedaiah, and Shenazzar, Jekamiah,
Hoshama, and Nedabiah. 19 And the sons of Pedaiah:
Zerubbabel, and Shimei. And the sons of Zerubbabel:
Meshullam and Hananiah; and Shelomith was their sister;

20 and Ashubah, and Ohel, and Berechiah, and Hasachiah, and Jushab-hesed. 21 And the sons of Hananiah: Pelatiah, and Jeshaiah; the sons of Rephaiah, the sons of Arnan, the sons of Obadiah, the sons of Shecaniah. 22 And the sons of Shecaniah: Shemaiah. And the sons of Shemaiah: Hattash, and Igal, amd Bariah, and Neariah, and Shaphat, six. 23 And the sons of Neariah: Elioenai, and Hizkiah, and Azrikam, three. 24 And the sons of Elioenai: Hodaviah, and Eliashib, and Pelaiah, and Akkub, and Johanan, and Delaiah, and Anani, seven.

Bathshua (v. 5). This is obviously just another name for Bathsheba. The LXX and the Vulgate render the word Bathsheba. Elmslie noted that,"This name is only a variant of the name Bathsheba."[1] Judging from the order of Bathsheba's sons as listed here,Solomon was the youngest; and one may wonder if David selected him because he himself was the youngest of Jesse's sons.

The appearance in this chapter of two sons of David named Elishama and two named Eliphelet was explained by Cook as, "Due to a corruption of the text in the first Elishama and to a confusion of the first Eliphelet with Elpelet (1C 14:5)."[2] The real marvel is that there are so few such problems in lists which are as old as these. Perhaps an even better explanation is that of DeHoff: "It is generally supposed that the first two of those named Elishama and Eliphelet died in infancy

---

[1] IB, Vol. 3, p. 357.

[2] AB, ***Chronicles,*** p. 321.

and that the names were repeated for children born later."[3]

And the sons of Shemaiah (v. 22). These five words are the second phrase in v. 22; and they apparently interrupt the enumeration of Shecaniah's six sons. Elmslie stated that they should be omitted.[4] Shemaiah would then be properly numbered among Shecanaih's six sons.

"Most of these genealogies are incomplete with many breaks in the lists; but the main line is there."[5] The line of the Davidic dynasty as well as other significant gnenealogies pertaining to the religious history of Israel, is here. "These genealogies are thundering proof that the Bible is history and not myth or legend."[6]

xxx

---

[3] GDH, Vol. 3, p. 360.

[4] IB, op. cit., p. 358.

[5] HHH, p. 203,

[6] Ibid.

CHAPTER 4

Verses 1-23, The sons of Judah: Perez, Hezron, and Carmi, and Hur, and Shobal. 2 And Reaiah the son of Shobal begat Jahath; and Jahath begat Ahumai and Lahad. These are the families of the Zorathites. 3 And these were the sons of the father of Etam: Jezreel, and Ishma, and Idbash; and the name of their sister was Hazzelelponi; 4 and Penuel the father of Gedor, and Ezer the father of Hushah. These are the sons of Hur, the first-born of Ephrathah, the father of Bethlehem. 5 And Ashur the father of Tekoa had two wives, Helah and Naarah. 6 And Naarah bare him Ahuzzam, and Hepher, and Temeni, and Haahashtari. These were the sons of Naarah. 7 And the sons of Helah were Zereth, Izhar, and Ethnan. 8 And Hakkoz begat Anub, and Zobebah, and the families of Aharhel the son of Harum. 9 And Jabez was more honorable than his brethren: and his mother called his name Jabez, saying I have borne him with sorrow. 10 And Jabez called on the God of Israel, saying, Oh that thou wouldest bless me indeed, and enlarge my border, and that thy hand might be with me, and that thou wouldest keep me from evil, that it be not to my sorrow! And God granted him that which he requested. 11 And Chelub the brother of Shuhah begat Mehir, who was the father of Eshton. 12 And Eshton begat Bethrapha, and Passeah, and Tenhinnah the father of Irnahash. These are the men of Recah. 13 And the sons of Kenaz: Othniel, and Seraiah. And the sons of Othniel: Hathath. 14 And Meonothai begat Ophrah: and Seraiah begat Joab the father of Geharashim; for they were craftsmen. 15 And the sons of Caleb the son of Jephunneh: Iru, Elah, and Naam; and the

sons of Elah; and Kenaz. 16 And the sons of Jehalelel: Ziph, and Ziphah, Tiria, and Azarel. 17 And the sons of Ezrah: Jether, and Mered, and Epher, and Jalon; and she bare Miriam, and Shammai, and Ishbah the father of Eshtemoa. 18 And his wife the Jewess bare Jared the father of Gedor, and Heber the father of Soco, and Jekuthiel the father of Zanoah. And these are the sons of Bithiah the daughter of Pharaoh whom Mered took. 19 And the sons of the wife of Hodiah, the sister of Naham, were the father of Keilah the Garmite, and Eshtemoa the Maacathite. 20 And the sons of Shimon: Amnon, and Rinnah, Bnenhanan, and Tilon. And the sons of Ishi: Zohethm and Benzoheth. 21 The sons of Shelah the son of Judah: Er the father of Lecah, and Laadah the father of Mareshah, and the families of the house of them that wrought fine linen, of the house of Ashbea; 22 and Jokim, and the men of Cozeba, and Joash, and Saraph,, who had dominion in Moab, and Jashubilehem. And the records are ancient. 23 These were the potters, and the inhabitants of Netaim and Gederah: there they dwelt with the king for his work.

Verses 24-43, The sons of Simeon: Nimuel, and Jamin, Jarib, Zerah, Shaul; 25 Shallum his son. Mibsam his son, Mishma his son. 26 And the sons of Mishma: Hammuel his son, Zaccur his son, Shimei his son. 27 And Shimei had sixteen sons and six daughters; but his brethren had not many children, neither did all their family multiply like to the children of Judah. 28 And they dwelt at Beersheba, and Moladah, and Hazarshual, 29 and at Bilhah, and at Ezem, and at Tolad, 30 and at Bethuel, and at Hormah, and at Ziklag. 31 and at Beth-marcaboth, and at Hazarsusim, and at Beth-bari, and at Shaaraim.

These were their cities unto the reign of David. 32 And their villages were Etham, and Ain, and Rimmon, and Tochen, and Ashan, five cities. 33 And all their villages which were round about the same cities, unto Baal. These were their habitations, and they have their genealogy. 34 And Meshobab, and Jamlech, and Joshah the son of Amaziah, 35 and Joel, and Jehu the son of Joshibiah, the son of Seraiah, the son of Asiel, 36 and Elioenai, and Jaakobah, and Jeshohaiah, and Asaiah, and Adiel, and Jesemiel, and Benaiah, 37 and Ziza the son of Shiphi, the son of Allon, the son of Jedaiah, the son of Shimri, the son of Shemaiah ---38 these mentioned by name were princes in their families: and their fathers' houses increased greatly. 39 And they went to the entrance of Gedor, even to the east side of the valley, to seek pasture for their flocks. 40 And they found fat pasture and good, and the land was wide, and quiet, and peaceable; for they that dwelt there aforetime were of Ham. 41 And these written by name came in the days of Hezekiah king of Judah, and smote their tents, and the Meunim that were found there, and destroyed them utterly unto this day, and dwelt in their stead; because there was pasture there for their flocks. 42 And some of them, even of the sons of Simeon, five hundred men, went to mount Seir, having for their captains Pelatiah, and Neariah, and Rephaiah, and Uzziel, the sons of Ishi. 43 And they smote the remnant of the Amalekites that escaped, and have dwelt there unto this day.

The sons of Simeon (v. 24). "This list differs from that in Genesis 46:10 and in Numbers 26:12; and this may have been occasioned by the same person having different names, one list giving one name, and another list giving the other. The matter is really of no importance."[1]

"In these chapters there is a sense of the grand sweep of human history and of the purpose of God which runs through it. None of us are mere creatures of today; we are the product of generations and generations of mankind; and in our lives there are tides of influence that began to move in the remotest antiquity. Our lives gain enormously in depth and meaning when we see our small existence as part of the whole adventure of man upon the earth."[2]

The first paragraph here (vv. 1-23) gives further genealogies connected with the tribe of Judah. It is by no means clear why these particular genealogies were kept or considered important enough to be included here.

Caleb the son of Jephunneh (v. 15). This man, along with Joshua, was one of the faithful spies sent out by Moses to spy out the land of Canaan.

Jabez...named in sorrow (v. 9). The mother's statement that she bore him in sorrow is "probably a reference to unusual suffering in childbirth."[3] Jabez's prayer is one of the noblest found in the OT, and has often been used as a sermon text. Basing his criticism on an alleged meaning of the word 'evil,' Elmslie called this prayer un-Christian. "His prayer was crude and

---

1 GDH, Vol. 3, p. 362.
2 LBC, Vol. 7, p. 131.
3 PC, Vol. 6a, p. 43.

selfish. His conscience was not troubled by the thought that others would suffer if he gained his wishes."[4] We do not agree with such opinions, because God's answering Jabez's prayer indicates the purity of the petitioner's motives.

The sons of Simeon (v. 24). "The genealogy of Simeon is fragmentary, reflecting the fact this tribe lost its identity quite early and was absorbed into the tribe of Judah."[5]

xxx

---

[4] IB, Vol. 3, p. 359.

[5] NLBC, p. 479.

CHAPTER 5

Verses 1-10, And the sons of Reuben the first-born of Israel (for he was the first-born; but, forasmuch as he defiled his father's couch, his birthright was given to Joseph the son of Israel; and the genealogy is not to be reckoned after the birthright. 2 For Judah prevailed above his brethren, and of him came the prince; but the birthright was Joseph's), 3 the sons of Reuben the first-born of Israel: Hanoch, and Pallu, Hezron, and Carmi. 4 The sons of Joel: Shemaiah his son, Gog his son, Shemei his son, 5 Micah his son, Reaiah his son, Baal his son, 6 Beerah his son, whom Tilgath-pilneser king of Assyria caried away captive: he was prince of the Reubenites. 7 And his brethren by their families, when the genealogy of their generations was reckoned: the chief Jeiel, and Zechariah, 8 and Bela the son of Azaz, the son of Shema, the son of Joel, who dwelt in Aroer, even unto Nebo, and Baal-meon: 9 and eastward he dwelt even unto the entrance of the wilderness from the river Euphrates, because their cattle were multiplied in the land of Gilead. 10 And in the days of Saul they made war with the Hagrites, who fell by their hand; and they dwelt in their tents throughout all the land east of Gilead.

Verses 11-17, And the sons of Gad dwelt over against them, in the land of Bashan unto Salecah: 12 Joel the chief, and Shapham the second, and Janai, and Shaphat in Bashan. 13 And their brethren of their father's houses: Michael, and Meshullam, and Sheba, and Jorai, and Jacan, and Zia, and Eber, seven. 14 These were the sons of Abihail, the son of Huri, the son of Jaroah, the son of Gilead, the son of Mishael, the son of Jeshishai the son of Hahdo, the son of Buz; 15 Ahi the son of Abdiel, the son of Guni, chief of their fathers' houses. 16 And they dwelt in Gilead in Bashan, and in its towns, and in all the suburbs of Sharon, as far as their borders. 17 All these were reckoned by genealogies in the days of Jotham king of Judah, and in the days of Jeroboam king of Israel.

Verses 18-22, The sons of Reuben, and the Gadites, and the half-tribe of Manasseh, of valiant men, men able to bear buckler and sword, and to shoot with bow, and skilled in war, were forty and four thousand seven hundred and threescore, that were able to go forth to war. 19 And they made war with the Hagrites, with Jetur, and with Naphish, and Nodab. 20 And they were helped against them, and the Hagrites were delivered into their hand, and all that were with them; for they cried to God in the battle, and he was entreated of them, because they put their trust in him. 21 And they took away their cattle; and of their camels fifty thousand, and of sheep two hundred and fifty thousand, and of asses two thousand, and of men a hundred thousand. 22 And there fell many slain, because the war was of God. And they dwelt in their stead until the captivity.

Verses 23-24, And the children of the half-tribe of Manesseh dwelt in the land: they increased from Bashan unto Baal-hermon and Senir and mount Hermon. 25 And these were the heads of their fathers' houses: even Epher, and Ishi, and Eliel, and Azriel, and Jeremiah, and Hodaviah, and Jahdiel, mighty men of valor, famous men, heads of their fathers' houses.

Verses 25-26, And they trespassed against the God of their fathers, and played the harlot after the gods of the

peoples of the land, whom God destroyed before them. 26 And the God of Israel stirred up the spirit of Pul king of Assyria, and of Tllgath-pilneser king of Assyria, and he carried them away, even the Reubenites, and the Gadites, and the half-tribe of Manasseh, and brought them unto Halah, and Habor, and to the river Gozan, unto this day.

Of him came the prince (v. 2). Despite the fact of the double portion, normally the right of the first-born, having been transferred to Joseph, "The Chronicler thought that the birthright of Joseph was nullified by the apostasy of North Israel,"[1] and that the blessing of the leadership of God's people was transferred to Judah.

Pul, and Tilgath-pilneser (vv. 6, 26). The name of this ruler is given as Tiglath-pileser in 2K 15:29. The variation in name could have come about by different pronunciations in diverse languages, or by difficulties some copyist might have found in copying it! If the latter had anything to do with it, this writer can identify with the problem; because copying all of these names has been indeed a painstaking and difficult assignment! "Pul and Tilgath-pilneser are the same man, Pul being his personal name which he retained as king of Babylon, and Tiglath-pileser his throne name as king of Assyria."[2]

The Hagrites (v. 10). "These were the same as the Arabs."[3]

---

1 AnBi, ***Chronicles,*** p. 36.

2 NBCR, p. 373.

3 AnBi, op. cit., p. 37.

Jeroboam (v. 17). "This was Jeroboam II."[4]

Verses 18-22 record an important victory over their enemies by the trans-Jordanic tribes, no record of which is found elsewhere in the Bible. This should warn us against assuming that the Bible records any such thing as a complete history of God's people. "There may be many other gaps in Samuel and Kings which Chronicles does not fill."[5]

Many of the events mentioned in this chapter are recorded in Genesis Chs. 25, 35, & 49, Exodus 6, Joshua 22:11, and in Numbers 1:20, 26:5.[6] See our comments under those references in our commentaries.

The king of Assyria ... carried them away (v. 26). This was the captivity of the tribes of Israel which inhabited the country east of Jordan. "It took place eleven years prior to the fall of Samaria (722 BC), that is, in 733 BC."[7]

---

[4] JRD, p. 251.

[5] Ibid.

[6] AnBi, ***Chronicles,*** p. 35.

[7] WYC, p. 372.

CHAPTER 6

Verses 1-15, The sons of Levi: Gershom, Kohath, and Merari. 2 And the sons of Kohath: Amram, Izhar, and Hebron, and Uzziel. 3 And the children of Amram: Aaron, and Moses, and Miriam. And the sons of Aaron: Nadab, and Abihu, Eleazar, and Ithamar. 4 Eleazar begat Phinehas, Phinehas begat Abishua, 5 and Abishua begat Bukki, and Bukki begat Uzzi, 6 and Uzzi begat Zerahiah, and Zerahiah begat Meraioth, 7 Meraioth begat Amariah, and Amariah begat Ahitub, 8 and Ahitub begat Zadok, and Zadok begat Ahimaaz, 9 and Ahimaaz begat Azariah, and Azariah begat Johanan, 10 and Johanan begat Azariah (he it is that executed the priest's office in the house that Solomon built in Jerusalem), 11 and Azariah begat Amariah, and Amariah begat Ahitub, 12 and Ahitub begat Zadok, and Zadok begat Shallum, 13 and Shallum begat Hilkiah, and Hilkiah begat Azariah, 14 And Azariah begat Seraiah, and Seraiah begat Jehozadak; 15 and Jehozadak went into captivity, when Jehovah carried away Judah and Jerusalem by the hand of Nebuchadnezzar.

Verses 16-30, The sons of Levi: Gershom, Kohath, and Merari. 17 And these are the names of the sons of Gershom: Libni, and Shimei. 18 And the sons of Kohath were Amram, and Izhar, and Hebron, and Uzziel. 19 The sons of Merari: Mahli, and Mushi. And these are the familes of the Levites according to their fathers' houses. 20 Of Gerhom: Libni his son, Jahath his son, Zimmah his son, 21 Joah his son, Iddo his son, Zerah his son, Jeatherai his son. 22 The sons of Kohath: Amminadab his son, Korah his son, Assir his son, 23 Elkanah his son, and Ebiasaph his son, and Assir his son, 24 Tahath his son, Uriel his son, Uzziah his son, and Shaul his son. 25 And the sons of Elkanah: Amasai, and Ahimoth. 26 As for

Elkanah, the sons of Elkanah: Zophai his son, and Nahath his son, 27 Eliab his son, Jeroham his son, Elkanah his son. 28 And the sons of Samuel: the first-born, Joel, and the second Abijah. 29 The sons of Merari: Mahli, Libna his son, Shimei his son, Samuel his son, Uzzah his son, 30 Shimea his son, Haggiah his son, Asaiah his son.

Verses 31-48, And these are they that David set over the service of song in the house of Jehovah, after that the ark had rest. 32 And they ministered with song before the tabernacle of the tent of meeting, until Solomon had built the house of Jehovah in Jerusalem: and they waited on their office according to their order. 33 And these are they that waited, and their sons. Of the sons of the Kohathites: Heman the singer, the son of Joel, the son of Samuel, 34 the son of Elkanah, the son of Jeroham, the son of Eliel, the son of Toah, 35 the son of Zuph, the son of Elkanah, the son of Mahath, the son of Amasai, 36 the son of Elkanah, the son of Joel, the son of Azariah, the son of Zephaniah, 37 the son of Tahath, the son of Assir, the son of Ebiasaph, the son of Korah, 38 the son Izhar, the son of Kohath, the son of Levi, the son of Israel. 39 And his brother Asaph, who stood on his right hand, even Asaph the son of Berechiah, the son of Shimea, 40 the son of Michael, the son of Baaseiah, the son of Malchijah, 41 the son of Ethni, the son of Zerah, the son of Adaiah, 42 the son of Ethan, the son of Zimmah, the son of Shimei, 43 the son of Jahath, the son of Gershom, the son of Levi. 44 And on their left hand their brethren the sons of Merari: Ethan the son of Kishi, the son of Abdi, the son of Malluch, 45 the son of Hashabiah, the son of Amaziah, the son of Hilkiah, 46 the son of Amzi, the son of Bani, the son of

Shemer, 47 the son of Mahli, the son of Mushi, the son of Merari, the son of Levi. 48 And their brethren the Levites were appointed for all the service of the tabernacle of the house of God.

Verses 49-53, But Aaron and his sons offered upon the altar of burnt-offering, and upon the altar of incense, for all the work of the most holy place, and to make atonement for Israel, according to all that Moses the servant of God had commanded. 50 And these are the sons of Aaron: Eleazar his son, Phinehas his son, Abishua his son, 51 Bukki his son, Uzzi his son, Zerahiah his son, 52 Meraioth his son, Amariah his son, 53 Zadok his son, Ahimaaz his son.

Verses 54-60, Now these are their dwelling places according to their encampments in their borders: to the sons of Aaron, of the families of the Kohathites (for theirs was the first lot), 55 to them they gave Hebron in the land of Judah, and the suburbs thereof round about it; 56 but the fields of the city, and the villages thereof, they gave to Caleb the son of Jephunneh. 57 And to the sons of Aaron they gave the cities of refuge, Hebron; Libnah also with its suburbs, and Jattir, and Eshtemoa with its suburbs, 58 and Hilen with its suburbs, Debir with its suburbs, 59 and Ashan with its suburbs, and Beth-shemesh with its suburbs; 60 and out of the tribe of Benjamin, Geba with its suburbs, and Allemeth with its suburbs, and Anathoth with its suburbs. All their cities throughout their families were thirteen cities.

Verses 61-65, And unto the rest of the sons of Kohath were given by lot, out of the family of the tribe, out of the half-tribe, the half of Manasseh, ten cities. 62 And the sons of Gershom, according to their families, out of the tribe of Isssachar, and out of the tribe of Ashur, and out of the tribe of Naphtali, and out of the tribe of Manasseh in Bashan, thirteen cities. 63 Unto the sons of Merari were given by lot according to their families,out of the tribe of Reuben, and out of the tribe of Gad, and out of the tribe of Zebulun, twelve cities. 64 And the children of Israel gave to the Levites the cities with their suburbs. 65 And they gave by lot out of the tribe of the children of Judah, and out of the tribe of the children of Simeon, and out of the tribe of the children of Benjamin, these cities which are mentioned by name.

Verses 66-70, And some of the families of the sons of Kohath had cities of their borders out of the tribe of Ephraim. 67 And they gave unto them the cities of refuge, Shechem in the hill country of Ephraim with its suburbs; Gezer also with its suburbs, 68 and Jokmeam with its uburbs, and Beth-horon with its suburbs, 69 and Aijalon with its suburbs, and Gath-rimmon with its suburbs; 70 and out of the half-tribe of Mansasseh, Aner with its suburbs, and Bileam with its suburbs, for the rest of the family of the sons of Kohath.

Verses 71-76, Unto the sons of Gershom were given, out of the family of the half-tribe of Manasseh, Golan in Bashan with its suburbs, and Ashtaroth with its suburbs; 72 and out of the tribe of Issachar, Kedesh with its suburbs, Daberath with its suburbs, 73 and Ramoth with its suburbs, and Anem with its suburbs, 74 and out of the tribe of Asher, Mashal with its suburbs, and Abdon with its suburbs, 75 and Hukok with its suburbs, and Rehob with its suburbs, 76 and out of the tribe of Naphtali,

Kedesh in Galilee with its suburbs, and Hammon with its suburbs, and Kiriathaim with its suburbs.

Verses 77-81, Unto the rest of the Levites, the sons of Merari, were given, out of the tribe of Zebulun, Rimmono with its suburbs, Tabor with its suburbs; 78 and beyond the Jordan at Jericho, on the east side of the Jordan, were given them, out of the tribe of Reuben, Bezer in the wilderness with its suburbs, and Jahzah, 79 and Kedemoth with its suburbs, and Mephaath with its suburbs; 80 and out of the tribe of Gad, Ramoth in Gilead with its suburbs, and Mahanaim with its suburbs, 81 and Heshbon with its suburbs, and Jazer with its suburbs.

By far the greater space was devoted to the genealogies of the Levites. "The reason for this, of course, was the importance of the priestly tribe in the religious life of Israel."[1]

An amazing feature of these is the use of the same names over and over from generation to generation. The time covered by these genealogies reaches all the way back to Israel (Jacob); and many of the names encountered here remind us of historical events centered around those names throughout the OT. Our comments on some of those occurrences are in Exodus 6th chapter, First Samuel chapters 1 and 8, and in chapter 21 of Joshua.

Nadab and Abihu (v. 3). Their offering strange fire before Jehovah and their untimely death are recorded in Leviticus 20:1-2, and in Numbers 3:4. They

---

[1] TBC, p. 221.

left no children.

A most significant fact that appears in this chapter is that all of the services of the tabernacle are presented as reaching all the way back to the Exodus; and the Chronicler tells us that their ceremonies were observed, "According to all that Moses the servant of God had commanded." (v. 49). Elmslie, speaking of this verse, declared it to be "emphatically stated."[2] The sacred author of Chronicles had evidently never heard of that fairy tale regarding that "D" Document allegedly discovered by Hilkiah in the days of Josiah. What is stated here could never have been written if that 'discovery' had been anything other than the Pentateuch (every single word of it).

All their cities were thirteen (v. 60). "Eleven of these are given here, and the other two are supplied in Joshua 21."[3]

The importance of these genealogies for the returning Israelites from their captivity in Babylon was stressed by Simmons: "It was important for them to realize that their captivity had been only an interruption of their religious and national life. These genealogies gave them a most significant link with their past. They created a continuity between the preexilic and postexilic Israel."[4]

XXX

---

[2] IB, Vol. 3, p. 369.
[3] WYC, p. 373.
[4] TBC, p. 221.

CHAPTER 7

Verses 1-5, And of the sons of Issachar: Tolah, and Puah, Jashib, and Shimron, four. 2 And the sons of Tolah: Uzzi, and Raphaiah, and Jeriel, and Jahmai, and Ibsam, and Shemuel, heads of their fathers' houses, to wit, of Tolah, mighty men of valor in their generations: their number in the days of David was two and twenty thousand and six hundred. 3 And the sons of Uzzi: Izrahiah. And the sons of Izrahiah: Michael, and Obadiah, and Joel, Isshiah, five; all of them chief men. 4 And with them, by their generations, after their fathers' houses, were bands of the host for war, six and thirty thousand; for they had many wives and sons. 5 And their brethren among all the families of Issachar, mighty men of valor, reckoned in all by genealogy, were fourscore and seven thousand.

Verses 6-12, The sons of Benjamin: Bel, and Becher, and Jediael, three. 7 And the sons of Bala:, Ezbon, and Uzzi, and Uzziel, and Jerimoth, and Itri, five; heads of fathers' houses, mighty men of valor; and they were reckoned by genealogy twenty and two thousand and thirty and four. 8 And the sons of Becher: Zemirah, and Joash, and Eliezer, and Elioenai, and Omri, and Jerimoth, and Abijah, and Anathoth, and Alemeth. All these were the sons of Becher. 9 And they were reckoned by genealogy, after their generations, heads of their fathers' houses, mighty men of valor, twenty thousand and two hundred. 10 And the sons of Jediael: Bilhan. And the sons of Bilhan: Jeush, and Benjamin, and Chenaanah, and Zethan, and Tarshish, and Ahishahar. 11 All these were sons of Jediael, according to the heads of their fathers' houses, mighty men of valor, seventeen thousand and two hundred,

that were able to go forth in the host for war. 12 Shuppim also, and Huppim, the sons of Ir (Iri), Hushim, the sons of Aher.

Verses 13, The sons of Naphtali: Jahziel, and Guni, and Jezer, and Shallum, the sons of Billah.

Verses 14-19, The sons of Manasseh: Asriel, whom his concubine the Aramitess bare; she bare Machir the father of Gilead. 15 And Machir took a wife of Huppim and Shuppim, whose sister's name was Maacah; and the name of the second was Zelophehad: and Zelophehad had daughters. 16 And Maacah the wife of Machir bare a son, and she called his name Peresh; and the name of his brother was Sheresh; and his sons were Ulam and Rakem. 17 And the sons of Ulam: Bedan. These were the sons of Gilead the son of Machir, the son of Manasseh. 18 And his sister Hammolecheth bare Ishhod, and Abiezer, and Mahlah. 19 And the sons of Shemidda were Ahian, and Shechem, and Likhi, and Aniam.

Verses 20-27, And the sons of Ephraim: Shuthelah, and Bered his son, and Tahath his son, 21 and Zabad his son, and Shuthelah his son, and Ezer, and Elead, whom the men of Gath that were born in the land slew, because they came down to take away their cattle. 22 And Ephraim their father mourned many days, and his brethren came to comfort him. 23 And he went in to his wife, and she conceived, and bare a son, and he called his name Beriah, because it went evil with his house. 24 And his daughter was Sheerah, who built Beth-horon the nether and the upper, and Uzzen-sheerah. 25 And Rephah was his son, and Resheph, and Telah his son, and Tahan his son, 26 Ladan his son, Ammihud his son, Elishama his son, 27

Nun his son, and Joshua his son.

Verses 28-29, And their possessions and habitations were Bethel and the towns thereof; Shechem also and the towns thereof, unto Azzah and the towns thereof; 29 and by the borders of the children of Manasseh, Beth-shean and its towns, Taanach and its towns, Megiddo and its towns. In these dwelt the children of Joseph the son of Israel.

Verses 30-40, The sons of Asher: Imnah, and Ishvah, and Ishva, and Beriah, and Serah their sister. 31 And the sons of Beriah: Heber, and Malchiel, who was the father of Birzaith. 32 And Heber begat Japhlet, and Shomer, and Hotham, and Shua their sister. 33 And the sons of Japhlet: Pasach, and Bimhal, and Ashvath. These are the children of Japhlet. 34 And the sons of Shemer (Shomer): Ahi, and Rohgah, Jehubbah, and Aram. 35 And the sons of Helem his brother: Zophah, and Imra, and Shelesh, and Amal. 36 The sons of Zophah: Suah, and Harnepher, and Shual, and Beri, and Imrah, 37 Bezer, and Hod, and Shamma, and Shilshah, and Ithran, and Beera. 38 And the sons of Jether: Jephunneh, and Pispa, and Ara. 39 And the sons of Ulla: Arah, and Hanniel, and Rizia. 40 All these were the children of Asher, heads of the fathers' houses, choice and mighty men of valor, chief of the princes. And the number of them reckoned by genealogy for service in war was twenty and six thousand men.

There are many discrepancies when these lists are compared with the lists cited in the marginal references to other scriptures; but it is no part of our purpose to attempt any explanation of them. The word ***son*** is used no less than nine different ways in the Bible.[1] Also, there was a mixing of the tribes, for examples, as when, "Becher's heiress married an Ephraimite which transferred his reckoning from the tribe of Benjamin to that of Ephraim."[2] We also have place-names such as ***Anathoth*** also used as the names of persons (v. 8). Cundall noted that we even have two different genealogies; "Nor is it possible to explain why two should have been given."[3] As Keil noted, "Verse 12 is unintelligible to us."[4]

Such problems as these do not concern us. The great purpose of the sacred author here was to forge a strong link between the preexilic and postexilic Israels; and these remarkable genealogies certainly accomplished that very thing. No doubt they were understood far more perfectly by the descendants of the twelve tribes than any one may understand them thousands of years later.

Also, as we have repeatedly stressed, these genealogies are incontrovertible proof that the OT deals, not with myth or legend, but with history. The power of this argument is indeed tremendous. Once, when this writer was minister of Manhattan Church of Christ, a group of several New York University students called upon him; and one of them asked if it was not a

---

[1] See our ***Commentary on II Samuel***, p. 269, for a list of these.

[2] FCC, ***Chronicles***, p. 331.

[3] NBCR, p. 374.

[4] CFK, Vol 3b, p. 134.

fact that Jesus Christ was merely a myth. This writer then quoted in its entirety the genealogy of Jesus Christ through his mother Mary as found in Luke 3:23ff, and concluded by asking, "Now, will some of you recite for me the genealogy of Paul Bunyon, Beowolf, Santa Claus, or any other myth"? One of these later obeyed the gospel.

These names stimulate our curiosity and our imagination. Many of these are described as mighty men of valor, heads of their fathers' houses, chief among the princes of Israel, etc. What wonderful deeds of faith and trust in God must have been done! What marvelous stories of heroism, tragedy, glory, defeat and victory were woven around the names written here. We shall never know the slightest thing about most of them; but as we gaze upon their names we are haunted by thoughts of those whose exploits lie buried under the silence of millenniums.

xxx

CHAPTER 8

Verses 1-28, And Benjamin begat Bela his first-born, Ashbel the second, and Aharah the third, 2 Nohah the fourth, and Rapha the fifth. 3 And Bela had sons: Addar, and Gera, and Abihud, 4 and Abishua, and Naaman, and Ahoah. 5 and Gera, and Shephuphan, and Huram. 6 And these are the sons of Ehud: these are the heads of the fathers' houses of the inhabitants of Geba, and they carried them captive to Manahath: 7 and Naaman, and Ahijah, and Gera, he carried them captive; and he begat Uzza, and Ahihud. 8 And Shaharaim begat children in the field of Moab, after he had sent them away; Hushim, and Baara were his wives. 9 And he begat of Hodesh his wife, Jobab, and Zibia, and Mesha, and Malcam, 10 and Jeuz, and Shachia, and Mirmah. These were his sons, heads of fathers' houses. 11 And of Hushim he begat Abitub and Elpaal. 12 And the sons of Elpaal: Eber, and Misham, and Shemed, who built Ono and Lod, with the towns thereof; 13 and Beriah and Shema, who were heads of fathers' houses of the inhabitants of Aijalon, who put to flight the inhabitants of Gath; 14 and Ahio, Shashak, and Jeremoth, 15 and Zebadiah, and Arad, and Eder, 16 and Michael, and Ishpah, and Johah, the sons of Beriah, 17 and Zebadiah, and Meshullam, and Hizki, and Heber, 18 and Ishmerai, and Izliah, and Jobab, the sons of Elpaal, 19 and Jakim, and Zichri, and Zabdi, 20 and Elienai, and Zillethai, and Eliel, 21 and Adaiah, and Beraiah, and Shimrath, the sons of Shimei. 22 and Ishpan, and Eber, and Eliel, 23 and Abdon, and Zichri, and Hanan, 24 and Hananiah, and Elam, and Anthothijah, 25 and Iphdeiah, and Penuel, the sons of Shashak, 26 and Shamsherai, and

Shehariah, and Athaliah, 27 and Jaareshiah, and Elijah, and Zichri, the sons of Jeroham. 28 These were heads of fathers' houses throughout their generations, chief men: these dwelt in Jerusalem.

Verses 29-40, And in Gibeon there dwelt the father of Gibeon, Jeiel, whose wife's name was Maacah; 30 and his first-born son Abdon, and Zur, and Kish, and Baal, and Nadab; 31 and Gedor, and Ahio, and Zecher. 32 And Mikloth begat Shimeah. And they dwelt with their brethren in Jerusalem, over against their brethren. 33 And Ner begat Kish, and Kish begat Saul; and Saul begat Jonathan, and Malcashua, and Abinadab, and Eshbaal. 34 And the son of Jonahtan was Meribbaal; and Meribbaal begat Micah. 35 And the sons of Micah: Pithon, and Melech, and Tarea, and Ahaz. 36 And Ahaz begat Jehoaddah; and Jehoaddah begat Alemeth, and Azmaveth, and Zimri, and Zimri begat Moza. 37 And Moza begat Binea; and Raphah was his son, Eleasah his son, Azel his son. 38 And Azel had six sons, whose names are these: Azrikam, Bocheru, and Ishmael, and Sheariah, and Obadiah, and Hanan. All these were the sons of Azel. 39 And the sons of Eshek his brother: Ulam his first-born, Jeush the second, and Eliphelet the third. 40 And the sons of Ulam were mighty men of valor, archers, and had many sons, and sons' sons, a hundred and fifty. All these were of the sons of Benjamin.

"The very full details given here as contrasted with most of the other tribes should not be put down as due to the availablility of more information, but should be regarded as a tribute to Benjamin's loyalty to David and his dynasty."[1] Also it appears that special attention was given to the line of David's friend Jonathan.

It is impossible to harmonize this with the parallel list in 7:6-12; and some scholars have believed that list to be a "corrupted genealogy of Zebulun and Dan."[2]

All of the names given thus far in Chronicles belonged to persons of preexilic Israel, "The first verse of the following chapter (9:1) states that what has gone before pertains only to the official register of the families ... ***when they were exiled.*** This clause separates the foregoing from what follows."[3] Payne did not agree with this interpretation. See further comment under 9:1.

Ono and Lod (v. 12). These cities were not mentioned in Joshua as part of Palestine originally assigned to Benjamin; but, "These places were built later. There is little doubt that Lod is the Lydda of Acts 9:22)."[4]

Curtis and Madsen disagreed with Myers (quoted above) by affirming the lists of this chapter as postexilic;[5] but the disagreement of scholars regarding such questions can be of little interest, since it really makes no difference at all ***exactly when*** the people of any of these lists actually lived.

---

1 NBCR, p. 374.

2 Ibid., p. 375.

3 AnBi, *Chronicles,* p. 62.

4 PC, Vol. 6a, p. 109.

5 ICC, *Chronicles,* p. 156.

Elmslie in ***IB*** devoted only sixteen lines to this whole chapter.[6]

There are many things in this chapter and in the entire OT that must forever remain in the realm of the mysterious and the unknown as far as modern men are concerned. For example, "Nothing is known about the exile mentioned in v 6. We do not know who exiled whom."[7] It is appropriate to remember in this connection that "The hidden things belong to God."

XXX

---

[6] IB, Vol. 3, p. 376.

[7] BBC, Vol. 3, p. 321.

CHAPTER 9

Verses 1-9, So all Israel were reckoned by genealogies; and, behold, they are written in the book of the kings of Israel. And Judah was carried away captive to Babylon for their transgression. 2 Now the first inhabitants that dwelt in their possessions in their cities were Israel, the priests, the Levites, and the Nethinem. 3 And in Jerusalem dwelt of the children of Judah, and of the children of Benjamin, and of the children of Ephraim and Manasseh: 4 Uthai the son of Ammihud, the son of Omri, the son of Imri, the son of Bani, of the children of Perez the son of Judah. 5 And of the Shilonites: Asaiah the first-born, and his sons. 6 And of the sons of Zerah: Jeuel and their brethren, six hundred and ninety. 7 And of the sons of Benjamin: Sallu the son of Meshullam, the son of Hodaviah, the son of Hassenuah, 8 and Ibneiah the son of Jeroham, and Elah the son of Uzzi, the son of Michri, and Meshullam the son of Shephatiah, the son of Reuel, the son of Ibnijah; 9 and their brethren according to their generations, nine hundred and fifty six. All these men were heads of father's houses by their fathers' houses.

Verses 10-13, And of the priests: Jedaiah, and Jehoiarib, Jachin, 11 and Azariah the son of Hilkiah, the son of Meshallam, the son of Zadok, the son of Meraioth, the son of Ahitub, the ruler of the house of God; 12 and Adaiah the son of Jeroham, the son of Pashhur, the son of Malchijah, and Maasai the son of Adiel, the son of Jahzerah, the son of Meshullam, the son of Meshillemith, the son of Immer; 13 and their brethren, heads of their fathers' houses, a thousand and seven hundred and threescore; very able men for the work of the service of the house of God.

Verses14-16, And of the Levites: Shemaiah the son of Hashub, the son of Azrikam, the son of Hashabiah, of the sons of Merari; 15 and Bakbakkar, Heresh, and Galal, and Mattaniah, the son of Mica, the son of Zichri, the son of Asaph, 16 the son of Obadiah, that dwelt in the villages of the Netophathites.

Verses 17-27, And the porters: Shallum, and Akkub, and Talmon, and Ahiman, and their brethren (Shallum was their chief), 18 who hitherto waited in the king's gate eastward: they were the porters for the camp of the children of Levi. 19 And Shallum the son of Kore, the son of Ebiasaph, the son of Korah, and his brethren, of his father's house, the Korahites, were over the work of the service, keepers of the thresholds of the tent: and their fathers had been over the camp of Jehovah, keepers of the entry. 20 And Phinehas the son of Eleazar was over them in time past, and Jehovah was with him. 21 Zechariah the son of Meshelemiah was porter of the door of the tent of meeting. 22 All these that were chosen to be porters in the thresholds were two hundred and twelve. These were reckoned by genealogy in their villages, whom David and Samuel the seer did ordain in their office of trust. 23 So they and their children had the oversight of the gates of the house of Jehovah, even the house of the tent, by wards. 24 On the four sides were the porters, on the east, west, north, and south. 25 And their brethren, in their villages, were to come in every seven days from time to time with them: 26 for the four chief porters who were Levites were in an office of trust, and were over the chambers and over the treasuries in the house of God, 27 and they lodged round about the house of God, because the charge thereof was upon them;

and to them pertained the opening thereof morning by morning.

*Verses 28-32, **And certain of them had charge of the vessels of service; or by count were these brought in and by count were these taken out. 29 Some of them also were appointed over the furniture, and over all the vessels of the sanctuary, and over the fine flour, and the wine, and the oil, and the frankincense, and the spices. 30 And some of the sons of the priests prepared the confection of the spices. 31 And Mattithiah, one of the Levites, who was the first-born of Shallum the Korahite, had the office of trust over the things that were baked in pans. 32 And some of their brethren, of the sons of the Kohathites, were over the showbread, to prepare it every sabbath.***

*Verses 33-34, **And these are the singers, heads of fathers' houses of the Levites who dwelt in the chambers and were free from other service; for they were employed in their work day and night. 34 These were heads of fathers' houses of the Levites, throughout their generations, chief men; these dwelt in Jerusalem.***

*Verses 35-44, **And in Gibeon there dwelt the father of Gibeon, Jeiel, whose wife was Maacah; 36 and his first-born son Abdon, and Zur, and Kish, and Baal, and Ner, and Nadab, 37 and Gedor,and Ahio, and Zechariah,and Mikloth. 38 And Mikloth begat Shimeam. And they also dwelt with their brethren in Jerusalem, over against their brethren. 39 And Ner begat Kish, and Kish begat Saul; and Saul begat Jonathan, and Malcashua, and Abinadab, and Eshbaal. 40 And the son of Jonathan was Meribbaal; and Meribbaal begat Micah. 41 And the sons of Micah: Pithon, and Melech, and Tahrea, and Ahaz. 42 And Ahaz***

begot Jarah; and Jarah begat Alemeth, and Azmaveth, and Zimri; and Zimri begat Moza; 43 and Moza begat Benia; and Rephaiah his son, Eleasah his son, and Azel his son. 44 And Azel had six sons, whose names are these: Azrikam, Bocheru, and Ishmael, and Sheriah, and Obadiah, and Hanan: these were the sons of Azel.

Verses 35-44 here are a duplicate of 8:29-38. Twelve generations of King Saul are listed here; and the reason for their being repeated would appear to be that they are an appropriate background for the record of the death of Saul, related in the very next chapter.

This brings us to the end of these amazing genealogies. Unbelieving scholars have levelled all kinds of critical allegations against these records; but the truth is that not any of them has been able to shed any light whatever upon these records.

"These genealogies are the skeletal framework of the entire OT. They bind the whole book together and afford the most convincing demonstration that the OT is genuine history as contrasted with myth or legend."[1]

"This chapter has a list of the postexilic inhabitants of Jerusalem, to which has been appended a list of the anncesters of king Saul as a fitting introduction to the story of Saul which immediately follows."[2] J. Barton Payne sharply disagreed with Dentan's statement here, affirming that, "This chapter enumerates the inhabitants of Jerusalem prior to the

---

[1] HHH, p. 203.

[2] LBC, Vol. 7, p. 131.

city's capture and the removal of its people to Babylon."[3] This writer believes that Payne's opinion is the more trustworthy. The principal support of Dentan's view comes, "From an emendation that changes the meaning of verse 2 in this chapter."[4] It is a weakness of the RSV that it follows that change of the sacred text without adequate authority.

The truly significant fact that comes to light here is that with the records before the Chronicler (whom we believe to have been Ezra) as revealed in this chapter, "It was possible for Ezra to restore the legitimate theocracy in Jerusalem after their return from Babylon."[5] This may have resulted from the detailed account in this chapter of the various services and responsibilities of the Levites.

These nine chapters, composed principally of genealogical tables, must, without doubt, be among the most neglected chapters in the Bible.

XXX

---

[3] WYC, p. 374.

[4] Ibid.

[5] Ibid., p. 375.

II. HISTORY OF DAVID'S REIGN
(Chapters 10-29)

CHAPTER 10

This chapter begins the record of the reign of David over all Israel, prefacing it with a brief account of Saul's death. (1000-960 BC)

The balance of 1 Chronicles is devoted to a review of the history of David, which falls into two parts. "Chapters 10-20 have an account of his reign; and chapters 21-29 give preparations for the building of the Temple and the orders and arrangements of those who would serve in it."[1]

Verses 1-14, Now the Philistines fought against Israel: and the men of Israel fled from before the Philistines, and fell down slain in mount Gilboa. 2 And the Philistines followed hard after Saul and after his sons; and the Philistines slew Jonathan, and Abinadab, and Malchishua, the sons of Saul. 3 And the battle went sore against Saul, and the archers overtook him; and he was distressed by reason of the archers. 4 Then said Saul unto his armorbearer, Draw thy sword, and thrust me through therewith, lest these uncircumcised come and abuse me. But his armorbearer would not, for he was sore afraid. Therefore Saul took his sword, and fell upon it. 5 And when his armorbearer saw that Saul was dead, he likewise fell upon his sword, and died. 6 So Saul died, and his three sons; and all his house died together.

7 And when all the men of Israel that were in the valley saw that they fled, and that Saul and his sons were

---

1 ICC, *Chronicles,* p. 180.

dead, they forsook their cities, and fled; and the Philistines came and dwelt in them. 8 And it came to pass on the morrow, when the Philistines came to strip the slain, that they found Saul and his sons fallen in mount Gilboa. 9 And they stripped him, and took his head, and his armor, and sent into the land of the Philistines round about, to carry the tidings unto their idols, and to the people. 10 And they put his armor in the house of their gods, and fastened his head in the house of Dagon. 11 And when all Jabesh-gilead heard all that the Philistines had done to Saul, 12 all the valiant men arose, and took away the body of Saul and the bodies of his sons, and brought them to Jabesh, and buried their bones under the oak in Jabesh, and fasted seven days.

13 So Saul died for his trespass which he committed against Jehovah, because of the word of Jehovah, which he kept not; and also for that he asked counsel of one that had a familiar spirit, to inquire thereby, 14 and inquired not of Jehovah: therefore he slew him, and turned the kingdom unto David the son of Jesse.

And all his house died together (v. 6). The picayune objection of some scholars that this is not strictly the truth, because Eshbaal (Ishbosheth), another son of Saul was left alive, and for awhile was made king over North Israel by Abner, is typical of the nit-picking hatred of the word of God by some writers. The reference is not to every single one of Saul's posterity, but merely to those just named. This is the same kind of hyperbole one uses when he says, "We gave a party, and everybody came."

They buried him under the oak in Jabesh (v. 12). This tree was called "a tamarisk tree" in 1S 31:13; and the marginal reference here gives "terebinth" as an alternative. If the trees were growing side by side, which is by no means impossible, the biblical accounts may both be absolutly accurate. No one has the right to deny what is here stated as a fact.

We shall not make line by line comments on this chapter, for we have already discussed it in the closing chapter of 1st Samuel and the opening chapter of 2nd Samuel. As Curtis (and Madsen) noted: "This account of the death of Saul is taken from 1 Samuel 31:1-13 with a few slight variations."[2]

XXX

[2] Ibid.

CHAPTER 11

David Made King Over All Israel; the Capture of Jerusalem; a List of David's Mighty men.

David Made King Over All Israel

Verses 1-3, Then all Israel gathered themselves together unto David at Hebron, saying, Behold, we are thy bone and flesh. 2 In times past, even when Saul was king, it was thou that leddest out and broughtest in Israel: and Jehovah thy God said unto thee, Thou shalt be shepherd of my people Israel, and thou shalt be prince over my people Israel. 3 So all the elders of Israel came to the king to Hebron; and David made a covenant with them in Hebron before Jehovah; and they anointed David king over Israel.

Our comments on these verses are in Vol. 4 of the historical books, (2 Samuel). pp. 53-55.

The Capture of Jerusalem

Verses 4-9, And David and all Israel went to Jerusalem (the same is Jebus); and the Jebusites, the inhabitants of the land, were there. 5 And the inhabitants of Jebus said to David, Thou shalt not come in hither. Nevertheless David took the stronghold of Zion; the same is the city of David. 6 And David said, Whosoever smiteth the Jebusites first shall be chief and captain. And Joab the son of Zeruiah went up first, and was made chief. 7 And David dwelt in the stronghold; therefore they called it the city of David. 8 And he built the city round about, from Millo even round about; and Joab repaired the rest of the city. 9

And David waxed greater and greater, for Jehovah of hosts was with him.

Second Samuel 5:4-10 is parallel with this paragraph; and our comments there are sufficient for what is written here.

Concerning the Names and Exploits of David's Mighty Men

Verses 10-47, Now these are the chief of the mighty men whom David had, who showed themselves strong with him in his kingdom, together with all Israel, to make him king, according to the word of Jehovah concerning Israel. 11 And this is the number of the mighty men whom David had: Jashobeam, the son of a Hachmonite, the chief of the thirty; he lifted up his spear against three hundred and slew them at one time. 12 And after him was Eleazar the son of Dodo, the Ahohite, who was one of the three mighty men. 13 He was with David at Pasdammim, and there the Philistines were gathered together to battle, where was a plot of ground full of barley; and the people fled from before the Philistines. 14 And they stood in the midst of the plot, and defended it; and slew the Philistines; and Jehovah saved them by a great victory.

15 And three of the thirty chief men went down to the rock to David, into the cave of Adullam; and the host of the Philistines were encamped in the valley of Rephaim. 16 And David was then in the stronghold, and the garrison of the Philistines was then in Bethlehem. 17 And David longed, and said, Oh that one would give me water to drink of the well of Bethlehem, which is by the gate! 18 And the three brake through the host of the Philistines, and drew water out of the well of Bethlehem, which is by the gate, and took it, and brought it to David: but David would not drink thereof, but poured it out unto Jehovah, 19 and said, My God forbid it me, that I should do this: shall I drink the blood of these men that have put their lives in jeopardy? for with the jeopardy of their lives they brought it. Therefore he would not drink it. These things did the three mighty men.

Verses 20-21, And Abishai, the brother of Joab, he was chief of the three; for he lifted up his spear against three hundred, and slew them, and had a name among the three. 21 Of the three, he was more honorable than the two, and was made their captain: howbeit he attained not to the first three.

Verses 22-25, Benaiah the son of Jehoiada, the son of a valiant man of Kabzeel, who had done mighty deeds, he slew the two sons of Ariel of Moab: he went down also and slew a lion in the midst of a pit in a time of snow. 23 And he slew an Egyptian, a man of great stature, five cubits high; and in the Egyptian's hand was a spear like a weaver's beam; and he went down to him with a staff, and plucked the spear out of the Egyptian's hand, and slew him with his own spear. 24 These things did Benaiah the son of Jehoiada, and he had a name among the three mighty men. 25 Behold, he was more honorable than the thirty, but he attained not to the first three: and David set him over his guard.

Verses 26-47, Also the mighty men of the armies: Asahel the brother of Joab, Elhanan the son of Dodo of

Bethlehem, 27 Shammoth the Harorite, Helez the Pelonite, 28 Ira the son of Ikkesh the Tekoite, Abiezer the Anathothite, 29 Sibbecai the Hushathite, Ilai the Ahohite, 30 Maharai the Netophathite, Heled the son of Baanah the Netophathite, 31 Ithai the son of Ribai of Gibeah of the children of Benjamin, Benaiah the Pirathonite, 32 Hurai of the brooks of Gaash, Abiel the Arbathite, 33 Azmaveth the Baharumite, Eliahba the Shaalbomite, 34 the sons of Hashem the Gizonite, Jonathan the son of Shagee the Hararite, 35 Ahiam the son of Sacar the Hararite, Eliphal the son of Ur, 36 Hepher the Mecherathite, Ahijah the Pelonite, 37 Hezro the Carmelite, Naarai the son of Ezbai, 38 Joel the brother of Nathan, Mibbar the son of Hagri, 39 Zelek the Ammonite, Naharai the Berothite, the armorbearer of Joab the son of Zeruiah, 40 Ira the Ithrite, Gareb the Ithrite, 41 Uriah the Hittite, Zabad the son of Ahlai, 42 Adina the son of Shiza the Reubenite, a chief of the Reubenites, and thirty with him, 43 Hanan the son of Maacah, and Joshaphat the Mithnite, 44 Uzzia the Ashterathite, Shama and Jeiel the sons of Hotham the Aroerite, 45 Jediael the son of Shimri, and Joha his brother, the Tizite, 46 Eliel the Mahavite, and Jeribai, and Joshaviah the sons of Elnaam, and Ithmah the Moabite, 47 Eliel and Obed, and Jaasiel the Mezobaite.

The parallel of these verses (10-47) is in 2 Samuel 23:8-35; and the variations are of no practical concern whatever. Our comments there will not be repeated here.

In the group of men called "The Thirty," there were most certainly casualties from time to time; and as men died, others were named in their places; thus there were possibly many lists of "The Thirty," that conformed, of course, to the particular date of any particular list.

And Abishai, the brother of Joab, he was chief of the three (v. 20). "The three" of which Abishai was chief may have been those three mentioned in the preceding paragraph who brought the water from the well of Bethlehem. However, Myers suggested that, "Abishai may have taken the place of Asahel after he was slain by Abner."[1]

The main list of David's Mighty Men actually ends with Uriah the Hittite (41a). There are thirty-one names, compared with exactly thirty in 2S 23:24-39. "There are some variations in names and spelling."[2] The same scholar spoke of both lists as "undoubtedly genuine."[3]

Beginning with verse 41b, sixteen other names are listed. These could have been others associated at one time or another with the "thirty"; or the Chronicler may have added them to emphasize the representatives of trans-Jordan who aided the cause of David. There are many such questions which shall remain unanswered.

"The variations between the parallel accounts of this chapter in Chronicles with that in 2 Samuel are few

---

1 AnBi, *Chronicles,* p. 89.

2 Ibid., p. 90.

3 Ibid., p. 88.

and unimportant."[4]

The intention of the Chronicler to emphasize David's commendable qualities and to ignore or downplay his terrible sins appears in the fact of his including the episode in vv. 15-19 and omitting altogether any mention of his adultery with Bathsheba and his murder of eighteen men along with Uriah the Hittite in a vain effort to hide it.

Further comment on this interesting chapter is given in our commentary on 2 Samuel.

xxx

---

[4] ICC, *Chronicles,* p. 188.

CHAPTER 12

The Men Who Came to David During His Days at Ziklag, and in His Days in the Wilderness Strongholds. Also the Military Strength that Came to Him at Hebron

The Gibeonites Come to David

Verses 1-7, Now these are they that came to David at Ziklag, while he yet kept himself close because of Saul the son of Kish; and they were among the mighty men, his helpers in war. 2 They were armed with bows, and could use both the right hand and the left in slinging stones and in shooting arrows from the bow: they were of Saul's brethren of Benjamin. 3 The chief was Ahiezer; then Joash, the sons of Shemaah the Gibeathite, and Jeziel, and Pelet, the sons of Azmaveth, and Beracah, and Jehu the Anathothite, 4 and Ishmaiah the Gibeonite, a mighty man among the thirty, and over the thirty, and Jeremiah, and Jahaziel, and Johanan, and Jozabad the Gederathite, 5 Eluzai, and Jerimoth, and Belaiah, and Shemariah, and Shephatiah the Haruphite, 6 Elkanah, and Isshiah, and Azarel, and Joezer, and Jashobeam, the Korahites, 7 and Joelah, and Zebadiah, the sons of Jeroham of Gedor.

The significance of this paragraph is that some of Saul's kinsmen defected to David at Ziklag, even a prominent citizen of Saul's home town, a Gibeonite. The material in this chapter is found nowhere else in the scriptures. The men named here were competent and able soldiers. We reject the snide unbelieving comment of Curtis and Madsen that, "Since on the death of Saul, the tribe of Benjamin remained faithful to his house, how much less can we believe that such desertions to David took place during his lifetime."[1] Such a comment is important only because it alerts us to the fact that the authors of it were unbelievers in the ultimate sense of the word. Foolish indeed are those who trust such writers to interpret the holy scriptures for them.

The occasions for these desertions to the cause of David was the period of David's residence at Ziklag, as related in 2 Samuel chapters 27-30. See our commentary under those references.

The Chronicler stressed the skill, training, competence and high social standing of several of the persons mentioned. Some writers have attempted to downgrade David's 'six hundred men' as "Debtors, discontented and desperate men,"[2] but this is merely a part of their evil campaign against the whole book of Chronicles. Why? Chronicles is an effective denial of their favorite fairy tale that denies the Books of Moses.

Myers pointed out the real reason for the desertion of many of the very best men in all Israel to the cause of David, as follows: "The best and most capable men became his followers, because they recognized in him the chosen vessel of Jehovah."[3]

---

1 ICC, ***Chronicles***, p. 195.

2 Ibid.. p. 194.

3 AnBi, ***Chronicles***, p. 97.

The Gadites Defect to David in His Wilderness Days

Verses 8-15, And of the Gadites there separated themselves unto David to the stronghold in the wilderness, mighty men of valor, men trained for war, that could handle shield and spear; whose faces were like the faces of lions, and they were as swift as the roes upon the mountains: 9 Ezer the chief, Obadiah the second, Eliab the third, 10 Mishmammah the fourth, Jeremiah the fifth, 11 Attai the sixth, and Eliel the seventh, 12 Johanan the eighth, Elzabad the ninth, 13 Jeremiah the tenth, Machbannai the eleventh. 14 These of the sons of Gad were captains of the host: he that was least was equal to a hundred, and the greatest to a thousand. 15 These are they that went over Jordan in the first month, when it had overflowed all its banks; and they put to flight all them of the valleys, both toward the east and toward the west.

To the stronghold in the wilderness (v. 8). This was prior to David's days at Ziklag. The particular stronghold is not mentioned, but it might have been either Engedi or Adullam.

Faces like the faces of lions ... as swift as the roes on the mountains (v. 8). No human being can outrun a deer; and the figures of speech used by the Chronicler here suggest that other figures of speech also appear in the chapter.

"The names of persons in these verses (9-13) are all found elsewhere in the Bible, but none of them as designating the same persons."[4]

They went over the Jordan in the first month (v. 15). "The time here was the same as our month of March/April."[5] The historical setting may have been that of the Conquest under Joshua; but the event here given is not elsewhere reported in the Bible.

Men of Benjamin and Judah Come to David in the Stronghold

Verses 16-18, And there came of the children of Benjamin and Judah to the stronghold unto David. 17 And David went out to meet them, and answered and said unto them, If ye be come peaceably unto me to help me, my heart shall be knit unto you; but if ye be come to betray me to mine adversaries, seeing there is no wrong in my hands, the God of our fathers look thereon, and rebuke it. 18 Then the Spirit came upon Amasai, who was chief of the thirty, and he said, Thine are we, David, and on thy side, thou son of Jesse: peace, peace be unto thee, and peace be on thy helpers; for thy God helpeth thee. Then David received them, and made them captains of the band.

David had every right to fear betrayal by those who approached him in this episode. He had suffered betrayal by Doeg the Edomite (1S Chs. 21,22), by citizens of Keilah (1S 23), and by the Ziphites (1S 26).

It is of special interest that the Holy Spirit

---

[4] PC, Vol. 6a, p. 175.

[5] Ibid.

reassured David in the words of Amasai.

Some of the Tribe of Manasseh Come to David

Verses 19-22, Of Manasseh also there fell away some to David, when he came with the Philistines against Saul to battle: but they helped them not; for the lords of the Philistines upon advisement sent him away, saying, He will fall away to his master Saul to the jeopardy of our heads. 20 As he went to Ziklag, there fell to him of Manasseh, Adnah, and Jozebad, and Elihu, and Zilethai, captains of thousands that were of Manasseh. 21 And they helped David against the band of rovers: for they were all mighty men of valor, and were captains in the host. 22 For from day to day men came to David to help him, until there was a great host, like the host of God.

When he (David) came with the Philistines against Saul (v. 19). A full account of what is here mentioned is given in 1S 29. See that reference for our notes regarding it. It was upon that occasion that some of the tribe of Manasseh united with David. It was a timely addition to David's forces, because he fought a battle against the Amalekites immediately afterward.

Captains of thousands (v. 20). This evidently refers to positions these defectors to David had with the tribe of Manasseh; but there is no statement here that they brought their 'thousands' with them to David's cause. Nevertheless, the death of Saul that followed very quickly very likely afforded an opportunity for adding many thousands to David's army.

They helped David against the band of rovers (v. 21). This band of rovers was that of the Amalekites who had plundered Ziklag during David's trip with the Philistines to mount Gilboa. See our commentary on 1S chapter 30 for a full discussion of that Amalekite raid on Ziklag and David's victory over them afterwards.

Until there was a great host, like the host of God (v. 22). This is a reference to the ultimate rally of all Israel to the kingship of David and should not be understood as applicable to the period of David's long contest against Saul.

The remaining verses of this chapter leap forward seven years and a half to the crowning of David as king over all Israel, completely ignoring his seven and a half years as king in Hebron.

The Establishment of David as King of All Israel

Verses 23-40, And these are the numbers of the heads of them that were armed for war, who came to David to Hebron, to turn the kingdom of Saul to him, according to the word of Jehovah. 24 The children of Judah that bare shield and spear were six thousand and eight hundred, armed for war. 25 Of the childen of Simeon, mighty men of valor for the war, seven thousand and one hundred. 26 Of the children of Levi four thousand and six hundred. 27 And Jehoiada was the leader of the house of Aaron; and with him were three thousand and seven hundred, 28 and Zadok, a young man mighty of valor, and of his father's house twenty and two captains. 29 And of the children of Benjamin, the brethren of Saul, three thousand:

for hitherto the greater part of them had kept their allegiance to the house of Saul. 30 And of the children of Ephraim twenty thousand and eight hundred, mighty men of valor, famous in their fathers' houses. 31 And of the half-tribe of Manasseh eighteen thousand who were mentioned by name, to come and make David king. 32 And of the children of Issachar, men that had understanding of the times, to know what Israel ought to do, the heads of them were two hundred; and all their brethren were at their commandment. 33 Of Zebulun, such as were able to go out in the host, that could set the battle in array, with all manner of instruments of war, and that could order the battle array, and were not of double heart. 34 And of Naphtali a thousand captains, and with them with shield and spear thirty and seven thousand. 35 And of the Danites that could set the battle in array, twenty and eight thousand and six hundred. 36 And of Asher, such as were able to go out in the host, that could set the battle in array, forty thousand. 37 And on the other side of the Jordan, of the Reubenites, and the Gadites, and of the half-tribe of Manasseh, with all manner of instruments of war for the battle, a hundred and twenty thousand.

38 All these, being men of war, that could order the battle array, came with a perfect heart to Hebron, to make David king over all Israel: and all the rest also of Israel were of one heart to make David king. 39 And they were there with David three days, eating and drinking; for their brethren had made preparations for them. 40 Moreover they that were nigh unto them, even as far as Issachar and Zebulun and Naphtali, brought bread on asses, and on camels, and on mules, and on oxen, victuals of meal, cakes

of figs, and clusters of raisins, and wine, and oil, and oxen, and sheep in abundance: for there was joy in Israel.

Critical writers, lacking any real reason to press their denials regarding the authenticity of Chronicles, seize upon the numbers of the armed men coming to Hebron to make David king, declaring them to be unreaonable, exaggerated, "magnified,"[6] unhistorical, inaccurate, etc. To all such allegations, there is one single word: ***NONSENSE!*** The conclusion announced by Curtis (Madsen) that, "Our chapter (this one) has no real historical worth,"[7] betrays the bias and essential ignorance of all such allegations. Curtis pointed out that the numbers given here in verses 23-40 come to a sum total of 339,600 men. There is nothing whatever suspicious, unreasonable, or difficult in the coming of such a crowd to Hebron for the coronatin of King David.

There are a number of historical references to the Jewish Passover, held every year in Jerusalem, indicating that in excess of 60,000 lambs were often slain at each celebration of the Passover; and there is one citation in which over 250,000 lambs were killed at the Passover.[8] Counting ten persons for each lamb, as prescribed in Exodus, indicates that crowds in Jerusalem were frequently in excess of half a million in number; and that in some instances, crowds of over a

---

[6] ICC, op. cit., p. 203.
[7] Ibid., p. 194.
[8] ISBE, Vol. 5. p. 2257.

million came to the Holy City. In this light, there is every reason to hold the numbers given here as absolutely accurate, nor should any Christian allow some unbelieving enemy of God's word to cast any doubt whatever upon them.

XXX

CHAPTER 13

David's First Attempt to Bring the Ark to Jerusalem

*Verses 1-14, And David consulted with the captains
of thousands and of hundreds, even with every leader. 2
And David said unto all the assembly of Israel, If it seem
good unto you, and if it be of Jehovah our God, let us send
abroad unto our brethren everywhere that are left in all the
land of Israel, with whom the priests and Levites are in
their cities that have suburbs, that they may gather
themselves unto us; 3 and let us bring again the ark of our
God to us: for we sought not unto it in the days of Saul. 4
And all the assembly said that they would do so; for the
thing was right in the eyes of all the people. 5 So David
assembled all Israel together, from the Shihor the brook of
Egypt even unto the entrance of Hamath, to bring the ark
of God from Kiriath-jearim. 6 And David went up, and all
Israel, to Baalah, that is, to Kiriath-jearim, which belonged
to Judah, to bring up thence the ark of God Jehovah that
sitteth above the cherubim, that is called by the Name. 7
And they carried the ark of God upon a new cart, and
brought it out of the house of Abinadab: and Uzza and
Ahio drove the cart. 8 And David and all Israel played
before God with all their might, even with songs, and with
harps, and with psalteries, and with timbrels, and with
cymbals, and with trumpets.*

*9 And when they came to the threshing floor of
Chidon, Uzza put forth his hand to hold the ark; for the
oxen stumbled. 10 And the anger of Jehovah was kindled
against Uzza, and he smote him, because he put forth his
hand to the ark; and there he died before God. 11 And
David was displeased, because Jehovah had broken forth*

against Uzza: and he called that place Perez-uzza, unto this day. 12 And David was afraid of God that day, saying, How shall I bring the ark of God home to me? 13 So David removed not the ark unto him into the city of David, but carried it aside into the house of Obed-edom the Gittite. 14 And the ark of God remained with the family of Obed-edom in his house three months: and Jehovah blessed the house of Obed-edom, and all that he had.

Second Samuel is parallel with this chapter in 6:11. See Vol. 4 of our commentaries on the historical books (2 Samuel), pp. 67-73, for comments on the events recorded here.

XXX

CHAPTER 14

David Builds Himself a Cedar House, Takes More Wives and Concubines, and Defeats the Philistines Twice

Verses 1-17, And Hiram king of Tyre sent messengers to David, and cedar trees, and masons, and carpenters, to build him a house. 2 And David perceived that Jehovah had established him king over Israel; for his kingdom was exalted on high, for his people Israel's sake.

3 And David took more wives at Jerusalem; and David begat more sons and daughters. 4 And these are the names of the children whom he had in Jerusalem: Shammua, and Shobab, Nathan, and Solomon, 5 and Ibhar, and Elishua, and Elpelet, 6 and Nogah, and Nepheg, and Japhia, 7 and Elishama, and Beeliada, and Eliphelet.

8 And when the Philistines heard that David was anointed king over all Israel, all the Philistines went up to seek David: and David heard of it, and went out against them. 9 Now the Philistines had come and made a raid in the valley of Rephaim. 10 And David inquired of God, Shall I go up against the Philistines? and wilt thou deliver them into my hand? And Jehovah said unto him, Go up; for I will deliver them into thy hand. 11 So they came up to Baal-perazim, and David smote them there; and David said, God hath broken mine enemies by my hand, like a breach of waters. Therefore they called the name of that place Baal-perazim. 12 And they left their gods there; and David gave commandment, and they were burned with fire.

13 And the Philistines yet again made a raid in the valley. 14 And David inquired again of God; and God said unto him, Thou shalt not go up after them: turn away from

them, and come upon them over against the mulberry trees. 15 And it shall be, that when thou hearest the sound of marching in the tops of the mulberry trees, that then thou shalt go out to battle; for God is gone out before thee to smite the host of the Philistines. 16 And David did as God commanded him: and they smote the host of the Philistines from Gibeon even to Gezer. 17 And the fame of David went out into all lands; and Jehovah brought the fear of him upon all nations.

Here also we have a chapter exactly parallel with 2 Samuel 5:11-25, where our commentary on these events is found on pp. 59-65, and where the slight and unimportant variations are also noted.

For his people Israel's sake (v. 2). David's life, like that of all mortals, was marred by many sins and mistakes; and this significant phrase indicates that David fully realized that God's blessings upon him were not for David's sake, but for the sake of God's people and the purpose of salvation for all men that was destined in the purpose of God to come through Israel.

Like a breach of waters (v. 11). The RSV renders this ambiguous phrase, ***like a bursting flood***.

In spite of the fact that David's notorious sins against Bathsheba and Uriah are not mentioned here, there is no effort whatever to conceal his multiplying unto himself wives and concubines specifically contrary to the Law of God.

XXX

CHAPTER 15

The Ark of God Brought to Jerusalem According to the Mosaic Law

Verses 1-15, And David made him houses in the city of David; and he prepared a place for the ark of God, and pitched for it a tent. 2 Then David said, None ought to carry the ark of God but the Levites: for them hath Jehovah chosen to carry the ark of God, and to minister unto him for ever. 3 And David assembled all Israel at Jerusalem, to bring up the ark of Jehovah unto its place, which he had prepared for it. 4 And David gathered together the sons of Aaron, and the Levites: 5 of the sons of Kohath, Uriel the chief, and his brethren a hundred and twenty; 6 of the sons of Merari, Asaiah the chief, and his brethren two hundred and twenty; 7 of the sons of Gershom, Joel the chief, and his brethren a hundred and thirty; 8 of the sons of Elizaphan, Shemaiah the chief, and his brethren two hundred; 9 of the sons of Hebron, Eliel the chief, and his brethren fourscore; 10 of the sons of Uziel, Amminadab the chief, and his brethren a hundred and twelve. 11 And David called for Zadok, and Abiathar the priests, and for the Levites, for Uriel, Asaiah, and Joel, Shemaiah, and Eliel, and Amminadab, 12 and said unto them, Ye are the heads of the fathers' houses of the Levites: sanctify yourselves, both ye and your brethren. that ye may bring up the ark of Jehovah the God of Israel, unto the place that I have prepared for it. 13 For because ye bare it not at the first, Jehovah our God made a breach upon us, for we sought him not according to the ordinance. 14 So the priests and the Levites sanctified themselves to bring up the ark of Jehovah, the God of Israel. 15 And the children of

the Levites bare the ark of God upon their shoulders with the staves thereon, as Moses commanded according to the word of Jehovah.

None ought to carry the ark of God except the Levites (v. 2). "This indicates that the severe lesson evident in the death of Uzzah had been earnestly laid to heart by David, and that he was extremely anxious to be more careful in observing the Law of God."[1]

Right here we have the certain, undeniable proof of the long prior existence of the Mosaic Law, which, in essence was the Constitution of the nation of Israel. The critical community has no recourse whatever against this chapter except to declare it fraudulent. But King David's careful observance in these verses of the directions laid down in the Mosaic books of Exodus, Leviticus and Numbers speaks in tones of thunder of the antiquity, authority and genuineness of the Mosaic Books, commonly called the Pentateuch.

Because ye bare it not at first, Jehovah made a breach upon us, for we sought him not according to the ordinance (v. 13). David did not here plead ignorance of the Mosaic Law, but his violation of its ordinances. The authentic record of this chapter removes for ever any doubt of the authenticty of the Books of Moses. The regulations mentioned here had existed throughout the entire history of Israel, from the times of the Exodus; and they were carefully observed during the wilderness wanderings and by those who carried the ark

---

[1] PC, Vol. 6a, p. 231.

during the Conquest under Joshua, and therefore had been universally known throughout Israel for at least four hundred years prior to the times of David.

It is also true that the regulation regarding "the place where God recorded his name," designated as the one and only authentic place of worship, was known throughout that whole period. The three annual pilgrimages to Jerusalem for the great festivals of Passover, Pentecost, and Tabernacles indicate that all Israel understood this.

The Levites Appoint Singers and Instrumentalists

Verses 16-24, And David spake to the chief of the Levites to appoint their brethren the singers, with instruments of music, psalteries, and harps, and cymbals, sounding aloud, and lifting up the voice with joy. 17 So the Levites appointed Heman the son of Joel; and of his brethren, Asaph the son of Berechiah; and of the sons of Merari, their brethren, Ethan the son of Kushaia; 18 and with them their brethren of the second degree, Zechariah, Ben, and Jaaziel, and Unni, Eliab, and Benaiah, and Maaseiah, and Mattithiah, and Eliphelehu, and Mikneiah, and Obed-edom, and Jeiel, the doorkeeprs. 19 So the singers, Heman, Asaph, and Ethan were appointed with cymbals of brass to sound aloud; 20 And Zechariah, and Aziel, and Shemiramoth, and Jehiel, and Unni, and Eliab, and Maaseiah, and Benaiah, with psalteries set to Alamoth; 21 and Mattithiah, and Eliphelehu, and Mikneiah, and Obed-edom, and Jeiel, and Azaziah, with harps set to the Sheminith, to lead. 22 And Chenaniah,

chief of the Levites, was over the song: he instructed about the song, because he was skilful. 23 And Berechiah, and Elkanah were doorkeepers for the ark. 24 And Shebaniah, and Joshaphat, and Nethanel, and Amasai, and Zechariah, and Benaiah, and Eliezer, the priests, did blow the trumpets before the ark of God; and Obed-edom and Jehiah were doorkeepers for the ark.

The psalteries set on Alamoth ... the harps set on Sheminith (vv. 20,21). It is not definitely known just what these instructions indicated.

The detailed description here of the ceremonies that accompanied David's bringing the ark to Jerusalem was the Chronicler's way of emphasizing the importance of that event. "The bringing of the ark into Jerusalem brought about a permanent centralization of the religion of Israel within Jerusalem."[2]

The Ark Enters Jerusalem

Verses 25-28, So David, and the elders of Israel, and the captains over thousands, went to bring up the ark of the covenant of Jehovah out of the house of Obed-edom with joy. 26 And it came to pass, when God helped the Levites that bare the ark of the covenant of Jehovah, that they sacrificed seven bullocks and seven rams. 27 And David was clothed with a robe of fine linen, and all the Levites that bare the ark, and the singers, and Chenaniah the master of the song with the singers: and David had

---

[2] WYC, p. 379.

upon him an ephod of linen. 28 Thus all Israel brought up the ark of the covenant of Jehovah with shouting, and sound of the cornet, and with trumpets, and with cymbals, sounding aloud with psalteries and harps.

Michal, Saul's Daughter, Despises David

Verse 29, And it came to pass, as the ark of the covenant of Jehovah came to the city of David, that Michal the daughter of Saul looked out at the window, and saw king David dancing and playing; and she despised him in her heart.

We have written several pages regarding this sad episode in our Commentary on 2 Samuel, pp. 75-77. Some may be surprised that we find many reasons to sympathize with the lonely, mistreated daughter of Saul. Also, this writer seriously questions the propriety of David's actions in dancing before the ark without his breeches.

We have continued to limit our comments on much of the material in Chronicles; because, important as it was to the participants, the ultimate significance of the detailed names and ceremonies outlined here is limited indeed.

XXX

CHAPTER 16

The Ark Placed in the Tent Prepared for it; David Appoints Ministers to Serve Before the Ark, and Delivers An Appropriate Psalm to Asaph

The Ark Brought Into Jerusalem

Verses 1-3. And they brought in the ark of God, and set it in the midst of the tent that David had prepared for it: and they offered burnt-offerings and peace-offerings before God. 2 And when David had made an end of offering the burnt-offerings and the peace-offerings, he blessed the people in the name of Jehovah. 3 And he dealt to every one of Israel, both man and woman, to every one a loaf of bread, a portion of flesh, and a cake of raisins.

These verses actually belong to the record of bringing the ark into Jerusalem in the previous chapter. "They make it clear that the sacrifices were presented by the whole community of Israel with the Levitical priests performing their proper functions. David appears here, not as a priest, but as the king who supervised the proper activities of worship."[1]

Levites Appointed to Minister Before the Ark

Verses 4-6, And he appointed certain of the Levites to minister before the ark of Jehovah, the God of Israel: 5 Asaph the chief, and second to him Zechariah, Jeiel, and Shemiramoth. and Jehiel, and Mattithai, and Eliab, and

---

[1] BBC, Vol. 3, p. 335.

Benaiah, and Obed-edom, and Jeiel, with psalteries, and with harps; and Asaph with cymbals, sounding aloud; 6 and Benaiah and Jahaziel the priests with trumpets continually, before the ark of the covenant of God.

It is not altogether clear just exactly what some of these appointments included; but, of course, the persons receiving these appointments and instructions understood them and carried out their duties as instructed. It is very significant that David was diligent to set up all of these provisions for establishing on a permanent basis the worship of God in Jerusalem.

David Establishes Regular Worship in Jerusalem

Verse 7, ***Then on that Day delivered first this psalm to thank the Lord into the hand of Asaph and his brethren (AV).***

We have, in this one verse, returned to the rendition in the Authorized Version, as that version seems better to convey the real meaning.

Barker gave the meaning of this verse as follows: "On that day did David first commit to the hand of Asaph and his brethren to render praises to Jehovah; i. e., after the following manner and words. The word ***first*** marks the solemn establishment of set public worship in the metropolis."[2]

Payne agreed with this meaning, rendering the

---

[2] PC, Vol. 6a, p. 247.

first clause here, "***David delivered first this Psalm.***"[3] He added that, "The following model song (psalm) that David provided them consists, with slight modifications, of Psalm 105:1-15, Psalm 96, and Psalm 106:1,47,48. All three Psalms are listed anonymously in the Psalter, but upon the basis of David's use of them here, it would appear that David was indeed the author of all three."[4]

The Model Psalm Delivered by David to Asaph
Verses 8-36

8 O give thanks unto Jehovah, call upon his name;
Make known his doings among the peoples.
9 Sing unto him, sing praises unto him;
Talk ye of all his marvelous works.
10 Glory be in his holy name;
Let the heart of them rejoice that seeketh Jehovah.
11 Seek ye Jehovah and his strength;
Seek his face evermore.
12 Remember his marvelous works that he hath done,
His wonders, and the judgments of his mouth,
13 O ye seed of Israel his servant,
Ye children of Jacob, his chosen ones.
14 He is Jehovah our God;
His judgments are in all the earth.
15 Remember his covenant for ever,
The word which he commanded to a thousand

---

[3] WYC, p. 380.
[4] Ibid.

generations,
16 The covenant which he made with Abraham,
And his oaths unto Isaac,
17 And confirmed the same unto Jacob for
a statute,
To Israel for an everlasting covenant,
18 Saying, Unto thee I give the land of Canaan,
The lot of your inheritance;
19 When ye were but a few men in number,
Yea, very few, and sojourners in it:
20 And they went about from nation to nation,
And from one kingdom to another people.
21 He suffered no man to do them wrong;
Yea, he reproved kings for their sakes,
22 Saying, Touch not mine anointed ones,
And do my prophets no harm.
23 Sing unto Jehovah, all the earth;
Show forth his salvation from day to day.
24 Declare his glory among the nations,
His marvelous works among all the peoples.
25 For great is Jehovah, and greatly to be praised:
He also is to be feared above all gods,
26 For all the gods of the peoples are idols:
But Jehovah made the heavens.
27 Honor and majesty are before him:
Strength and gladness are in his place.
28 Ascribe unto Jehovah, ye kindred of the peoples,
Ascribe unto Jehovah glory and strength;
29 Ascribe unto Jehovah the glory due unto his
name:
Bring an offering, and come before him;

Worship Jehovah in holy array.
30 Tremble before him, all the earth:
The world also is established that it cannot be moved.
31 Let the heavens be glad, and let the earth rejoice;
And let them say among the nations, Jehovah reigneth.
32 Let the sea roar, and the fulness thereof;
Let the fields exult, and all that is therein;
33 Then let the trees of the wood sing for joy before Jehovah;
For he cometh to judge the earth.
34 O give thanks unto Jehovah; for he is good;
For his lovingkindness endureth for ever.
35 And say ye, Save us, O God of our salvation,
And gather us together and deliver us from the nations,
To give thanks unto thy holy name,
And to triumph in thy praise.
36 Blessed be Jehovah, the God of Israel, from everlasting even to everlasting.

And all the people said, Amen, and praised Jehovah.

Verses 8-22 correspond almost exactly with Psalm 105:1-15; and our comments are found on pages 255-259 of our Commentary on Pslams II.

Verses 23-33 correspond almost exactly with Pslam 96 in its entirety. Our full comments on that Psalm are in Psalms II, pp. 193-200.

The concluding verses of the Model Psalm are found in Psalm 106:1,47 & 48. Our comments on Psalm 106 are found in our Commentary on Psalms II, pp. 267-279.

A Permanent Worship Set up in Jerusalem

Verses 37-38, So he left there, before the ark of the covenant of Jehovah, Asaph and his brethren to minister before the ark continually, as every day's work required; 38 and Obed-edom, with their brethren, threescore and eight; Obed-edom also the son of Jeduthun and Hosah to be doorkeepers.

"These verses reveal that a permanent ministry and choir were established in Jerusalem for the purpose of carrying forward the worship of God continually on a regular schedule, an achievement hitherto unattainable."[5]

Tabernacle and Ark, at this Time, Separated

Verses 39-43, And Zadok the priest, and his brethren the priests, before the tabernacle of Jehovah in the high place that was at Gibeon, 40 to offer burnt-offerings unto Jehovah upon the altar of burnt-offerings continually morning and evening, even according to all that is written in the law of Jehovah, which he commanded unto Israel; 41 and with them Haman and Jeduthun, and the rest that

---

[5] PC, op. cit., p. 248.

were chosen, who were mentioned by name, to give thanks to Jehovah, because his lovingkindness endureth for ever; 42 and with the Haman and Jeduthun with trumpets and cymbals for those that should sound aloud, and with instruments for the songs of God; and the sons of Jeduhun to be at the gate. 43 And all the people departed every man to his house: and David returned to bless his house.

"It is here brought into prominence that the ark and the tabernacle were in two separate places. The great ordinary sacrifices, including the morning and evening sacrifices as commanded in Exodus 38:2, were now resumed in the tabernacle, 'according to all that is written in the law of the Lord.' "[6]

The significance of what David accomplished here is great indeed; and the Chronicler has provided in verse 39, "An explanation of where the tabernacle had been after it was removed from Nob."[7]

"During the times of the Judges, the tabernacle had been at Shiloh (Joshua 18:1); during the reign of Saul, it was at Nob (1S 21); and it was later at Gibeon (1C 16:39); and later Solomon laid it up in the temple (1K 8:4)."[8]

Of course, the ark belonged in the tabernacle, in the Holy of Holies; and, although David was here unable to bring about the restoration of their true relation to each other, he did set in motion the events

---

6 Ibid.

7 Ibid.

8 D. W. Goodman in NBD, p. 1231.

that would eventually lead to their being together when the temple was erected by Solomon to replace the tabernacle. The purpose of the Chronicler in what is written in these chapters is clear enough. He is telling us how the true worship of God eventually came to be reestablished according to God's original instructions in the Pentateuch. This, of course, is precisely why radical critics pretend to find so much fault with Chronicles.

xxx

CHAPTER 17

God Rejects David's Purpose to Build a Temple But Promises the Messiah Whose Throne Would Last For Ever; David's Prayer of Response

Verses 1-15, And it came to pass, when David dwelt in his house, that David said to Nathan the prophet, Lo, I dwell in a house of cedar, but the ark of the covenant of Jehovah dwelleth under curtains. 2 And Nathan said unto David, Do all that is in thy heart; for God is with thee. 3 And it came to pass the same night, that the word of God came to Nathan, saying, 4 Go and tell David my servant, Thus saith Jehovah. Thou shalt not build me a house to dwell in: 5 for I have not dwelt in a house since the day that I brought up Israel, unto this day, but have gone from tent to tent, and from one tabnernacle to another. 6 In all places wherein I have walked with all Israel, spake I a word with any of the judges of Israel, whom I commanded to be shepherd of my people, saying, Why have ye not built me a house of cedar? 7 Now therefore thus shalt thou say to my servant David, Thus saith Jehovah of hosts, I took thee from the sheepcote, from following the sheep, that thou shouldest be prince over my people Israel: 8 and I have been with thee whithersoever thou hast gone, and have cut off all thine enemies from before thee; and I will make thee a name, like unto the name of the great ones that are in the earth. 9 And I will appoint a place for my people Israel, and will plant them, that they may dwell in their own place, and be moved no more; neither shall the children of wickedness waste them any more, as at the first, 10 and as from the day that I commanded judges to be over my people

Israel; and I will subdue all thine enemies. Moreover I tell thee that Jehovah will build thee a house. 11 And it shall come to pass, when thy days are fulfilled that thou must go to be with thy fathers, that I will set up thy seed after thee, who shall be of thy sons; and I will establish his kingdom. 12 He shall build me a house; and I will establish his throne for ever. 13 I will be his father, and he shall be my son: and I will not take my lovingkindness away from him, as I took it from him that was before thee; 14 but I will settle him in my house and in my kingdom for ever; and his throne shall be established for ever. 15 According to all these words, and according to all this vision, so did Nathan speak unto David.

Second Samuel 7:1-17 is parallel to these fifteen verses; and we have written fourteen pages of comments on them in Vol. 4 (2 Samuel) of the Historical Books in our series of commentaries, pp. 81-94.

The variations in the two accounts are not significant. God's prohibition against David's intention of building God a house was stated in the form of a question in 2 Samuel, but appears here as a positive commandment forbidding it. The meaning is the same either way. The Hebrew method of making a negative statement frequently took the form of a question as in Luke 18:8.

Also, both accounts make it absolutely certain that the passage has no reference whatever to Solomon. This, of course, is disputed. Jacob M. Myers, for example, wrote that, "Verse 11 must not be made to bear too much weight ... it seems to refer only to

Solomon."[1] However, it is impossible to put "too much weight" on verse 11! It thunders the message, found also in the parallel, that the Great One who would build God a house would appear ***after*** (yes, that's the word, ***AFTER***) David's death; and Solomon did not appear after David's decease, but during his lifetime and was co-regent with him for a period. See our extensive comment on this in the parallel.

David's Prayer of Response

Verses 16-27, Then David the king went in, and sat before Jehovah; and said, Who am I, O Jehovah God, and what is my house, that thou hast brought me thus far? 17 And this was a small thing in thine eyes, O God; but thou hast spoken of thy servant's house for a great while to come, and hast regarded me according to the estate of a man of high degree, O Jehovah God. 18 What can David say yet more unto thee concerning the honor which is done to thy servant? for thou knowest thy servant. 19 O Jehovah, for thy servant's sake, and according to thine own heart, hast thou wrought all this greatness, to make known all these great things. 20 O Jehovah, there is none like thee, neither is there any god besides thee, according to all that we have heard with our ears, 21 and what one nation in the earth is like thy people Israel, whom God went to redeem unto himself for a people, to make thee a name by great and terrible things, in driving out nations from before thy people, whom thou redeemedst out of Egypt? 22 For thy

---

[1] AnBi, Chronicles, p. 126.

people Israel didst thou make thine own people for ever; and thou Jehovah becamest their God. 23 And now, O Jehovah, let the word that thou hast spoken concerning thy servant, and concerning his house, be established for ever, and do as thou hast spoken. 24 And let thy name be established and magnified for ever, saying, Jehovah of hosts is the God of Israel, aven a God to Israel: and the house of David thy servant is established before thee. 25 For thou, O my God, hast revealed to thy servant that thou wilt build him a house: therefore hast thy servant found in his heart to pray before thee. 26 And now, O Jehovah, thou art God, and hast promised this good thing unto thy servant: 27 and now it hath pleased thee to bless the house of thy servant, that it may continue for ever before thee: for thou, O Jehovah, hast blessed, and it is blessed for ever.

These verses are parallel to 2 Samuel 7:18-29; and, "The Chronicler followed his source quite closely, with insignificant variations."[2]

We have written three pages of comments on these verses in our Commentary on 2 Samuel, pp. 85-97.

There is a strong likelihood that David, at first, understood that "house" which the Lord said would be built as a reference to the physical temple later erected by Solomon; but there is every reason to believe that David later realized that the promise included the coming of one much Greater than Solomon, that the true temple of God was in heaven, and that God's Israel was in no manner whatever limited to any race of men.

---

[2] Ibid., p. 130

The Messianic promises of the Psalms, especially in many of them that were written by David, abundantly prove this ultimate understanding on David's part.

The critical notion that this text teaches that Solomon would be the builder of that promised "house" is effectively refuted by verse 25, above, in which David made it crystal clear that he understood the builder of that house to be, not Solomon, or any other mortal, but God himself.

xxx

CHAPTER 18

David's God-given Victories of His Enemies

Victory Over the Philistines and the Moabites

Verses 1-2, And after this it came to pass, that David smote the Philistines, and subdued them, and took Gath and its towns out of the hands of the Philistines. 2 And he smote Moab; and the Moabites became servants to David, and brought tribute.

Defeat of the King of Zobab

Verses 3-4, And David smote Hadarezer king of Zobah unto Hamath, as he went to establish his dominion by the river Euphrates. 4 And David took from him a thousand chariots, and seven thousand horsemen, and twenty thousand footmen; and David hocked all the chariot horses, but reserved of them for a hundred chariots.

Defeat of the Syrian Allies of Hadarezer

Verses 5-8, And when the Syrians came to succor Hadarezer king of Zobah, David smote of the Syrians two and twenty thousand men. 6 Then David put garrisons in Syria of Damascus; and the Syrians became servants of David, and brought tribute. And Jehovah gave victory to David whithersoever he went. 7 And David took the shields of gold that were on the servants of Hadarezer, and brought them to Jerusalem. 8 And from Tibhath and from Cun, cities of Hadarezer, David took very much brass, wherewith Solomon made the brazen sea, and the pillars, and the

vessels of brass.

Tolu Accepts the Dominion of David

Verses 9-11, And when Tolu king of Hamath heard that David had smitten all the host of Hadarezer king of Zobah, 10 he sent Hadoram his son to king David, to salute him, and to bless him, because he had fought against Hadarezer and smitten him (for Hadarezer had wars with Tolu); and he had with him all manner of vessels of gold and silver and brass. 11 These also did king David dedicate unto Jehovah, with the silver and the gold that he carried away from all the nations; from Edom, and from Moab, and from the children of Ammon, and from the Philistines, and from Amalek.

Other Victories of David by Abishai

Verses 12-13, Moreover Abishai the son of Zeruiah smote of the Edomites in the Valley of Salt eighteen thousand. 13 And he put garrisons in Edom; and all the Edomites became servants to David. And Jehovah gave victory to David whithersoever he went.

These verses are parallel with 2 Samuel 8:1-14; and we have devoted nine pages to a discussion of these verses in our Commentary on Second Samuel, pp. 99-108. The Chronicler made no mention of David's extreme cruelty to the Moabites; but otherwise there are few variations.

A List of David's Administrators

Verses 14-17, And David reigned over all Israel; and he executed justice and righteousness unto all his people. 15 And Joab the son of Zeruiah was over the host; and Jehoshaphat the son of Ahilud was recorder; 16 and Zadok the son of Ahitub, and Abimelech the son of Abiathar were priests; and Shavsha was scribe; 17 and Benaiah the son of Jehoiada was over the Cherethites and the Pelethites; and the sons of David were chief about the king.

These verses are parallel with 2 Samuel 8:15-18; and we have written five pages of comments on these verses in that commentary, pp. 108-112. Special attention is there devoted to the apparent conflict of v, 17 here with verse 18 in 2 Samuel. It is resolved in the fact that there was an early meaning of the word incorrectly translated 'priest," in 2 Samuel, which was sometimes used for ***administrator,*** which is the office meant in both references.

xxx

CHAPTER 19

Ammonites and Syrians Make War Against David

David's Messengers of Good Will Insulted

Verses 1-5, ***And it came to pass after this, that Nahash the king of the children of Ammon died, and his son reigned in his stead. 2 And David said, I will show kindness unto Hanun the son of Nahash, because his father showed kindness to me. So David sent messengers to comfort him concerning his father. And David's messengers came into the land of the children of Ammon to Hanun, to comfort him. 3 But the princes of the children of Ammon said to Hanun, Thinkest thou that David doth honor thy father, in that he hath sent comforters unto thee? are not his servants come unto thee to search, to overthrow, and to spy out the land? 4 Then Hanun took David's servants, and shaved them, and cut off their garments in the middle, even to their buttocks, and sent them away. 5 Then there went certain persons, and told David how the men were served. And he sent to meet them; for the men were greatly ashamed. And the king said, Tarry at Jericho until your beards be grown, and then return.***

Hanun Prepares for War Against David

Verses 6-9, ***And when the children of Ammon saw that they had made themselves odious to David, Hanun and the children of Ammon sent a thousand talents of silver to hire them chariots and horsemen out of Mesopotamia, and out of Aram-Maacah,and out of Zobah. 7 So they hired them thirty and two thousand chariots, and***

the king of Maacah and his people, who came and encamped before Medeba. And the children of Ammon gathered themselves from their cities, and came to battle. 8 And when David heard of it, he sent Joab, and all the host of the mighty men. 9 And the children of Ammon came out, and put the battle in array at the gate of the city: and the kings that were come were by themselves in the field.

The Initial Defeat of the Ammonites

Verses 10-15, Now when Joab saw that the battle was set against him before and behind, he chose of all the choice men of Israel, and put them in array against the Syrians. 11 And the rest of the people he committed into the hand of his brother Abishai; and they put themselves in array against the children of Ammon. 12 And he said, If the Syrians be too much for me, then thou shalt help me; but if the children of Ammon be too strong for thee, then I will help thee. 13 Be of good courage, and let us play the man for our people, and for the cities of our God: and Jehovah do that which seemeth to him good. 14 So Joab and the people that were with him drew nigh before the Syrians unto the battle; and they fled before him. 15 And when the children of Ammon saw that the Syrians were fled, they likewise fled before Abishai his brother, and entered into the city. Then Joab came to Jerusalem.

The Syrian Allies of Ammon Crushed by David

Verses 16-19, And when the Syrians saw that they were put to the worse before Israel, they sent messengers,

and drew forth the Syrians that were beyond the River, with Shophach the captain of the host of Hadarezer at their head. 17 And it was told David; and he gathered all Israel together, and passed over the Jordan, and came upon them, and set the battle in array against them. So when David had put the battle in array against the Syrians, they fought with him. 18 And the Syrians fled before Israel; and David slew of the Syrians the men of seven thousand chariots, and forty thousand footmen, and killed Shophach the captain of the host. 19 And when the servants of Hadarezer saw that they were put to the worse before Israel, they made peace with David, and served him: neither would the Syrians help the children of Ammon any more.

We have thoroughly discussed these nineteen verses in chapter 10 of 2 Samuel, where they are found parallel to all that is written here. These comments are on pp. 123-132 of our Commentary on Second Samuel. There is nothing further which we wish to add here.

XXX

CHAPTER 20

David's Barbarous Treatment of the Ammonites; More War with the Philistines; More Information Regarding the Giants of Gath

Tragic End of the Siege of Rabbah

Verses 1-3, And it came to pass at the time of the return of the year, at the time when kings go out to battle, that Joab led forth the army, and wasted the country of the children of Ammon, and came and besieged Rabbah. 2 But David tarried at Jerusalem. And Joab smote Rabbah, and overthrew it. And David took the crown of their king from off his head, and found in it the weight of a talent of gold; and there were precious stones in it; and it was set upon David's head: and he brought forth the spoil of the city, exceeding much. 3 And he brought forth the people that were therein, and cut them with saws and harrows of iron, and with axes. And thus did David to all the cities of the children of Ammon. And David and all the people returned to Jerusalem.

These verses are parallel with 2 Samuel 11:1 and 12:26, 30-31; and our comments on what is written here are on pages 135, 163-166. We might add here that this chapter marks a terrible turning point in David's life. Not only is there the matter of his torturing the Ammonites, but his adultery with Bathsheba, and his heartless murder of Uriah the Hittite and seventeen of his fellow-soldiers in a vain effort to hide his sin ---all took place in connection with this siege of Rabbah. The bad days of David's life began right here.

War with the Philistines; More About the Giants

Verses 4-8, And it came to pass after this, that there arose a war at Gezer with the Philistines: the Sibbecai the Hushathite slew Sippai of the sons of the giants; and they were subdued. 5 And there was again war with the Philistines; and Elhanan the son of Jair slew Lahmi the brother of Goliath the Gittite, the staff of whose spear was like a weaver's beam. 6 And there was again war at Gath, where was a man of great stature, whose fingers and toes were four and twenty, six on each hand, and six on each foot; and he also was born unto the giant. 7 And when he defied Israel, Jonathan the son of Shimea David's brother slew him. 8 These were born unto the giant in Gath; and they fell by the hand of David, and by the hand of his servants.

There was not merely one Goliath (or giant); there was an entire family of them; and there is no reason whatever to question the accuracy of what the Chronicler has written here. See our further comments on the Giants of Gath in our commentary on Second Samuel, pp. 302-303. Critical objections to the Chronicler's report here are grounded in their prior hatred of the witness borne in the Chronicles to the authenticity of the Books of Moses. The Chronicler did not "create" this record of several giants; he merely reported the truth.

XXX

CHAPTER 21

David's Numbering the People, the Pestilence, and Purchase of the Site for the Temple

David's Sin in Numbering the people

Verses 1-8, ***And Satan stood up against Israel, and moved David to number Israel. 2 And David said to Joab and to the princes of the people, Go, number Israel from Beersheba even to Dan; and bring me word that I may know the sum of them. 3 And Joab said, Jehovah make his people a hundred times as many as they are: but, my lord the king, are they not all my lord's servants? why doth my lord require this thing? why will he be a cause of guilt unto Israel? 4 Nevertheless the king's word prevailed against Joab. Wherefore Joab departed, and went throughout all Israel, and came to Jerusalem. 5 And Joab gave up the sum of the numbering of the people unto David. And all they of Israel were a thousand thousand and a hundred thousand that drew sword: and Judah was four hundred threescore and ten thousand men that drew sword. 6 But Levi and Benjamin he counted not among them; for the king's word was abominable to Joab. 7 And God was displeased with this thing; therefore he smote Israel. 8 And David said unto God, I have sinned greatly, in that I have done this thing: but now put away, I beseech thee, the iniquity of thy servant; for I have done very foolishly.***

God Offers David a Choice of Three Punishments

Verses 9-17, ***And Jehovah spake unto Gad, David's seer, saying, 10 Go and speak unto David, saying, Thus***

saith Jehovah, I offer thee three things: choose thee one of them, that I may do it unto thee. 11 So Gad came unto David, and said unto him, Thus saith Jehovah, Take which thou wilt: 12 either three years of famine; or three months to be consumed before thy foes, while the sword of thine enemies overtaketh thee; or else three days the sword of Jehovah, even pestilence in the land, and the angel of Jehovah destroying throughout all the borders of Israel. Now therefore consider what answer I shall return to him that sent me. 13 And David said unto Gad, I am in a great strait: let me fall, I pray thee, into the hand of Jehovah; for very great are his mercies: and let me not fall into the hand of man. 14 So Jehovah sent a pestilence upon Israel; and there fell of Israel seventy thousand men. 15 And God sent an angel unto Jerusalem to destroy it: and as he was about to destroy, Jehovah beheld, and he repented of the evil, and said to the destroying angel, It is enough; now stay thy hand. And the angel of Jehovah was standing by the threshing floor of Ornan the Jebusite. 16 And David lifted up his eyes, and saw the angel of Jehovah, standing between earth and heaven, having a drawn sword in his hand stretched out over Jerusalem. Then David and the elders, clothed in sackcloth, fell upon their faces. 17 And David said unto God, Is it not I that commanded the people to be numbered? even I that have sinned and done very wickedly; but these sheep, what have they done? let thy hand, I pray thee, O Jehovah my God, be against me, and against my fathers' house; but not against thy people, that they should be plagued.

The Purchase of the Threshing Floor of Ornan

Verses 18-27, Then the angel of Jehovah commanded Gad to say to David, that David should go up and rear an altar unto Jehovah in the threshing floor of Ornan the Jebusite. 19 And David went up at the saying of Gad, which he spake in the name of Jehovah. 20 And Ornan turned back, and saw the angel; and his four sons that were with him hid themselves. Now Ornan was threshing wheat. 21 And as David came to Ornan, Ornan looked and saw David, and went out of the threshing floor, and bowed himself to David with his face to the ground. 22 Then David said to Ornan, Give me the place of this threshing floor, that I may build thereon an altar unto Jehovah: for the full price shalt thou give it me, that the plague may be stayed from the people. 23 And Ornan said unto David, Take it to thee, and let my lord the king do that which is good in his eyes: lo, I give thee the oxen for burnt-offerings, and the threshing instruments for wood, and the wheat for the meal-offering; I give it all. 24 And king David said to Ornan, Nay but I will verily buy it for the full price; for I will not take that which is thine for Jehovah, nor offer a burnt-offering without cost. 25 So David gave to Ornan for the place six hundred shekels of gold by weight. 26 And David built there an altar unto Jehovah, and offered burnt-offerings and peace-offerings, and called upon Jehovah; and he answered him from heaven by fire upon the altar of burnt-offering. 27 And Jehovah commanded the angel: and he put up his sword again into the sheaf thereof.

David Continues to Sacrifice on the Threshing Floor

Verses 28-30, At that time, when David saw that Jehovah had answered him in the threshing floor of Ornan the Jebusite, then he sacrificed there. 29 For the tabernacle of Jehovah, which Moses made in the wilderness, and the altar of burnt-offering, were at that time in the high place at Gibeon. 30 But David could not go before it because of the sword of the angel of Jehovah.

This chapter is parallel with 2 Samuel 24; and we have written thirteen pages of commentary there, pp. 326-339. The variation regarding the price paid to Ornan is explained.

Keil has explained the significance of the last paragraph here, which is not in 2 Samuel.

God's answering David's sacrifice with fire from heaven taught David that the altar built upon the threshing floor of Ornan had been chosen by the Lord as the place where Israel should always thereafter offer their burnt-offerings and sacrifices.[1]

This explains why David was afraid thereafter to go to the high place at Gibeon. The events of this chapter explain why Solomon's temple was placed at that very location where God had answered David with fire from heaven. A few other variations in the parallels are of no importance.

XXX

---

[1] CFK, Vol. 3b, p. 240

CHAPTER 22

David's Preparation to Build the Temple

Verses 1, Then David said, This is the house of Jehovah God, and this is the altar of burnt-offering for Israel.

Practically all of the rest of First Chronicles is devoted to a discussion of David's extensive preparations to build the temple. There is no parallel elsewhere for what is given in this chapter, aside from obvious references to the Law of Moses, to Joshua and to Nathan's prophecy delivered to David in 2 Samuel 7. This verse indicate's David's decision to have the temple built in Jerusalem, on the site purchased from Ornan the Jebusite.

This was that very place called, "one of the mountains of Moriah," upon which Abraham prepared to offer Isaac as a burnt-offering (Genesis 22:22), as confirmed by our Chronicler in 2C 3:1. "Today it is occupied by the Dome of the Rock Mosque."[1]

David Gathers Material for the Temple's Construction

Verses 2-5, And David commanded to gather together the sojourners that were in the land of Israel; and he set masons to hew wrought stones to build the house of God. 3 And David prepared iron in abundance for the nails for the doors of the gates, and for the couplings; and brass in abundance without weight; 4 and cedar trees

---

[1] BBC, Vol. 3, p. 346.

without number: for the Sidonians and they of Tyre brought cedar trees in abundance to David. 5 And David said, Solomon my son is young and tender, and the house that is to be builded by Jehovah must be exceedingly magnificent, of fame and of glory throughout all countries; I will therefore make preparations for it. So David prepared abundantly before his death.

David commanded to gather together the sojourners (v. 2). These were the aliens, the original Canaanites, whom Israel enslaved, contrary to God's commandments. The complete record of this is found in the first chapter of Judges. See our Vol. 2, of the Historical Books, ***Judges and Ruth,*** pp. 9-22. "Second Samuel 20:24 indicates that David used forced labor."[2]

These verses indicate that David proceeded to gather vast quantities of materials with which the temple would be constructed.

God Did Not Command David to Do This

There can be no doubt whatever that David missed the significant point in the words of God to him through the prophet Nathan (2 Samuel 7), in which it was certainly clear enough that God did not desire the erection of any earthly temple whatever. David understood, of course, that he was commanded not to build it, which by any fair interpretation of the prohibition laid upon David would also have included

---

[2] Ibid.

the extensive preparations which David made to have it done, even commanding it most emphatically to be done by Solomon. And upon the principle that any man does, what he commands others to do, David must be charged with violation of God's commandment in this particular.

The Chronicler, King David, Solomon, all the princes of Israel, and the entire nation nevertheless looked upon this temple as the most wonderful thing that ever happened to Israel. That God indeed allowed it, accomodated to it, used the temple in many ways to further the achievement of God's purpose, even sending a special manifestation of his Eternal Presence to dwell within the Holy of Holies upon the occasion of its dedication ---none of this can be denied; but God's destruction of Solomon's temple, and also his destroying the one constructed by Israel upon their return from captivity, cannot be harmonized with the proposition that the Jewish temple was, in any sense, the complete will of God.

Allowed, tolerated, used by God himself, yes; but it still stands as a thing David conceived, promoted, commanded, planned, prepared for and projected in its entirety. From its conception in the mind of David, and throughout its entire history, the temple, in a sense, similar to pagan temples all over the world, was the conception and project of a mortal human being, not of God.

Furthermore, David was grossly mistaken about that temple's being the "house" that God promised to build for David; and he was also totally in error in his conception that Solomon was the mighty one of his posterity whose throne God would establish for ever.

In this light, the following paragraph must be read as the Chronicler's true and accurate statement of the things David did and said, but not as proof that David was totally correct either in his words or deeds.

David Commands Solomon to Build the Temple

Verses 6-11, Then he called for Solomon his son, and charged him to build a house for Jehovah, the God of Israel. 7 And David said to Solomon his son, As for me, it was in my heart to build a house for the name of Jehovah my God. 8 But the word of Jehovah came to me, saying, Thou hast shed blood abundantly, and hast made great wars: thou shalt not build a house unto my name, because thou hast shed much blood upon the earth in my sight. 9 Behold, a son shall be born to thee, who shall be a man of rest; and I will give him rest from all his enemies round about him; for his name shall be Solomon, and I will give peace and quietness to Israel in his time. 10 He shall build a house for my name; and he shall be my son, and I will be his father; and I will establish the throne of his kingdom over Israel for ever. 11 Now, my son, Jehovah be with thee; and prosper thou, and build the house of Jehovah thy God, as he hath spoken concerning thee.

David charged him (Solomon) to build a house for Jehovah (vv. 6,11). Throughout the Bible, the principle that one actually does what he commands others to do is fully established; and in this command, David went beyond God's word.

Thou hast shed blood abundantly (v. 8). Great significance attaches to this verse. It presupposes that war is sinful, wrong, contrary to God's will. This cannot mean that David's wars were not justified. God commanded his people to fight wars; but here shines the eternal truth that bloodshed is inherently evil, no matter how necessary it may be at times

Behold, a son shall be born unto thee (v. 9). The words used here show that David was referring to the words of God through Nathan (2S 7:12-14). Yes, God promised that son, all right, but David failed to understand what God said about ***WHEN*** that son would be born. It would not happen during David's lifetime, but ***when thou shalt sleep with thy fathers*** (2S 7:12).

Furthermore, the kingdom of that son would be ***established after David*** (2S 7:12); but Solomon's kingdom was established during David's lifetime. "Solomon was made king before David's death (1K 1:32-40; 1C 23:1) ... there was a co-regency of four years."[3]

His name shall be called Solomon (v. 9). We believe this to be a mistranslation, because all scholars agree that the Hebrew word here rendered Solomon is ***peace***, or ***peaceful***; and on the basis that the word Solomon is supposed to mean peaceful, the translators have incorrectly injected the proper name ***Solomon*** into this verse.

---

3 NLBC, p. 489.

Regarding the Name SOLOMON

1. ***For his name shall be Solomon (v. 9)***. It is a mistake to read these words as revealing the name that God himself gave to that Great One who would build David a house. This clause is the word of David, not the word of God. God indeed gave Solomon a name, but that name was Jedidah (2S 12:25). God certainly did not name Solomon twice!

2. The word in the Hebrew text is not Solomon ***(SLMH)***, but peace ***(SLWM)***.[4] There are two different words here; and there is no authority for changing the word ***PEACE*** to ***SOLOMON***. The conviction of this writer is that the passage in 2 Samuel 7 is focussed, not upon Solomon at all, but upon Jesus Christ the Messiah. Certainly the word ***PEACE*** is far more applicable to the Prince of Peace (Isaiah 9:6) than it is to Solomon with his legions of slave-laborers.

3. God did not name David's successor ***Solomon***; Bathsheba did so. "The name corresponds to ***Irenaeus*** in Greek, ***Friedrich*** in German, (***Frederick*** in English), and ***Selim*** in Arabian. The name should be pronounced ***Shillumah***, meaning ***compensation***, because Solomon was given to her (Bathsheba) in the place of a child who had died."[5]

He shall be my son, and I shall be his father (10). This is a direct quotation of 2S 12:14. "It refers to

---

[4] Ibid.

[5] Thomas H. Weir in ***ISBE***, p. 2824.

Christ,"[6] fully in keeping with our interpretation of the entire passage. Solomon, a 'son of God'? Ridiculous! Where, in all the Bible is any passage that supports such a notion as that? He built more pagan temples than any other man in human history.

In this light, we must discern David's mistaken interpretation of God's prophecy through Nathan. Those magnificent messianic passages of the Psalms, written by David under the inspiration of the Holy Spirit, may not have been fully understood, even by David himself, as an apostle stated (1 Peter 1:10-12).

Now my son, ... build the house of Jehovah thy God (v. 11). Thus David, in effect, by his previous preparations, and by direct orders to his son and successor, did the very thing God had prohibited him from doing.

Of course, God forgave David for this misunderstanding and mistake. As a forerunner and type of Messiah himself, David's temple was overruled and utilized by the Lord in the ultimate achievement of the divine purpose of providing salvation to be made available for all men. God allowed it to stand under the old covenant as a type of the true temple of God, namely, the holy Church of Jesus Christ. Such a thing was possible only because the temple incorporated so many features of the tabernacle which it replaced (As conclusively indicated in the Book of Hebrews).

Thus God allowed to stand for the time then present David's mistake regarding the nature of God's

---

[6] WYC, p. 385.

true temple; but over and beyond David's application of God's word through Nathan to the building of Solomon's temple, there still stood, ***and it still stands,*** the immortal prophecy of the Son of God himself.

David's Further Charge to Solomon

Verses 12-16, Only Jehovah give thee discretion and understanding, and give the charge concerning Israel; that so thou mayest keep the law of Jehovah thy God. 13 Then shalt thou prosper, if thou observe to do the statutes and the ordinances which Jehovah charged Moses with concerning Israel: be strong and of good courage; fear not, neither be dismayed. 14 Now, behold, in my affliction I have prepared for the house of Jehovah a hundred thousand talents of gold, and a thousand thousand talents of silver, and of brass and iron without weight; for it is in abundance: timber also and of stone have I prepared; and thou mayest add thereto. 15 Moreover there are workmen with thee in abundance, hewers and workers of stone and timber, and all men that are skilful in every manner of work: 16 of the gold, the silver, and the brass, and the iron, there is no number. Arise and be doing, for Jehovah is with thee.

The significance here is the reference to the Law of God through Moses, a reference to Exodus 20:1, and the direct quotations from Exodus 3:4 and Joshua 1:6-9 and Deuteronomy 31:24, thus providing incontrovertible evidence of the prior existence of the Pentateuch long centuries prior to the discovery of that allegedly 'false document' in the reign of Josiah. No wonder the radical critics hate Chronicles. An example of that hatred is the following.

> This chapter is full of general and exaggerated statements. No statement suggests a trustworthy historian. That David contemplated building a temple is likely, and he might have made some preparations for it; but the Chronicler's description must have been drawn by inference ... assisted by a vivid imagination ... a careless list of such things as happened to occur to the writer.[7]

Regarding the tremendous amounts of gold and silver mentioned here, Elmslie referred to the passage as hyperbole.[8] There is also the question of exactly what constituted a talent in the times of Solomon. "Any accurate calculation of the value of the silver and gold mentioned here is a hopeless task, because of the uncertainy of our data, our uncertain knowledge of the Hebrew weights of money, and our total ignorance of the relative value of those precious metals to the commodities of life."[9]

The Roman historian Pliny, "Wrote that Cyrus in his subjugation of Asia took half a million talents of silver and 34,000 lbs of gold,"[10] a sum not too very far from the immense amount mentioned here.

---

[7] ICC, Chronicles, p. 255.

[8] IB, Vol. 3, p. 420.

[9] PC, Vol. 6b, p. 355.

[10] Ibid., op. cit., p. 356.

David's Command for the Princes of Israel to Aid Solomon

Verses 17-19, David also commanded all the princes of Israel to help Solomon his son, saying, 18 Is not Jehovah your God with you? and hath he not given you rest on every side? for he hath delivered the inhabitants of the land into my hand; and the land is subdued before Jehovah, and before his people. 19 Now set your heart and your soul to seek after Jehovah God, to bring the ark of the covenant of Jehovah, and the holy vessels of God, into the house that is to be built to the name of Jehovah.

XXX

CHAPTER 23

David Prescribes the Offices of the Levites

Three Divisions of the Levites

Verses 1-6, Now David was old and full of days; and he made Solomon his son king over Israel. 2 And he gathered together all the princes of Israel, with the priests and the Levites. 3 And the Levites were numbered from thirty years old and upward: and their number by their polls, man by man, was thirty and eight thousand. 4 Of these, twenty and four thousand were to oversee the work of the house of Jehovah; and six thousand were officers and judges; 5 and four thousand were doorkeepers; and four thousand praised Jehovah with the instruments which I made, said David, to praise therewith. 6 And David divided them into courses according to the sons of Levi: Gershon, Kohath, and Merari.

Now David was old ... and made Solomon his son king over Israel (v. 1). The truth here makes it impossible to receive Nathan's prophecy in 2 Samuel 7 as a primary reference to Solomon. The Great One mentioned there was prophesied to be born after David slept with his fathers. This verse clearly indicates that Solomon enjoyed a co-regency for an unspecified time with David his father.

Levites were numbered from thirty years old and upward (v. 3). David's actions here in numbering the Levites conformed exactly to the instructions of Moses given in Numbers 4:23.

Four thousand praised Jehovah with the

instruments that I (David) made (v. 5). David's actions in this had no prior command of God to justify it. He violated the divine instructions that, "Ye shall not add unto the word which I command you, neither shall ye diminish from it" (Deuteronomy 4:2). David's invention of instruments of music and his introduction of them into the worship of God was specifically condemned by the prophet Amos (5:23, 6:5). We have discussed this in Vol. 1 of our Commentaries on the Minor Prophets, ***Joel, Amos and Jonah***, pp. 163-169, 180-183.

The Sons of Gershon

Verses 7-11, Of the Gershonites: Ladan and Shimei. 8 The sons of Ladan: Jehiel the chief, and Zetham, and Joel, three. 9 The sons of Shimei: Shelomoth, and Haziel, and Haran, three. These were the heads of the fathers' houses of Ladan. 10 And the sons of Shimei: Jahash, and Zina, and Jeush, and Beriah. These four were the sons of Shimei. 11 And Jahash was the chief, and Zizah the second: but Jeush and Beriah had not many sons; therefore they became a fathers' house in one reckoning.

The Sons of Kohath

Verses 12-20, The sons of Kohath: Amram, Izhar, Hebron, and Uzziel, four. 13 The sons of Amram: Aaron and Moses; and Aaron was separated, that he should sanctify the most holy things, he and his sons, for ever, to burn incense before Jehovah, to minister unto him, and to

bless in his name, for ever. 14 But as for Moses the man of God, his sons were named among the tribe of Levi. 15 The sons of Moses: Gershom and Eliezer. 16 The sons of Gershom: Shebuel the chief. 17 And the sons of Eliezer were: Rehabiah the chief; and Eliezer had no other sons; but the sons of Rehabiah were very many. 18 The sons of Izhar: Shelomith the chief. 19 The sons of Hebron: Jeriah the chief, Amariah the second, Jahaziel the third, and Jekameam the fourth. 20 The sons of Uzziel: Micah the chief, and Isshiah the second.

The Sons of Merari

Verses 21-23, ***The sons of Merari: Mahli and Mushi. The sons of Mahli: Eleazar and Kish. 22 And Eleazar died, and had no sons, but daughters only: and their brethren the sons of Kish took them to wife. 23 The sons of Mushi: Mahli, and Eder, and Jeremoth, three.***

The Levitical Heads of Fathers' Houses

Verses 24-32, ***These were the sons of Levi after their fathers' houses, even the heads of the fathers' houses of those of them that were counted, in the number of names by their polls, who did the work of the house of Jehovah, from twenty years old and upward. 25 For David said, Jehovah, the God of Israel, hath given rest unto his people; and he dwelleth in Jerusalem for ever: 26 and also the Levites shall no more have need to carry the tabernacle and all the vessels of it for the sevice thereof. 27 For by the last words of David the sons of Levi were numberd, from twenty***

years old and upward. 28 For their office was to wait on the sons of Aaron for the service of the house of Jehovah, in the courts, and in the chambers, and in the purifying of all holy things, even the work of the service of the house of God; 29 for the showbread also, and for the fine flour for the meal-offering, whether of unleavened wafers, or of that which is baked in the pan, or of that which is soaked, and for all manner of measure and size; 30 and to stand every morning to thank and praise Jehovah, and likewise at even; 31 and to offer all burnt-offerings unto Jehovah, on the sabbaths, on the new moons, and on the set feasts, in number according to the ordinances concerning them, continually before Jehovah; 32 and that they should keep the charge of the tent of meeting, and the charge of the holy place, and the charge of the sons of Aaron their brethren, for the service of the house of Jehovah.

The Gargantuan significance of this chapter lies in the proof that during the life of David king of Israel, all of the extensive instructions and details written in the Book of Moses (The Pentateuch) were well known in Israel. As any good reference Bible will demonstrate, there is hardly a line in this chapter that does not tie in specifically with instructions in the Pentateuch. Furthermore, all of these instructions (except David's use of instruments of music) were ***ancient***, dating back to the times of Moses. They were not ***invented*** by David but ***honored*** by him.

Here is the complete frustration of the efforts of radical critics to late-date the Pentateuch. And, as for the allegation that some late Chronicler falsely attributed all these words and activities to King David, such a theory is just as unreasonable and impossible of acceptance as would be the allegation of some alleged 'scholar' someone named Smith or Brown discovered America instead of Christopher Columbus.

xxx

CHAPTER 24

Courses of the Sons of Aaron and Other Levites

How Their Relative Positions Were Chosen

***Verses 1-6,** And the courses of the sons of Aaron
were these. The sons of Aaron: Nadab and Abihu, Eleazar
and Ithamar. 2 But Nadab and Abihu died before their
father, and had no children: therefore Eleazar and Ithamar
executed the priest's office. 3 And David with Zadok of the
sons of Eleazar, and Ahimelech of the sons of Ithamar,
divided them according to their ordering in the service. 4
And there were more chief men found of the sons of Eleazar
than of the sons of Ithamar; and thus were they divided: of
the sons of Eleazar there were sixteen, heads of fathers'
houses, and of the sons of Ithamar, according to their
fathers' houses, eight. 5 Thus were they divided by lot, one
sort with another; for there were princes of the sanctuary,
and princes of God, both of the sons of Eleazar, and of the
sons of Ithamar. 6 And Shemiah the son of Nethanel the
scribe, who was of the Levites, wrote them in the presence
of the king, and the princes, and Zadok the priest, and
Ahimelech the son of Abiathar, and the heads of the
fathers' houses of the priests and of the Levites; one fathers'
house being taken for Eleazar, and one taken for Ithamar.*

Due to the fact that many thousands of the Levites were eligible to participate in the temple services, it was necessary that some systematic manner of determining the order in which they would serve was required. One must be impressed with the manner of David's making such a determination by lot, duly witnessed by all parties concerned.

Princes of the sanctuary, and princes of God (v. 5). "The distinction between these is not clear."[1] Curtis (Madsen) wrote that, "The two terms are probably synonymous."[2]

Assignment of the Sons of Aaron

Verses 7-19, Now the first lot came forth to Jehoiarib, the second to Jedaiah, 8 the third to Harim, the fourth to Seorim, 9 the fifth to Malchijah, the sixth to Mijamin, 10 the seventh to Hakkoz, the eighth to Abijah, 11 the ninth to Jeshua, the tenth to Shecaniah, 12 the eleventh to Eiashib, the twelfth to Jakim, 13 the thirteenth to Huppah, the fourteenth to Jeshebeab, 14 the fifteenth to Bilgah, the sixteenth to Immer, 15 the seventeenth to Hezir, the eighteenth to Hapizzer, 16 the nineteenth to Pethahiah, the twentieth to Jehezkel, 17 the one and twentieth to Jachin, the two and twentieth to Gamul, 18 the three and twentieth to Delaiah, the four and twentieth to Maaziah. 19 This was the ordering of them in their service, to come into the house of Jehovah according to the ordinance given unto them by Aaron their father, as Jehovah, the God of Israel, had commanded him.

Ordering of the Other Levites

Verses 20-31, And of the rest of the sons of Levi: of

---

1 PC, Vol. 6a, p. 389.

2 ICC, *Chronicles*, p. 270.

the sons of Amram, Shubael; of the sons of Shubael, Jehdeiah. 21 Of Rehabiah: of the sons of Rehabiah, Isshiah the chief. 22 Of the Izharites, Shelomoth; of the sons of Shelomoth, Jahath. 23 And of the sons of Hebron: Jeriah the chief, Amariah the second, Jahaziel the third, Jekemeam the fourth. 24 The sons of Uzziel, Micah; of the sons of Micah, Shamir. 25 The brother of Micah, Isshiah; of the sons of Isshiah, Zechariah. 26 The sons of Merari: Mahli and Mushi; the sons of Jaaziah, Beno. The sons of Merari: of Jaaziah, Beno and Shoham, and Zaccri, and Ibri. 28 Of Mahli: Eleazar, who had no sons. 29 Of Kish; the sons of Kish: Jerahmeel. 30 And the sons of Mushi: Mahli, and Eder, and Jerimoth. These were the sons of the Levites after their fathers' houses. 31 These likewise cast lots even as their brethren the sons of Aaron in the presence of David the king, and Zadok, and Ahimelech, and the heads of the fathers' houses of the priests and of the Levites; the fathers' houses of the chief even as those of his younger brother.

"It should be remembered that these lists of names represent families rather than individuals, and that a number of these families continued into NT times (for example, Zacharias was of the line of Abijah, Luke 1:5)."[3]

Interesting as the omission is, we can give no reason for the omission of the family of Gershon.

The variations in these lists is of no importance. "Some of these courses died out, or had to be

---

[3] NLBC, p. 400.

consolidated with others; and new ones were formed to take their place. At the time of the return from exile, 538 BC, only four of these courses were operative."[4]

Any intelligent criticism of any of these lists would therefore have to begin with the exact date of it.

xxx

[4] WYC, p. 386.

CHAPTER 25

David's Instrumentalists and Singers

The Principal Familes of Them that Served

Verses 1-8, Moreover David and the captains of the host set apart for the service certain of the sons of Asaph, and of Heman, and of Jeduthun, who should prophesy with harps, with psalteries, and with cymbals: and the number of them that did the work according to their service was: 2
of the sons of Asaph: Zaccur, and Joseph, and Nethaniah, and Asharelah, the sons of Asaph, under the hand of Asaph, who prophesied after the order of the king. 3 Of
Jeduthun; the sons of Jeduthun: Gedaliah, and Zeri, and Jeshaiah, Hashabiah, and Mattithiah, six, under the hands of their father Jeduthun with the harp, who prophesied in giving thanks and praising Jehovah. 4 Of Heman; the sons
of Heman: Bukkiah, Mattaniah, Uzziel, Shebuel, and Jerimoth, Hananiah, Hanani, Eliathah, Giddalti, and Romamtiezer, Joshbekashah, Mallothi, Hothir, Mahazioth.
5 All these were the sons of Heman the king's seer in the words of God, to lift up the horn. And God gave to Heman fourteen sons and three daughters. 6 All these were under
the hands of their father for song in the house of Jehovah, with cymbals, psalteries, and harps, for the service of the house of God; Asaph, Jeduthun, and Heman being under the order of the king. 7 And the number of them, with their
brethren, that were instructed in singing unto Jehovah, even all that were skilful, was two hundred fourscore and eight. 8 And they cast lots for their officers, all alike, as
well the small as the great, the teacher as the scholar.

Who should prophesy with harps, psalteries, etc (v.1). The Good News Bible probably has the correct meaning here: "They were to proclaim God's messages accompanied by the music of harps and cymbals."

The Casting of Lots for Their Positions

Verses 9-31, Now the first lot came forth to Asaph for Joseph: the second to Gedaliah; he and his brethren and sons were twelve: 10 the third to Zaccur, his sons and his brethren, twelve: 11 the fourth to Izri, his sons and his brethren, twelve: 12 the fifth to Nethaniah, his sons and his brethren, twelve: 13 the sixth to Bukkiah, his sons and his brethren, twelve: 14 the seventh to Jesharelah, his sons and his brethren, twelve: 15 the eighth to Leshaiah, his sons and his brethren, twelve: 16 the ninth to Mattaniah, his sons and his brethren, twelve: 17 the tenth to Shimei, his sons and his brethren, twelve: 18 the eleventh to Azarel, his sons and his brethren, twelve: 19 the twelfth to Hashabiah, his sons and his brethren, twelve: 20 for the thirteenth, Shubael, his sons and his brethren twelve: 21 for the fourteenth, Mattithiah, his sons and his brethren, twelve: 22 for the fifteenth to Jeremoth, his sons and his brethren, twelve: 23 for the sixteenth to Hananiah, his sons and his brethren, twelve: 24 for the seventeenth to Joshbekashah, his sons and his brethren, twelve: 25 and for the eighteenth to Hanani, his sons and his brethren twelve: 26 and for the nineteenth to Mallothi, his sons and his brethren, twelve: 27 for the twentieth to Eliathah. his sons and his brethren, twelve: 28 for the one and twentieth to Hothir, his sons and his brethren, twelve: 29 for the two

and twentieth to Giddalti, his sons and his brethren, twelve: 30 for the three and twentieth to Mahazioth, his sons and his brethren, twelve: 31 for the four and twentieth to Romantiezer, his sons and his brethren, twelve.

Regarding David's injecting the use of mechanical instruments of music, and other noise-makers, into God's worship, see our notes on the preceding chapters 23 and 24.

xxx

CHAPTER 26

The Doorkeepers, Treasurers and Civil Officers

Distinguished Families of the Doorkeepers

***Verses 1-11,** For the courses of the doorkeepers: of the Korahites, Meshelemiah the son of Kore, of the sons of Asaph. 2 And Meshelemiah had sons: Zechariah the first-born, Jediael the second, Zebadiah the third, Jathniel the fourth, 3 Elam the fifth, Jehohanan the sixth, Eliehoenai the seventh. 4 And Obed-edom had sons: Shemaiah the first-born, Jehozabad the second, Joah the third, and Sacar the fourth, and Nethanel the fifth, 5 Ammiel the sixth, Issachar the seventh, Peullethai the eighth; for God blessed him. 6 Also unto Shemaiah his son, were sons born, that ruled over the house of their father; for they were mighty men of valor. 7 The sons of Shemaiah: Othni, and Rephael, and Obed, Elzabad, whose brethren were valiant men, Elihu, and Semachiah. 8 All these were of the sons of Obed-edom: they and their sons and their brethren, able men in strength for the service; threescore and two of Obed-edom. 9 And Meshelemiah had sons and brethren, valiant men, eighteen. 10 Also Hosah, of the children of Merari, had sons: Shimri the chief (for though he was not the first-born, yet his father made him chief), 11 Hilkiah the second, Tebaliah the third, Zechariah the fourth: all the sons and brethren of Hosah were thirteen.*

Their Assignment by Casting Lots

***Verses 12-19,** Of these were the courses of the doorkeepers, even of the chief men, having offices like their* *brethren, to minister in the house of Jehovah. 13 And they cast lots, as well the small as the great, according to their fathers' houses, for every gate. 14 And the lot eastward fell to Shelemiah. Then for Zechariah his son, a discreet counsellor, they cast lots; and his lot came out northward. 15 To Obed-edom southward; and to his sons the store-house. 16 To Shuppim and Hosah westward, by the gate of Shallecheth, at the causeway that goeth up, watch against watch. 17 Eastward were six Levites, northward four a day, southward four a day, and for the store-house two and two. 18 for Parbar westward, four at the causeway, and two at Parbar. 19 These were the courses of the doorkeepers; of the sons of the Korahites, and of the sons of Merari.*

Regarding the Keepers of the Treasures

Verses 20-28, And of the Levites, Ahijah was over the treasures of the house of God, and over the treasures of the dedicated things. 21 The sons of Ladan, the sons of the Gershonites belonging to Ladan, the heads of the fathers; houses belonging to Ladan the Gershonite: Jehieli. 22 The sons of Jehieli: Zetham, and Joel his brother, over the treasures of the house of Jehovah. 23 Of the Amramites, of the Izharites, of the Hebronites, of the Uzzielites: 24 and Shebuel the son of Gershom, the son of Moses, was ruler over the treasures. 25 And his brethren: of Eliezer came Rehabiah his son, and Jeshaiah his son, and Joram his son, and Zichri his son, and Shelomoth his son. 26 This Shelemoth and his brethren were over all the treasures of the dedicated things, which David the king, and the heads of the fathers' houses, the captains over thousands and hundreds, and the captains of the host had dedicated. 27 Out of the spoil won in battles did they dedicate to repair the house of Jehovah. 28 And all that Samuel the seer, and Saul the son of Kish, and Abner the son of Ner, and Joab the son of Zeruiah, had dedicated, whosoever had dedicated anything, it was under the hand of Shelomoth, and of his brethren.

And Others Involved in the King's Business

Verses 29-32, Of the Izharites, Chenaniah and his sons were for the outward business over Israel, for officers and judges. 30 Of the Hebronites, Hashabiah and his brethren, men of valor, a thousand and seven hundred, had the oversight of Israel beyond the Jordan westward, for all the business of Jehovah, and for the business of the king. 31 Of the Hebronites was Jerijah the chief, even of the Hebronites, according to their generations by fathers' houses. In the fortieth year of the reign of David they were sought for, and there were found among them mighty men of valor at Jazer of Gilead. 32 And his brethren, men of valor, were two thousand and seven hundred, heads of fathers' houses, whom David made overseers over the Reubenites, and the Gadites, and the half-tribe of the Manassites, for every matter pertaining to God, and for the affairs of the king.

None of the commentaries we have consulted with regard to this chapter has provided us with anything we wish to quote. Many of them wrote only a few brief lines on this chapter; and the Interpreters' Bible barely has a hundred words on it.

The pursuit of variations in this list as compared with others, speculations about things that are ambiguous, conflicting guesses about the "date when" this or that list might have been 'added,' and fanciful charges that some or all of these chapters in Chronicles are 'artificial,' etc., etc., ---the pursuit of such problems constitutes an exercise in futility, in which we choose not to participate.

Accurate and dogmatic answers to many questions and problems that may be found in these chapters are simply impossible. For example, the word ***SON,*** which occurs hundreds of times in Chronicles, has no less than nine meanings as used in the Bible.[1]

Nevertheless, the value of Chronicles to Christians is very great. Here is the irresistible proof that the OT deals, not with myth, legend, or folklore, but with fact, with history, with flesh and blood events in the long and turbulent story of God's people Israel, through whom Almighty God brought redemption in Jesus Christ to Adam's lost and ruined descendents.

XXX

---

[1] Vol. 4, ***Second Samuel,*** of our Commentaries on the historical books, p. 269.

CHAPTER 27

The Men Who Headed the Military Structure, Heads of Each of the Twleve Tribes, And Other High Officers

Heads of the Courses Month by Month

***Verses 1-15, Now the children after their number,
to wit, the heads of fathers' houses and the captains of
thousands and of hundreds, and their officers that served
the king, in any matter of the courses that went in and went
out month by month throughout all the months of the year
---of every course were twenty and four thousand. 2 Over
the first course for the first month was Jashobeam the son
of Zabdiel: and in his course were twenty and four
thousand. 3 He was of the children of Perez, the chief of all
the captains of the host for the first month. 4 And over the
course of the second month was Dodai the Ahohite, and his
course; and Mikloth the ruler: and in his course were
twenty and four thousand. 5 The third captain of the host
for the third month was Benaiah, the son of Jehoiada the
priest, chief: and his course were twenty and four thousand.
6 This is that Benaiah, who was the mighty man of the
thirty, and over the thirty: and of his course was
Ammizabad his son. 7 The fourth captain for the fourth
month was Asahel the brother of Joab, and Zebadiah his
son after him: and in his course were twenty and four
thousand. 8 The fifth captain for the fifth month was
Shamuth the Izrahite: and in his course were twenty and
four thousand. 9 The sixth captain for the sixth month was
Ira the son of Ikkesh the Tekoite: and in his course were
twenty and four thousand. 10 The seventh captain for the***

seventh month was Helez the Pelonite, of the children of Ephraim: and in his course were twenty and four thousand. 11 The eighth captain for the eighth month was Sibbecai the Hushathite, of the Zerahites: and in his course were twenty and four thousand. 12 The ninth captain for the ninth month was Abiezer the Anathothite, of the Benjamites: and in his course were twenty and four thousand. 13 The tenth captain for the tenth month was Meharai the Netophathite, of the Serahites: and in his course were twenty and four thousand. 14 The eleventh captain for the eleventh month was Benaiah the Pirathonite, of the children of Ephraim: and in his course were twenty and four thousand. 15 The twelfth captain for the twelfth month was Heldai the Netophathite, of the children of Ephraim: and in his course were twenty and four thousand.

These verses present the structure of David's military establishment, which consisted of a standing army of 288,000 men, rotated 24,000 at a time, month by month, under the commanders here mentioned.

The commanders were, "Men of extraordinary personal activity, strength and valor, reminding us of the heroes of King Arthur or Charlemagne, except that the armor of the feudal chieftains gave them their superiority, while in the forces of David, it was main strength of body and dauntless fortitude of mind."[1]

Apparently, this arrangement continually surrounded David with 24,000 armed men, month by

---

1 PC, Vol. 6a, p. 409.

month, and made available for any emergency the entire 288,000. It also left the soldiery practically free eleven months in the year to pursue their own interests. The monotonous repetition is characteristic of ancient records and denies the notion that "The Chronicler" invented these records.

The Tribal Heads in David's Reign

Verses 16-24, Furthermore over the tribes of Israel: of the Reubenites was Eliezer the son of Zichri the ruler: of the Simeronites, Shephatiah the son of Maacah: 17 of Levi, Hashabiah the son of Kemuel: 18 of Judah, Elihu, one of the brethren of David: of Issachar, Omri the son of Michael: 19 of Zebulun, Ishmaiah the son of Obadiah: of Naphtali, Jeremoth the son of Azriel: 20 of the children of Ephraim, Hoshea the son of Azaziah: of the half-tribe of Manasseh, Joel the son of Pedaiah: 21 of the half-tribe of Manasseh in Gilead, Iddo the son of Zechariah: of Benjamin, Jaasiel the son of Abner: 22 of Dan, Azarel the son of Jeroham. These were the captains of the tribes of Israel. 23 But David took not the number of them from twenty years old and under, because Jehovah had said he would increase Israel like to the stars of the heaven. 24 Joab the son of Zeruiah began to number, but finished not; and there came wrath for this upon Israel; neither was the number put into the account in the chronicles of king David.

It is strange that neither Gad nor Asher of the Twelve Tribes is mentioned. Curtis supposed that this was because, "The list of twelve was complete without them"![2]

David took not the number of them from twenty years old and under (v. 22). There is a hint here as to the reason why God was displeased with David's numbering Israel. Curtis (Madsen) believed that, "David refrained from counting them, because such an act would have implied a doubt on David's part of God's promise in Genesis 22:17."[3] Evidently, his efforts to find out exactly how many able-bodied soldiers Israel had likewise exhibited a sinful doubt on David's part. He was apparently tempted to trust in the number of his troops, instead of relying upon the promise of God.

David's Departmental Overseers

Verses 25-32, And over the king's treasures was Azmaveth the son of Adiel: and over the treasures in the fields, in the cities, and in the villages, and in the castles, was Jonathan the son of Uzziah: 26 and over them that did the work of the field for tillage of the ground was Ezri the son of Chelub: 27 and over the vineyards was Shimei the Ramathite: and over the increase of the vineyards for the wine-cellars was Zabdi the Shiphmite: 28 and over the olive-trees and the sycamore-trees that were in the lowland was Baal-hanan the Gederite: and over the cellars of oil was Joash: 29 and over the herds that fed in Sharon was Shitrai the Sharonite: and over the herds that were in the

---

[2] ICC, *Chronicles*, p. 291.

[3] Ibid., p. 292.

valleys was Shaphat the son of Adlai: 30 and over the camels was Obil the Ishmaelite: and over the asses was Jehdeiah the Meronothite: and over the flocks was Jaziz the Hagrite. 31 All these were the rulers of the substance which was king David's.

These officials were, in a sense, stewards of the king's vast properties.

Other Very Important Officers of the King

Verses 32-34, Also Jonathan, David's uncle, was a counsellor, a man of understanding, and a scribe: and Jehiel the son of Hachmoni was with the king's sons: 33 And Ahithophel was the king's counsellor: and Hushai the Archite was the king's friend: 34 and after Ahithophel was Jehoiada the son of Benaiah, and Abiathar: the captain of the king's host was Joab.

It is of interest that the Chronicler passed over the treachery of Ahithophel during the rebellion of Absalom. He did, however, give the names of David's counsellors following the suicide of Ahithophel.[4]

xxx

---

[4] See our Commentary, ***Second Samuel***, pp. 204-205, 227-234, for discussion of Ahithophel.

CHAPTER 28

This and the following chapter conclude First Chronicles and are devoted to the final words and instructions of king David, especially as they related to Solomon and the construction of the temple. David freely confessed here that God had told him, "Thou shalt not build a house for my name" (v. 3); but David nevertheless proceeded to build it, making all the necessary preparations for doing so, accumulating the necessary supplies, and vigorously commanding Solomon and all Israel to build it. Throughout human history, every man has been credited with doing what he commanded others to do, a principle illustrated a hundred times in the Bible; and we must therefore accept the truth that David's actions with reference to Solomon's temple were sinful. He violated the prohibition that God laid upon him.

The inspired Chronicler has given us in these chapters a faithful and accurate record of what was said and done; but many of the things David said and did in these two chapters were not based upon what God had commanded but upon David's sincere and honest misunderstanding of the prophecy of the Lord through Nathan the prophet.

Once the die was cast and all Israel had enthusiastically accepted the idea of building a temple, God indeed accomodated to it, continuing to bless Israel, and even overruling their sins and mistakes, bending them to contribute toward the Eternal Purpose of Redemption for all mankind.

Yes, God even commanded the temple to be rebuilt under Ezra and Nehemiah; but at that stage in Israel's long and rebellious history of sin and apostasy, the heavenly command to build again the temple must be viewed as exactly the equivalent of Jesus's command for Judas Iscariot to betray him (John 13:27), or the command of God's angel to Balaam, "Go with the men" (Numbers 22:35).

Solomon's temple, in every real sense, was the project conceived and achieved by David. It was in the same category as the monarchy, used and overruled by God toward the achievement of his Eternal Purpose; but neither of them, in the ultimate sense, was actually the will of God, except in the sense that he permitted them.

This background review of the Jewish temple should be kept continually in mind in our study of these two chapters.

David's Public Announcement that Solomon Would Build the Temple

Verses 1-8, And David assembled all the princes of Israel, the princes of the tribes, and the captains of the companies that served the king by course, and the captains of thousands, and the captains of hundreds, and the rulers over all the substance and possessions of the king and of his sons, with the officers, and the mighty men, even all the mighty men of valor, unto Jerusalem. 2 Then David the king stood up upon his feet, and said, Hear me, my brethren, and my people: as for me, it was in my heart to

build a house of rest for the ark of the covenant of Jehovah, and for the footstool of our God; and I made ready for the building. 3 But God said unto me, "Thou shalt not build a house for my name, because thou art a man of war, and hast shed much blood. 4 Howbeit Jehovah, the God of Israel, chose me out of all the house of my father to be king over Israel for ever: for he hath chosen Judah to be prince; and in the house of Judah, the house of my father; and among the sons of my father he took pleasure in me to make me king over all Israel; 5 and of all my sons (for Jehovah hath given me many sons) he hath chosen Solomon my son to sit upon the throne of the kingdom of Jehovah over Israel. 6 And he said unto me, Solomon thy son, he shall build my house and my courts; for I have chosen him to be my son, and I will be his father. 7 And I will establish his kingdom for ever, if he be constant to do my commandments and mine ordinances, as at this day. 8 Now therefore, in the sight of all Israel, the assembly of Jehovah, and in the audience of our God; observe and seek out all the commandments of Jehovah your God; that ye may possess this good land, and leave it for an inheritance to your children after you for ever.

I have chosen him to be my son, and I will be his father (v. 6). This and the following verse positively indicate that David was here basing what he said upon his understanding of the prophecy in 2S:7; however, that prophecy said nothing at all resembling what David here declared. Solomon, in no sense whatever, was God's son, nor did God establish Solomon's throne for ever. All that was happening in this chapter was taking place during David's lifetime, absolutely contrary to the specific declaration in 2S 7:12 that the promised Great One who would build that house for the name of God would do so, "When thou (David) shalt sleep with thy fathers, and that the Promised One would be ***SET UP AFTER THEE***" (2S 7:12). Solomon was not set up after David but during David's reign; and God did not do it, as the prophecy indicated, but David did it! See our extensive comment on this in 2 Samuel.

David's Order for Solomon to Build the Temple

Verses 9-10, And thou, Solomon my son, know thou the God of thy father, and serve him with a perfect heart and with a willing mind; for Jehovah searcheth all hearts, and understandeth all the imaginations of the thoughts. If thou seek him, he will be found of thee; but if thou forsake him, he will cast thee off for ever. 10 Take heed now; for Jehovah hath chosen thee to build a house for the sanctuary: be strong, and do it.

Here, in the presence of all Israel, David laid the solemn charge upon his son Solomon to build the Jewish temple, which thus became, in every particular, what David did through his son Solomon. It should have been called ***David's Temple.***

God's Overruling Providence in the Temple's Construction

Verses 11, Then David gave to Solomon his son the

pattern of the porch of the temple, of the houses thereof, and of the treasuries therof, and of the upper rooms thereof, and of the place of the mercy-seat.

David himself did not invent this pattern, but God gave it to him, having first given it to Moses; and David learned all about it from Exodus 25:10, 17-22, 31:7, 40:20, and in Numbers 7:89. The statement in the next verse that David had this pattern "by the Spirit" is a reference to the fact that God's Spirit revealed all of these things to Moses.

Many Other Details Given by David to Solomon

Verses 12-19, And the pattern of all that he had by the Spirit for the courts of the house of Jehovah, and for all the chambers round about, for the treasuries of the house of God, and for the treasuries of the dedicated things; 13 also for the courses of the priests and the Levites, and for all the work of the service of the house of Jehovah; 14 of gold by weight for the vessels of gold, for all vessels for every kind of service; 15 by weight also for the candlesticks of gold, and for the lamps thereof, of gold, by weight for every candlestick and for the lamps thereof; and for the candlesticks of silver, silver by weight for every candlestick and for the lamps thereof, according to the use of every candlestick; 16 and the gold by weight for the tables of show-bread, for every table; and silver for the tables of silver; 17 and the flesh-hooks, and the basins, and the cups, of pure gold; and the golden bowls by weight for every bowl; 18 and for the altar of incense refined gold by

weight; and gold for the pattern of the chariot, even the cherubim, that spread out their wings, and covered the ark of the covenant of Jehovah. 19 All this, said David, have I been made to understand in writing from the hand of Jehovah, even all the works of this pattern.

The very names, descriptions and instructions regarding all of these things were derived by David from the Mosaic Law as given in the Pentateuch. Any good reference Bible lists the following references in this single paragraph to the Law of Moses: Exodus 20:16; 25:9, 18-22, 37; 26:31-39; 28:16; 30:1-19, 34; and 36:9; Leviticus 16:2, 14, 15; and Numbers 1:47. Thus what we have here is David's relay of the instructions Moses received from God for the building of the tabernacle accomodated to the requirements of the temple. We know that Solomon did not strictly follow David's instructions; and there were enough departures from the true pattern to justify the author of the Book of Hebrews in by-passing the Jewish Temple altogether and going back to the tabernacle for all of true symbolism supposed to be in the temple.

David said, I have been made to understand in writing from the hand of Jehovah all the works of this pattern (v. 19). These words are another reference to the Mosaic Law where David read the pattern of the tabernacle, and which pattern Solomon was supposed to follow in the construction of the temple. The proof of this is in the general correspondence of the temple in all of its truly important features to the ancient tabernacle.

The variations and changes imposed upon the temple by Solomon should not be charged to David.

David's Admonition for Solomon

Verses 20-21, And David said to Solomon his son, Be strong and of good courage, and do it: fear not, nor be dismayed; for Jehovah God, even my God is with thee; he will not fail thee, or forsake thee, until all the work for the service of the house of Jehovah be finished. 21 And, behold, there are the courses of the priests and the Levites, for all the service of the house of God: and there shall be with thee in all manner of work every willing man that hath skill for any manner of service: also the captains and all the people will be wholly at thy commandment.

The absolute sincerity and total devotion of king David in his love of God and his enthusiasm for building the temple shine in every word of these wonderful sentences. How tragic it is that his son Solomon failed so wretchedly to honor the admonition of this wonderful father.

Special Note on Verse 5

He (God) hath chosen Solomon ... to sit upon the throne of the KINGDOM OF JEHOVAH over Israel (v. 5). There is not a more preposterous statement in all the Bible than this one. David truly believed, as did all Israel, that the earthly kingdom that God had given them was the ***kingdom of heaven.***

In a certain sense, of course, the people of Israel were a type of that 'kingdom of heaven' which is the Church; but in no sense whatever was the secular, political kingdom of David and Solomon ***the kingdom of God.*** The ancient inhabitants of Canaan were not driven out of Palestine, as God commanded; but they were enslaved by Israel. See the opening chapters of our Commentary on Judges.

"Second Samuel 20:24 indicates that David used forced (slave) labor; that passage does not say who composed the labor gangs";[1] and, although David might not have forced Israeites into his forced labor gangs, the enslaved Canaanites were certainly used; and Solomon quickly extended them to include Israelites also. There is no way that the evil, secular and political kingdom of Israel could have been the kingdom of heaven. Of course, the multitudes who were living off the sweat of other peoples' faces liked doing so; and no doubt many thought it was wonderful. See further comment on this in our introduction to chapter 4 in 1 Kings

The political Jewish kingdom was never anything other than what the prophet of God called it; "***THE SINFUL KINGDOM***" (Amos 9:8).

xxx

---

[1] BBC, Vol. 3, p. 346.

CHAPTER 29
Conclusion of the Reign of David

David Gives His Great Wealth for the Temple

Verses 1-5, And David the king said unto all the assembly, Solomon my son whom God alone hath chosen, is yet young and tender, and the work is great; for the palace is not for man, but for Jehovah God. 2 Now I have prepared with all my might for the house of my God the gold for the things of gold, and the silver for the things of silver, and the brass for the things of brass, the iron for the things of iron, and wood for the things of wood; onyx stones, and stones to be set, stones for inlaid work, and of divers colors, and all manner of precious stones, and marble stones in abundance. 3 Moreover also, because I have set my affection on the house of my God, seeing that I have a treasure of mine own of gold and silver, I give it unto the house of my God, over and above all that I have prepared for the holy house, 4 even three thousand talents of gold, of the gold of Ophir, and seven thousand talents of refined silver, wherewith to overlay the walls of the house; 5 of gold for the things of gold, and of silver for the things of silver, and for all manner of work to be made by the hands of artificers. Who then offereth willingly to consecrate himself this day unto Jehovah?

Due to the uncertainty that prevails with respect to the numbers given here, and to our equal uncertainty as to the exact value of the talent used in these calculations, we are not able to assign any exact value to the amount in dollars of David's magnificent gift; but there is no doubt that many millions of dollars should be assigned as the value of his gift. He gave it publicly in order to inspire others to do likewise.

The big point here is not the actual cash value of David's gift, but the principle propounded here in the last sentence.

Who then offereth willingly to consecrate himself this day unto Jehovah (v. 5c). This is indeed a profound proposition. What David gave and urged others to give to the house of the worship of God was, in the last analysis, ***unto Jehovah.*** How much more is it true that what men freely give to the holy Church of Jesus Christ is actually the consecration of the giver unto God in Christ.

Honestly mistaken as David certainly was about some things, his sincere love of God was the central passion of his life; and, in that light, there can be no wonder that God accepted his loving gift of the temple and continued to use it throughout Israel's history.

The Princes of Israel Respond to David's Challenge

Verses 6-9, Then the princes of the fathers' houses, and the princes of the tribes of Israel, and the captains of thousands and of hundreds, with the rulers over the king's work, offered willingly; 7 and they gave for the service of the house of God of gold five thousand talents and ten thousand darics, and of silver ten thousand talents, and of brass eighteen thousand talents, and of iron a hundred thousand talents. 8 And they with whom precious stones were found gave them to the treasure of the house of

Jehovah, under the hand of Jehiel the Gershonite. 9 Then the people rejoiced, for they offered willingly, because with a perfect heart they offered willingly to Jehovah: and David the king also rejoiced with great joy.

The people rejoiced (v. 5c). The greatest happiness that human beings may have comes from a clear conscience and generous giving to further the cause of truth and righteousness upon earth by contributions to the work of God through his church.

Ten thousand darics (v. 7). "These were Persian gold coins worth about $5.00 each."[1]

David's Blessing of Jehovah Before the People

Verses 10-19, Wherefore David blessed Jehovah before all the assembly; and David said, Blessed be thou, O Jehovah, the God of Israel our father, for ever and ever. 11 Thine, O Jehovah, is the greatness, and the power, and the glory, and the victory, and the majesty: for all that is in the heavens and in the earth is thine; thine is the kingdom, O Jehovah, and thou art exalted as head above all. 12 Both riches and honor come of thee, and thou rulest over all; and in thy hand is power and might; and in thy hand it is to make great, and to give strength unto all. 13 Now therefore, our God, we thank thee, and praise thy glorious name. 14 But who am I, and what is my people, that we should be able to offer so willingly after this sort? for all things come of thee, and of thine own have we given thee.

---

[1] WYC, p. 389.

15 For we are strangers before thee, and sojourners, as all our fathers were: our days on earth are as a shadow, and there is no abiding. 16 O Jehovah our God, all this store that we have prepared to build thee a house for thy holy name cometh of thy hand, and is all thine own. 17 I know also, my God, that thou triest the heart, and hast pleasure in uprightness. As for me, in the uprightness of my heart I have willingly offered all these things: and now I have seen with joy thy people, that are present here, offer willingly unto thee. 18 O Jehovah, the God of Abraham, of Isaac, and of Israel, our fathers, keep this for ever in the imagination of the thoughts of the heart of thy people, and prepare their heart unto thee; 19 and give unto Solomon my son a perfect heart, to keep thy commandments, thy testimonies, and thy statutes, and to do all these things, and to build the palace, for which I have made provision.

The palace (vv. 1, 19). Only in these two verses is this term applied to the temple. "It is the Hebrew form of a Persian word used generally to designate the residence of the Persian monarch, as in Esther 1:2, 5; 2:3, 8; Nehemiah 1:1; and in Daniel 8:2."[2]

David blessed Jehovah (v. 10). We normally think of God's blessing men, not the other way around; but we learn from verse 20, below, that when David commanded the people to "Bless Jehovah," they did so by worshipping God and offering sacrifices, all of this being exactly what David did here. Thus we conclude that those who truly worship God indeed do "bless

---

[2] AB, Chronicles, p. 366.

God."

Dentan said of this paragraph, "It is an excellent illustration of the Chronicler's high conception of God, and of man's proper relation to him."[3] This is a fair example of the views of critical scholars who deny the authenticity of Chronicles, treating it as an invention of the Chronicler, and not as a record of events that really happened. We believe that David spoke the words which the writer of Chronicles attributed to him, there being no good reason whatever for denying them to David.

As we have frequently noted, the real reason behind the rejection, by some writers, of Chronicles is the effective denial it provides for the radical critics' late-dating of the Pentateuch.

Chronicles is not a fabrication. "A fabrication would have fitted more neatly (with few variations). The differences found in Chronicles are due to the independence of traditions (authorities); and recent archaeological finds further authenticate this."[4]

All the People Bless God by Worshipping Him

Verses 20-22, And David said to all the assembly, Now bless Jehovah your God. And all the assembly blessed Jehovah, the God of their fathers, and bowed down their heads and worshipped Jehovah, and the king. 21 And they sacrificed sacrifices unto Jehovah, and offered burnt-

---

[3] LBC, Vol. 7, pp. 139, 140.

[4] BBC, Vol. 3, p. 360.

offerings unto Jehovah, on the morrow, after that day, even a thousand bullocks, a thousand rams, and a thousand lambs, with their drink-offerings, and sacrifices in abundance for all Israel, 22 and did eat and drink before Jehovah on that day with great gladness.

And they bowed down their heads and worshipped Jehovah, and the king (v. 20). The worship of any man is sinful, even the worship of a great king like David; and this verse should be translated as in the RSV, "All the assembly bowed their heads and worshipped the Lord, and did obeisance to the king."

The reason that older translations are like our version (the ASV) here is that, "The word normally translated ***worship*** in the OT means ***to prostrate one's self.***"[5] In those days, it was customary thus to honor kings ; but in the NT, Christians are forbidden to honor any man in such a manner. See elaboration of this principle in our Commentary on Revelation.[6]

Solomon Made King the Second Time

Verses 22b-25, And they made Solomon the son of David king the second time, and anointed him unto Jehovah to be prince, and Zadok to be priest. 23 Then Solomon sat on the throne of Jehovah as king instead of David his father, and prospered; and all Israel obeyed him. 24 And all the princes, and the mighty men, and all the sons likewise of king David, submitted themselves unto

---

[5] NBCR, p. 384.

[6] Vol. 12 of the NT Series, pp. 511-513.

Solomon. 25 And Jehovah magnified Solomon exceedingly in the sight of all Israel, and bestowed upon him much royal majesty as had not been on any king before him in Israel.

Solomon sat on the throne of Jehovah (v. 23). The Chronicler here spoke of Solomon in the terms of the popular acclaim that greeted this second coronation. Solomon was already king and had been co-regent with his father David a number of years preceding this second crowning. It cannot be accepted as a literal fact that the wicked Solomon actually "sat on the throne of Jehovah."

The Death of King David

Verses 26-30, Now David the son of Jesse reigned over all Israel. 27 And the time that he reigned over Israel was forty years; seven years reigned he in Hebron, and thirty and three years reigned he in Jerusalem. 28 And he died in a good old age, full of days, riches, and honor; and Solomon his son reigned in his stead. 29 Now the acts of David the king, first, and last, behold, they are written in the history of Samuel the seer, and in the history of Nathan the prophet, and in the history of Gad the seer, 30 with all his reign and his might, and the times that went over him, and over Israel, and over all the kingdoms of the countries.

See our introduction to Chronicles for a discussion of the extensive documentation behind what is herein written. This is an appropriate place indeed to separate First Chronicles from Second Chronicles, since Second Chronicles deals with the reign of Solomon, the rebellion of the ten northern tribes, the affairs of the divided kingdom, the rapid corruption of Israel that led to their captivity, and with their history until Cyrus' decree for the rebuilding of the temple.

xxx

2 Chronicles

I. THE UNITED KINGDOM FROM SOLOMON TO THE DIVISION (Chapters 1-10)

CHAPTER 1

Solomon at Gibeon; God Appears in a Dream

***Verses 1-6,** And Solomon the son of David was strengthened in his kingdom, and Jehovah his God was with him, and magnified him exceedingly. 2 And Solomon spake unto all Israel, to the captains of thousands and of hundreds, and to the judges, and to every prince in all Israel, the heads of the fathers' houses. 3 So Solomon and all the assembly with him, went to the high place that was at Gibeon; for there was the tent of meeting of God, which Moses the servant of God had made in the wilderness. 4 But the ark of God had David brought up from Kiriath-jearim to the place that David had prepared for it; for he had pitched a tent for it at Jerusalem. 5 Moreover the brazen alter that Bezalel the son of Uri, the son of Hur, had made, was there before the tabernacle of Jehovah: and Solomon and the assembly sought unto it. 6 And Solomon went up thither to the brazen altar before Jehovah, which was at the tent of meeting, and offered a thousand burnt-offerings upon it.*

The brazen altar that Bezalel ... had made (v. 5). Continually throughout Chronicles we find an acute consciousness of all that was written in the Pentateuch in the times of Moses. The references here are from

Exodus 17:10, 28:1-8, 31:2.

Solomon offered a thousand burnt-offerings upon it (v. 6). This means that Solomon provided the burnt-offerings, not that he offered them personally, a duty that pertained to the priests. "This altar is mentioned as assurance that Gibeon was the proper place for sacrifice and worship."[1]

By beginning his record of Solomon's reign in this manner, the Chronicler apparently sought to focus the attention of Israel upon their ancient heritage of the favor and blessing of God, and upon his deliverance of them from Egypt by the hand of Moses.

God's Appearance to Solomon in a Dream

Verses 7-13, In that night did God appear to Solomon, and said unto him, Ask what I shall give thee. 8 And Solomon said unto God, Thou hast showed great lovingkindness to David my father, and hast made me king in his stead. 9 Now, O Jehovah God, let thy promise unto David my father be established; for thou hast made me king over a people like the dust of the earth in multitude. 10 Give me now wisdom and knowledge, that I may go out and come in before this people; for who can judge this thy people, that is so great? 11 And God said to Solomon, Because this was in thy heart, and thou hast not asked riches, wealth, nor honor, nor the life of them that hate thee, neither yet hast asked long life; but hast asked wisdom and knowledge for thyself, that thou mayest judge my

---

[1] PC, Vol. 6b. p. 3.

people, over whom I have made thee king: 12 wisdom and knowledge is granted unto thee; and I will give unto thee riches, and honor, such as none of the kings have had that have been before thee; neither shall any after thee have the like. 13 So Solomon came from the high place that was at Gibeon, from before the tent of meeting, unto Jerusalem; and he reigned over Israel.

That night God appeared unto Solomon (v. 7). First, we should dispose of the critical suggestion that this is a contradiction of the statement in 1K 3:5 that, "Jehovah appeared unto Solomon that night in a dream." Curtis (Madsen) commented that, "The dream has disappeared, and the revelation is a more direct one."[2] Such a comment is totally in error. There's not a word here about the dream's disappearance, nor any suggestion that the revelation was in any manner 'more direct' than what was mentioned in 1 Kings. The very fact of the appearance having been at night made it unnecessary to add the fact that all Israel already knew, namely, that the appearance was in a dream.

The Chronicler's account here is more brief than that in Kings; and, "The principal point of omission was the conditional promise of long life to Solomon,"[3] This omission was probably because the Chronicler knew that Solomon's wickedness had voided that promise. "Otherwise there is no essential difference of any

---

2 ICC, ***Chronicles***, p. 317.

3 AB, ***Chonicles,*** p. 370.

importance in the parallel accounts."[4]

Solomon's Wicked Multiplication of His Horses

Verses 14-17, And Solomon gathered chariots and horsemen: and he had a thousand and four hundred chariots, and twelve thousand horsemen, that he placed in the chariot cities, and with the king at Jerusalem. 15 And the king made silver and gold to be in Jerusalem as stones, and cedars made he to be as the sycamore trees that are in the lowland, for abundance. 16 And the horses which Solomon had were brought out of Egypt; the king's merchants received them in droves, each drove at a price. 17 And they fetched up and brought out of Egypt a chariot for six hundred shekels of silver, and a horse for a hundred and fifty; and so for all the kings of the Hittites, and the kings of Syria, did they bring them out by their means.

It is evident to this writer that some have missed altogether the Chronicler's intention. The allegation that, "It was contrary to the Chronicler's purpose to convey a too unfavorable impression of Solomon,"[5] has often been cited; but how could that be true, in the light of this very first chapter, where practically the first thing Solomon did was to violate in the most contemptuous and wholesale manner the divine prohibition in Deuteronomy?

Thou shalt surely set a king over thee ... Only he

---

[4] PC, op. cit., p. 4.

[5] ICC, op. cit., p. 313.

shall not multiply horses to himself, nor cause the people to return to Egypt to ... multiply horses. --- Deut. 17:15-16.

This shameful violation of God's word by Solomon has been remarkably confirmed by archaeological discoveries in recent times. There were many of these 'chariot cities'; and, "At Megiddo, southeast of mount Carmel, has been excavated the ruins of a single extensive stone stable capable of housing about four hundred horses."[6]

"This passage (vv. 14-17) is very nearly identical with 1K 10:26-29."[7]

xxx

---

6 WYC, p. 392.

7 AB, op. cit., p. 371.

CHAPTER 2

Final Preparations for Building the Temple and the Palace

Verses 1-2, Now Solomon purposed to build a house for the name of Jehovah, and a house for his kingdom. 2 And Solomon counted out threescore and ten thousand men to bear burdens, and fourscore thousand men were hewers in the mountains, and three thousand six hundred to oversee them.

And a house for his kingdom (v. 1). This refers to the house Solomon would build for himself.'[1] The Chronicler omitted many details that are found in Kings, simply because those details were already widely known. "Knowledge of the temple (and many other things) from Kings and other sources is taken for granted."[2] Therefore, we reject as worthless the speculations of scholars regarding alleged "reasons" why this or that was abbreviated or left out altogether.

The 153,600 men mentioned here were slaves, composed of, "Descendants of those Canaanites whom the children of Israel did not drive out."[3] From Kings it is clear that Israelites were also conscripted by Solomon for such slave labor and required to devote one month of every three to his service.

---

1 PC, Vol. 6b, p. 17.

2 AnBi, *2 Chronicles*, p. 11.

3 AB, *Chronicles*, p. 373.

Solomon Requests Help of the King of Tyre

Verses 3-4. And Solomon sent to Huram the king of Tyre, saying, As thou didst deal with David my father, and didst send him cedars to build him a house to dwell therein, even so deal with me. 4 Behold, I am about to build a house for the name of Jehovah my God, to dedicate it to him, and to burn before him incense of sweet spices, and for the continual showbread, and for the burnt-offerings morning and evening, on the sabbaths, and on the new moons, and on the set feasts of Jehovah our God. This is a set ordinance for ever for Israel.

Huram the king of Tyre (v. 3). This person is called Hiram in Kings; "But throughout Chronicles he is called Huram (except in 1C 14:1)."[4]

Verse 4 here is a summary of the principal rituals of the ancient tabernacle and an indication of their continued observance in the projected temple. The entire Pentateuch is, in a sense, summarized in this single verse, in keeping with the entire religious constitution of ancient Israel. Extensive sections of Exodus, Leviticus, Numbers and Deuteronomy are reflected in this single verse. No wonder the critics hate it. Elmslie looked at it, and wrote, "It looks like a heavy-handed addition."[5] However, there is absolutely no evidence of any kind that this verse is an interpolation. It is the previous mind-set of critics that

---

[4] AB, op. cit., p. 371.
[5] IB, Vol. 3, p. 445.

causes them to make such an allegation.

Verses 5-10, And the house which I build is great; for great is our God above all gods. 6 But who is able to build him a house, seeing heaven and the heaven of heavens cannot contain him? who am I then, that I should build him a house, save only to burn incense before him? 7 Now therefore send me a man skilful to work in gold, and in silver, and in brass, and in iron, and in purple, and crimson, and blue, and that knoweth how to grave all manner of gravings, to be with the skilful men that are with me in Judah and in Jerusalem, whom David my father did provide. 8 Send me also cedar-trees, fir-trees, and algum-trees,out of Lebanon; for I know that thy servants know how to cut timber in Lebanon. And, behold, my servants shall be with thy servants, 9 even to prepare me timber in abundance; for the house which I am about to build shall be great and wonderful. 10 And, behold, I will give to thy servants, the hewers that cut timber, twenty thousand measures of beaten wheat, and twenty thousand measures of barley, and twenty thousand baths of wine, and twenty thousand baths of oil.

The heaven of heavens cannot contain him (God) (v. 6). "The notion that God could be confined in a house or a box is an error which skeptics have falsely attributed to the people of God during the OT period; but they knew that God was Lord of heaven and earth, and so declared it many times, as Solomon did here."[6]

---

[6] GDH, Vol. 11, p. 405.

Moreover, it was not a discovery by Solomon. He had most certainly learned it from David, whose Psalms often gave voice to the same truth. The Chronicler's accurate record here of Solomon's words refutes the critic's allegations on this matter also, as well as denying their foolish fairy tale regarding a late date for the Pentateuch.

That knoweth how to grave all manner of gravings (v. 7). The words here rendered ***grave*** and ***gravings*** are read as ***engrave*** and ***engravings*** in the RSV.

And in purple, and crimson, and blue (v. 7) Thus, in the color scheme, "The temple, in this respect, as well as in others, conformed to the pattern of the tabernacle (Exodus 25:4, 26:1, etc.)."[7] See our Commentary, Vol. 8, of the NT Series (Hebrews), p. 172, for a discussion of the significance of these colors.

Algum-trees out of Lebanon (v. 8). Curtis wrote that these were probably, "Sandalwood or ebony."[8]

Wheat ... barley ...wine ... and oil (v. 10). The translation of the quantities of all these supplies into their modern equivalent is of no importance, and is also impossible.

The Response of the King of Tyre

Verses 11-17, Then Huram the king of Tyre answered in writing, which he sent to Solomon, Because Jehovah loveth his people, he hath made thee king over

---

[7] AB, op. cit., p. 372.

[8] ICC, op. cit., p. 321.

them. 12 Huram said moreover, Blessed be Jehovah, the God of Israel, that made heaven and earth, who hath given to David a wise son, endued with discretion and understanding, that should build a house for Jehovah, and a house for his kingdom. 13 And now I have sent a skilful man, endued with understanding, of Huram my father's, 14 the son of a woman of the daughters of Dan; and his father was a man of Tyre, skilful to work in gold, and in silver, in brass, in iron, in stone, and in timber, in purple, and blue, and in fine linen, and in crimson, also to grave any manner of graving, and to devise any device; that there may be a place appointed unto him with thy skilful men, and with the skilful men of my lord David thy father. 15 Now therefore the wheat and the barley, the oil and the wine, which my lord hath spoken of, let him send unto his servants: 16 and we will cut wood out of Lebanon, as much as thou shalt need; and we will bring it to thee by floats to Joppa; and thou shalt carry it up to Jerusalem.

Blessed be Jehovah ... lord of heaven and earth (v. 12). Critics find fault here, as they do at every possible excuse, because of Huram's apparent belief in Jehovah; but anyone should be able to see that the king of Tyre said this in the same lack of sincerity with which he even called Solomon his 'lord' in v. 15. "In a polytheistic society politeness to a neighbor's god cost nothing."[9]

Of Huram my father's (v. 13). The RSV should be followed here, "I have sent a skilful man ... Huramabi."

The son of a woman of the daughters of Dan (v.

---

[9] NBCR, p. 384.

14). Critics love to cite this as a discrepancy with 1K 7:14, which refers to her as "a widow of the tribe of Naphtali," some even calling it a contradiction. Of course, the two passages teach that Huramabi's mother was, by birth, of the tribe of Dan, and by residence of the tribe of Napthtali.

Let him send unto his servants (v. 15). Huram, in these words, surely suggests that the supplies for the upkeep of all the workmen Solomon requested was expected to be paid in advance.

In floats by sea to Joppa, and thou shalt carry it up to Jerusalem (v. 16). This was the nearest seaport to Jerusalem, located about 35 miles east of Joppa, with rugged territory in between. Solomon indeed needed many workmen to transport shiploads of lumber over that distance.

Solomon's Census of His Forced Labor Gangs

Verses 17-18, And Solomon numbered all the sojourners that were in the land of Israel, after the numbering wherewith David his father had numbered them; and they were found a hundred and fifty thousand and three thousand and six hundred. 18 And he set threescore and ten thousand of them to bear burdens, and fourscore thousand that were hewers in the mountains, and three thousand and six hundred overseers to set the people at work.

After the numbering wherewith David his father had numbered them (v. 17). This means that Solomon's

numbering was sinful exactly as was David's (1C 21:1-17).

There is no device by which this paragraph could be construed as the Chronicler's compliment to king Solomon. In fact, right here we have the clue to what was wrong with David's 'numbering Israel' (1C 22:2f). Both he and Solomon were actually in the business of enslaving all of the aliens and sojourners in Israel, (descendants of the original Canaanites whom Israel did not drive out), for one purpose only, that of forcing them to labor in the building of the temple. Here is also the explanation of that total number given at the head of this chapter, namely, 150,000 workers and 3,600 overseers. The census came first, and Solomon compelled all those numbered to enter his forced labor gangs.

To set the people at work (v. 18). "This means ***to compel them to work***. Probably like the Egyptian and Assyrian overseers of forced labor, these officers carried whips to quicken the movement of the sluggish."[10]

It was the brutal and heartless wickedness of Solomon in this very particular that precipitated the rebellion of the ten northern tribes in the reign of Solomon's son Rehoboam. It happened, when Rehoboam sent the hated slave-driver Adoram to negotiate with the dissatisfied northern tribes (1K 12:18). See our further comment on this in I Kings.

XXX

---

10 AB, op. cit., p. 273.

CHAPTER 3

Instructions Solomon Received for Building the Temple, And Things He did Sinfully

The chief problem in this chapter relates to verse 3, which in our version states that,

> ***These are the foundations which Solomon laid for the building of the house of God.***

Yet the foundations are not even mentioned in this chapter. Furthermore, the **RSV** states that "These are Solomon's measurements." The **GNB** omits the statement, and James Moffat has; "Here is the ground-plan drawn up by Solomon." It is quite evident that the the true meaning of the verse is disputed.

This writer believes that the **KJV** should be followed in verse 3. The translators of that version believed that they were translating God's word, but that conviction no longer guides the renditions of many modern translators; and their fanciful 'emendations,' given for the purpose of giving 'what the Spirit intended to say,' or 'what He really meant.' are frequently inaccurate.

> ***Now these are the things wherein Solomon was instructed for the building of the house of God---* KJV.**

This rendition is undoubtedly the best one; and it has the utility of clearing up what would otherwise be an impossible contradiction later in v. 14. Also the **ASV** honored this translation of the passage by including it in the marginal reference.

What is the significance of this? Verse 14 below

mention's Solomon's making the veil of the temple; but we have already noted that Solomon actually made two doors of olive-wood for the entrance to the oracle, and not a veil; therefore the reference here to his 'making the veil' should be understood, not as what he did, but as what he was instructed to do, as plainly indicated in v. 3. See our comment on this in the commentary on I Kings, p. 76.

Of course, there is another way of reconciling Kings and Chronicles regarding the two olive-wood doors (Kings) and the veil (Chronicles), namely, by the conclusion that the temple had both! While such is possible, that idea will not appeal to very many people.

Contrary to the usual opinion of commentators that the Chronicler was attempting to glorify Solomon in these chapters, this writer believes he had a totally different purpose, including here, not what Solomon had done with those olive-wood doors, but what he had been instructed to do by his father David, namely, to make the veil.

This was by no means all of Solomon's violations of God's word. Those extravagantly large cherubim, the graven images of lions on each side of his throne, and the twelve brazen oxen that supported the laver, and the pagan pillars Jachin and Boaz ---all of which violations are mentioned by the Chronicler, and to indicate, contrary to what many suppose, that the Chronicler was not attempting to glorify Solomon.

Solomon Begins Actual Construction of the Temple

Verses 1-7, Then Solomon began to build the house of Jehovah at Jerusalem on mount Moriah, where Jehovah appeared unto David his father, which he made ready in the place which David had appointed, in the threshing-floor of Ornan the Jebusite. 2 And he began to build in the second day of the second month, in the fourth year of his reign. 3 Now these are the foundations which Solomon laid for the building of the house of God. The length by cubits after the first measure was threescore cubits, and the breadth twenty cubits. 4 And the porch that was before the house, the length of it, according to the breadth of the house, was twenty cubits, and the height a hundred and twenty; and he overlaid it within with pure gold. 5 And the greater house he ceiled with fir-wood; which he overlaid with fine gold, and wrought thereon palm-trees and chains. 6 And he garnished the house with precious stones for beauty: and the gold was gold of Parvaim. 7 And he overlaid also the house, the beams, the thresholds, and the walls thereof, and the doors thereof, with gold; and graved cherubim on the walls.

And he began to build ... in the fourth year of his reign (v. 2). "The delay to the fourth year may have been duc to the problems of collecting materials, or it may represent a four-year co-regency of Solomon with his father Daivd."[1]

Verses 3. See chapter heading for discussion of

---

[1] NLBC, p. 495.

this.

And the porch ... the height a hundred and twenty (cubits) (v. 4). "This height which so much exceeds the height of the main building (1K 6:2) should probably be corrected by the reading of the Arabic version and by the Alexandrian Septuagint, which read twenty cubits."[2]

In this connection, we wonder why the **RSV** failed to make this obviously indicated correction. They have not failed to make many other changes with even less authority.

Regarding the Holy of Holies

Verses 8-9, And he made the most holy house: the length thereof, according to the breadth of the house, was twenty cubits, and the breadth thereof twenty cubits; and he overlaid it with fine gold, amounting to six hundred talents. 9 And the weight of the nails was fifty shekels of gold. And he overlaid the upper chambers with gold.

The upper chambers mentioned here do not conform to any architectural description, either of their utility, or their exact location. The whole chapter appears to have a strange mixture of things that Solomon was instructed to do, and did not do, and of things which he did contrary to God's will.

---

[2] AB, *Chronicles*, p. 373.

Those Gargantuan Cherubim

Verses 10-13, And in the most holy house he made two cherubim of image work; and they overlaid them with gold. 11 And the wings of the cherubim were twenty cubits long. The wing of the one cherub was five cubits, reaching to the wall of the house; and the other wing was likewise five cubits, reaching to the wing of the other cherub. 12 And the wing of the other cherub was five cubits, reaching to the wall of the house; and the other wing was five cubits also, joining to the wing of the other cherub. 13 The wings of the cherubim spread themsleves forth twenty cubits; and they stood on their feet; and their faces were toward the house.

These colossal figures violated all of Moses' instructions regarding their use in the tabernacle. They were not supposed to fill up the house, but were intended to decorate the mercy seat, which was in fact a lid for the ark of the covenant. Furthermore, they were not supposed to "face the house" but to be in a posture of peering down intently into the mercy seat. One may find what these figurines were supposed to be in Exodus 25. They were to face each other, with their wings overshadowing the mercy seat, not to be standing side by side facing the outer sanctuary. Their wings were to pertain not to the whole Holy of Holies, but to the mercy seat alone. The apostle Peter referred to the symbolical significance of these cherubim in 1Peter 1:12.

Verse 14, And he made the veil of blue, and purple, and crimson, and fine linen, and wrought cherubim theron.

See chapter heading for our perplexity regarding this verse. Significantly, it is not stated that this veil sealed off the Holy of Holies, although it may be implied. Certainly that is what should have been done; but 1 Kings 6 indicates that olive-wood doors were used. One thing is certain, the Herodian temple had the veil.

Another One of Solomon's Sins: Jachin and Boaz

Verses 15-17, And he made before the house two pillars of thirty and five cubits high, and the capital that was upon each of them was five cubits. 16 And he made chains in the oracle, and put them on the tops of the pillars; and he made a hundred pomegranates, and put them on the chains. 17 And he set up the pillars before the temple, one of the right hand, and the other on the left; and he called the name of that on the right hand Jachin, and the name of that on the left Boaz.

See our full discussion of these pagan pillars which Solomon put in front of the temple in our commentary on 1Kings, pp. 83-85.

The accounts in Kings and Chronicles vary as to the exact dimensions of those pillars; but so what? they were sinful innovations anyway.

xxx

CHAPTER 4

More of Solomon's Sinful Changes

The Sinful Laver and the Sinful Images Placed Under the Laver

Verses 1-6, Moreover he made an altar of brass, twenty cubits the length thereof, and twenty cubits the breadth thereof, and ten cubits the height thereof.
2 Also he made the molten sea of ten cubits from brim to brim, round in compass; and the height thereof was five cubits; and a line of thirty cubits compassed it round about.
3 And under it was the likeness of oxen, which did compass it round about, for ten cubits, compassing the sea round about. The oxen were in two rows, cast when it was cast.
4 It stood upon twelve oxen, three looking toward the north, and three looking toward the west, and three looking toward the south, and three looking toward the east: and the sea was set upon them, above, and all their hinder parts were inward.
5 And it was a handbreadth thick; and the brim thereof was wrought like the brim of a cup, like the flower of a lily: it received and held three thousand baths.
6 He made also ten lavers, and put five on the right hand, and five on the left, to wash in them; such things as belonged to the burnt-offering they washed in them; but the sea was for the priests to wash in.

He made an altar of brass ... the height thereof ten cubits (v. 1). What was wrong with this? Ten cubits was a height of something like fifteen feet, which required that steps would have to be used by the priests in making sacrifices upon it; and God had specifically commanded Israel, ""Neither shalt thou go up by steps unto my altar" (Exodus 20:26).

Not only did Solomon's temple and all that it contained violate many of God's specific commandments, such as this one; but there were also countless concessions to paganism, as seen in the images of the bulls (politely called oxen here) placed under the laver. The bulls, calves, oxen, whatever they were called, were the usual images under which the old Canaanite fertitlity god Baal was worshipped. Even the Jewish historian Josephus condemned Solomon for what he did in this.[1] It is an unqualified mystery to us why "Christian" writers attempt to justify it! Besides that, the Decalogue specifically forbade the making of images, or 'likenesses' of anything either in heaven or on earth, the sacred images of the cherubim commanded by Moses, having been one exception to this.

It ... held three thousand baths (v. 5). The bath was a Jewish measure, being the equivalent of about 4 and 7/8 gallons.[2] The very size of this laver was a testimonial to the type of 'washing' to which the priests submitted. It was by immersion,[3] being in that particular typical of Christian baptism. For further elaboration of this, see our ***Commentary on Exodus,*** pp. 404,405.

---

[1] JOSA, p. 255.

[2] NBCR, p. 331.

[3] Michael Esses, ***Jesus in Exodus,*** (Plainfield, N. J.: Logos International,1977, p. 205.

Solomon's Corruped Version of the the Golden Candlesticks

Verses 7-11, And he made the candlesticks of gold according to the ordinance concerning them; and he set them in the temple, five on the right side, and five on the left. 8 He made also ten tables, and placed them in the temple, five on the right side, and five on the left. And he made a hundred basins of gold. 9 Furthermore he made the court of the priests, and the great court, and doors for the court, and overlaid the doors of them with brass. 10 And he set the sea on the right side of the house eastward, toward the south. 11 And Huram made the pots, and the shovels, and the basins.

There was hardly anything that Solomon touched that he did not corrupt it in one way or another. The candlestick he perverted from the divine pattern of seven branches, and made it into ten. Instead of putting it on the south side of the holy place, he put five on one side, and five on the other. The table of the showbread was changed into ten tables with five on the north side and five on the south (v. 19).

He made the candlesticks of gold according to the ordinance concerning them (v. 7). This should not mislead us. God had indeed required the calndlesticks to be of gold; and, in that alone did Solomon heed the divine ordinance. That this is true is proved by the fact that when the second temple was constructed, the golden candlestick was again conformed to the pattern in the tabernacle, as proved by the bas relief depicting it upon the Arch of Titus in Rome, where it is visible today.

The Conclusion of the Work of Huram of Tyre

Verses 11b-18, So Huram made an end of doing the work that he wrought for king Solomon in the house of God: 12 the two pillars, and the bowls, and the two capitals which were on the tops of the pillars, and the two networks to cover the two bowls of the capitals that were on the top of the pillars, 13 and the four hundred pomegranates for the two networks; two rows of pomegranates for each network, to cover the two bowls of the capitals that were upon the pillars. 14 He made also the bases, and the lavers made he upon the bases; 15 one sea, and the twelve oxen under it. 16 The pots also, and the shovels, and the flesh-hooks, and all the vessels thereof, did Huram his father make for king Solomon, for the house of Jehovah, of bright brass. 17 In the plain of the Jordan did the king cast them, in the clay ground between Succoth and Zeredah. 18 Thus Solomon made all these vessels in great abundance; for the weight of the brass could not be found out.

Huram his father (v. 16). **According to Payne, Solomon had conferred the title 'father' upon Huram in recognition of his skilled craftsmanship; and the reference here means Solomon's** *Father Huram*.[4]

[4] WYC, p. 395.

Before leaving this chapter, we should also point out that another interpretation of Solomon's Ten Candlesticks views them as ten complete candlesticks (of seven branches each). Either was a violation of the true pattern given by Moses. In support of that view, it is clear enough that ten tables of the showbread were used, but not, "one at a time" as Payne thought, for they were on opposite sides of the holy place, five on each side.

And King Solomon Did all This

Verses 19-22, And Solomon made all the vessels that were in the house of God, the golden altar also, and the tables whereon was the showbread; 20 and the candlesicks with their lamps, to burn according to the ordinance before the oracle, of pure gold; 21 and the flowers, and the lamps, and the tongs, of gold, and that perfect gold; 22 and the snuffers, and the basins, and the spoons, and the firepans, of pure gold. And as for the entry of the house, the inner doors thereof for the most holy place, and the doors of the house, to wit, of the temple, were of gold.

And Solomon made all these vessels (v. 19). Yet, it was stated above that Huram made all these things. Thus we have another example of the biblical conception that a man does what he commands or employs another to do. We have referred to this in our contention that David indeed built the temple contrary to God's prohibition.

As for the inner doors ... of the most holy place ... they were of gold (v. 22). Several commentators have stated that the olive-wood doors of the Holy of Holies were not mentioned by the Chronicler, but here they are, the meaning being that they were overlaid with gold. This is further evidence that the veil was omitted.

XXX

CHAPTER 5

The Ark Placed in Temple; God's Glory Fills House

Dedicated Things Deposited in Temple

Verse 1, Thus all the work that Solomon wrought for the house of Jehovah was finished. And Solomon brought in the things that David his father had dedicated, even the silver, and the gold, and all the vessels, and put them in the treasuries of the house of God.

The Ark Brought Into the Holy of Holies

Verses 2-10, Then Solomon assembled the elders of Israel, and all the heads of the tribes, the princes of the fathers' houses of the children of Israel, unto Jerusalem, to bring up the ark of the covenant of Jehovah out of the city of David, which is Zion. 3 And all the children of Israel assembled themselves unto the king at the feast, which was in the seventh month. 4 And all the elders of Israel came: and the Levites took up the ark; 5 and they brought up the ark, and the tent of meeting, and all the vessels that were in the Tent; these did the priests the Levites bring up. 6 And king Solomon and all the congregation of Israel, that were assembled unto him, went before the ark, sacrificing sheep and oxen, that could not be counted nor numbered for multitude. 7 And the priests brought in the ark of the covenant of Jehovah unto its place, into the oracle of the house, to the most holy place, even under the wings of the cherubim. 8 For the cherubim spread forth their wings over the place of the ark, and the cherubim covered the ark and the staves thereof above. 9 And the staves were so long

that the ends of the staves were seen from the ark before the oracle; but they were not seen without: and there it is unto this day. 10 There was nothing in the ark save the two tables that Moses put there at Horeb, when Jehovah made a covenant with the children of Israel, when they came out of Egypt.

"All of chapters 5, 6 & 7 is virtually identical with 1 Kings 8:1-9:9, the few additions giving mainly liturgical information."[1] Our ***Commentary on 1 Kings*** has our discussion of what is contained in this section.

The city of David, which is Zion (v. 2). Zion was the old citadel and stronghold of the Jebusites which David captured. The temple was located north of Zion on the elevation known as Moriah.

And there it is unto this day (v. 9). These words are from the ancient source quoted by the Chronicler (Ezra); because the temple no longer stood when Chronicles was written.

A Cloud Symbolizing God's Glory Filled the Temple

Verses 11-14, And it came to pass, when the priests were come out of the holy place (for all the priests that were present had sanctified themsleves, and did not keep their courses; 12 also the Levites who were the singers, all of them, even Asaph, Heman, and Jeduthun, and their sons and their brethren, arrayed in fine linen, with cymbals and psalteries and harps, stood at the east end of the altar, and

---

[1] NBCR, p. 385.

with them a hundred and twenty priests sounding with trumpets); 13 and it came to pass, when the trumpeters and the singers were as one, to make one sound to be heard in praising and thanking Jehovah; and when they lifted up their voice with the trumpets and cymbals and instruments of music, and praised Jehovah, saying, For he is good; for his lovingkindness endureth for ever; that the house was filled with a cloud, even the house of Jehovah, 14 so that priests could not stand to minister by reason of the cloud: for the glory of Jehovah filled the house of God.

"The significnce of the temple is made specific in the ceremonies that accompanied its dedication. They designated the Temple to be the lineal successor to Israel's previous sanctuaries."[2] The ark of the covenant and the tent of meeting were brought into the temple, and God recognized the temple as the place where his name was recorded and where a manifestation of his earthly presence would dwell.

In view of all the sins and rebellions of Israel, and of the sins and failures of David, and especially of Solomon, and in consideration of the basic truth that God never commanded the building of the temple in the first place ----in spite of all this, God remained firm and immovable in his promise to Abraham that, "in him and in his seed (singular) "(Genesis 12:3), all the familes of mankind would be blessed. To fulfill that glorious promise to the patriarchs, it was impossible for God to reject their physical descendants until the

---

[2] WYC, p. 395.

Messiah had been delivered, no matter what misunderstandings or outright sins and rebellions marked the behavior of the Chosen People. We may state it bluntly that, God was stuck with Israel until He had achieved the Grand Objective, namely, that of bringing the Prince of Life into our lost and ruined race. This simple truth explains ***why*** God accepted the temple, honored it with his presence, and sent fire from heaven as another positive indication of his approval (7:1-10).

"The cloud of God's glory that filled the temple (vv. 11-14), was called the ***SHEKINAH.***"[3]

XXX

---

[3] Ibid., p. 395.

CHAPTER 6

Solomon Addresses Israel; His Dedicatory Prayer

His Address

Verses 1-11, Then spake Solomon, Jehovah hath said he that would dwell in the thick darkness. 2 But I have built thee a house of habitation, and a place for thee to dwell in for ever. 3 And the king turned his face, and blessed all the assembly of Israel: and all the assembly of Israel stood.

4 And he said, Blessed be the God of Israel, who spake with his mouth to David my father, and with his hands hath fulfilled it, saying, 5 Since the day that I brought forth my people out of the land of Egypt, I chose no city out of all the tribes of Israel to build a house in, that my name might be there; neither chose I any man to be prince over my people Israel: 6 but I have chosen Jerusalem, that my name might be there, and have chosen David to be over my people Israel. 7 Now it was in the heart of David my father to build a house for the name of Jehovah, the God of Israel. 8 But Jehovah said unto David my father, Whereas it was in thy heart to build a house for my name, thou didst well that it was in thy heart: 9 nevertheless thou shalt not build the house; but thy son that shall come forth out of thy loins, he shall build the house for my name. 10 And Jehovath hath performed the word that he spake; for I am risen up in the room of David, and sit on the throne of Israel, as Jehovah promised, and have built the house for the name of Jehovah, the God of Israel. 11 And therein have I set the ark, wherein is the covenant of Jehovah, which he made with the children of Israel.

Without supposing for a moment that Solomon was insincere in this address, we must nevertheless conclude that he was profoundly mistaken in his positive identification of himself as that descendant who would build God a house for his name for ever. That Person was none other than Jesus Christ our Lord. That Holy One was to be God's Son, and God would be his father. On the other hand David, not God, was Solomon's father; and also, that Great Builder of the true Temple of God, namely, the Church of Jesus Christ, was one who would rise up ***after David.*** Solomon rose up ***with David*** and was co-regent with David for an unknown number of years. See 2S 8.

The Dedicatory Prayer

a. An appeal for God to keep his promises:

Verses 12-17, And he stood before the altar of Jehovah in the presence of all the assembly of Israel, and spread forth his hands 13 (for Solomon had made a brazen scaffold, five cubits long, and five cubits broad, and three cubits high, and had set it in the midst of the court; and upon it he stood, and kneeled down upon his knees before all the assembly of Israel, and spread forth his hands toward heaven); 14 and he said, O Jehovah, the God of Israel, there is no god like thee, in heaven, or on earth; who keepest covenant and lovingkindness with thy servants, that walk before thee with all their heart; 15 who hast kept with thy servant David my father that which thou didst promise

him: yea, thou spakest with thy mouth, and hast fulfilled it with thy hand, as it is this day. 16 Now therefore, O Jehovah, the God of Israel, keep with thy servant David my father that which thou hast promised him, saying, There shall not fail thee a man in my sight to sit on the throne of Israel, if only thy children take heed to their way, to walk in my law as thou hast walked before me. 17 Now therefore, O Jehovah, the God of Israel, let thy word be verified, which thou spakest unto thy servant David.

b. Solomon prays for forgiveness for himself and Israel:

Verses 18-21, But will God in very deed dwell with men on the earth? behold, heaven and the heaven of heavens cannot contain thee; how much less this house which I have builded! 19 Yet have thou respect unto the prayer of thy servant, and to his supplication, O Jehovah, my God, to hearken unto the cry and to the prayer which thy servant prayeth before thee; 20 that thine eyes be open toward this house day and night, even toward the place whereof thou hast said that thou wouldest put thy name there; to hearken unto the prayer which thy servant shall pray toward this place. 21 And hearken thou to the supplication of thy servant, and of thy people Israel, when they shall pray toward this place: yea, hear thou from thy dwelling place, even from heaven; and when thou hearest, forgive.

c, A prayer for God to execute justice against evil-doers:

Verses 22-23, If a man sin against his neighbor, and an oath be laid upon him to cause him to swear, and he come and swear before thine altar in this house; 23 then hear thou from heaven, and do, and judge thy servants, requiting the wicked, to bring his way upon his own head; and justifying the righteous, to give him according to his righteousness.

d, A prayer that even after sin and defeat Israel may find forgiveness if they repent, confess, and pray:

Verses 24-25, And if thy people Israel be smitten down before the enemy, because they have sinned against thee, and shall turn again, and confess thy name, and pray and make supplication before thee in this house; 25 then hear thou from heaven, and forgive the sin of thy people Israel, and bring them again unto the land which thou gavest to them and to their fathers.

e, --- that Israel through repentance and prayer may end a drouth:

Verses 26-28, When the heavens are shut up, and there is no rain, because they have sinned against thee; if they pray toward this place, and confess thy name, and turn from their sin, when thou dost afflict them: 27 then hear thou in heaven, and forgive the sin of thy servants, and of thy people Israel, when thou teachest them the good way wherein they should walk; and send rain upon thy

land, which thou hast given to thy people for an inheritance.

f, ---that Israel through repentance and prayer may find relief from any kind of calamity:

Verses 28-31, If there be in the land famine, if there be pestilence, if there be blasting or mildew, locust or caterpillar; if their enemies besiege them in their cities; whatsoever plague or whatsoever sickness there be; 29 what prayer and supplication soever be made by any man, or by all thy people Israel, who shall know every man his own plague and his own sorrow, and shall spread forth his hands toward this house: 30 then hear thou from heaven thy dwelling place, and forgive, and render unto every man according to all his ways, whose heart thou knowest (for thou, even thou only, knowest the hearts of the children of men): 31 that they may fear thee, to walk in thy ways, so long as they live in the land which thou gavest unto our fathers.

g, ---that non-Israelites also may be heard and blessed of God:

Verses 32-33, Moreover concerning the foreigner, that is not of thy people Israel, when he shall come from a far country for thy great name's sake, and thy mighty hand, and thine outstretched arm; when they shall come and pray toward this house: 33 then hear thou from heaven, even from thy dwelling place, and do according to all that the foreigner calleth to thee for; that all the peoples of the earth

may know thy name, and fear thee, as doth thy people Israel, and that they may know that this house which I have built is called by thy name.

h, ---that Israel in battle may have victory through prayer:

Verses 34-35, If thy people go out to battle against their enemies, by whatsoever way thou shalt send them, and they pray unto thee toward this city which thou hast chosen, and the house which I have built for thy name; 35 then hear thou from heaven their prayer and their supplication, and maintain their cause.

i, ---that even if carried away captive Israel still may be heard and blessed of God:

Verses 36-39, If they sin against thee (for there is no man that sinneth not), and thou be angry with them, and deliver them to the enemy, so that they carry them away captive unto a land far off or near; 37 yet if they shall bethink themselves in the land whither they are carried captive, and turn again, and make supplication unto thee in the land of their captivity, saying, We have sinned, we have done perversely, and have dealt wickedly; 38 if they return unto thee with all their heart and with all their soul in the land of their captivity, whither they have carried them captive, and pray toward their land, which thou gavest unto their fathers, and the city which thou hast chosen, and toward the house which I have built for thy name: 39 then hear thou from heaven, even from thy dwelling place, their prayer and their supplications, and

maintain their cause, and forgive thy people who have sinned against thee.

j, Conclusion of Solomon's dedicatory prayer:

Verses 40-42, Now, O my God, let, I beseech thee, thine eyes be open, and let thine ears be attent, unto the prayer that is made in this place. 41 Now therefore, arise, O Jehovah God, into thy resting place, thou, and the ark of thy strength: let thy priests, O Jehovah God, be clothed with salvation, and let thy saints rejoice in goodness. 42 O Jehovah God, turn not away the face of thine anointed: remember thy lovingkindness to David thy servant.

The theology of this prayer is glorious indeed. (a) God dwells not in any earthly place, "the heaven of heavens cannot contain him." (b) Forgiveness of sins is available only for those who repent (turn again), confess, and pray. (c) The blessing of God is not for any race alone, not even for Israel; but it is also for those who are not of Israel. (d) All have sinned. (e) Disasters of various kinds come upon men because of their wickedness. (e) The great need of every man is ***forgiveness.*** Note how often the plea for God to forgive is uttered. (f) The omniscience of God who knows the hearts of all men, etc.

No fault may be found in this magnificent prayer. It probably represents the very zenith of Solomon's spiritual life. What a pity that the great man who prayed this prayer became the prime builder of pagan temples in his generation! We shall not attempt to make excuse for Solomon's disastrous failure, other than to point out that the ancient proverb, namely, that ***POWER CORRUPTS, AND TOTAL POWER CORRUPTS TOTALLY,*** was amazingly verified in the life of Solomon.

As we have already pointed out, these chapters are virtually identical with the account in First Kings, where what comments we have on this are written.

XXX

CHAPTER 7

Fire from Heaven; the Great Feast; God warns Solomon

The Fire from Heaven

Verses 1-3, Now when Solomon had made an end of praying, the fire came down from heaven, and consumed the burnt-offering and the sacrifices; and the glory of Jehovah filled the house. 2 And the priests could not enter the house of Jehovah, because the glory of Jehovah filled Jehovah's house. 3 And all the children of Israel looked on, when the fire came down, and the glory of Jehovah was upon the house; and they bowed themselves down with their faces to the ground upon the pavement, and worshipped, and gave thanks unto Jehovah, saying, For he is good; for his lovingkindness endureth for ever.

Other biblical accounts of fire coming down from heaven to consume sacrifices are: (1) at the Mosaic tabernacle (Leviticus 9:24), (2) before Manoah (Judges 13:20), and (3) at the Davidic altar on mount Moriah (1 C 21:26). Curtis (Madsen) believed that the Chronicler "invented" this;[1] but the mystery to this writer is not the the fire from heaven, which is not any more wonderful than a hundred other things recorded in the OT, but, ***WHY WOULD ANY SCHOLAR WHO DOES NOT BELIEVE WHAT IS WRITTEN, WASTE A LIFETIME OF STUDY ON WHAT HE THINKS IS A FALSEHOOD?*** The attention that unbelievers bestow upon the sacred text is a tacit confession that they ***do believe it.*** If they think the Bible is false, why do

---

1 ICC, *Chronicles,* p. 347.

they bother themselves about it? As Shakespeare stated it, "Methinks (he) dost protest too much."[2]

Sacrifices prepared for the Great Feast

Verses 4-7, Then the king and all the people offered sacrifices before Jehovah. 5 And king Solomon offered a sacrifice of twenty and two thousand oxen, and a hundred and twenty thousand sheep. So the king and all the people dedicated the house of God. 6 And the priests stood according to their offices; the Levites also with instruments of music of Jehovah, which David the king had made to give thanks unto Jehovah (for his lovingkindness endureth for ever), when David praised by their ministry: and the priests sounded trumpets before them; and all Israel stood. 7 Moreover Solomon hallowed the middle of the court that was before the house of Jehovah; for there he offered the burnt-offerings, and the fat of the peace-offerings, because the brazen altar which Solomon had made was not able to receive the burnt-offering, and the meal-offering, and the fat.

Solomon evidently felt free to make any changes in the sacred rituals that came to his mind. The use here of another altar, other than the official one, is only one of many innovations and changes initiated by Solomon. The tremendous numbers of animals sacrificed on this occasion is a problem in the minds of some; but there is no honest device by which men in the

---

[2] William Shakespeare, ***Hamlet,*** Act III, S c. 2, Line 149.

20th century, three thousand years afterwards, can make any dependable corrections for what is written. Our comment is simply: "That must have been some big barbecue"!

The Feast Lasted Three Weeks

Verses 8-10, So Solomon held the feast at that time seven days, and all Israel with him, a very great assembly, from the entrance of Hamath to the brook of Egypt. 9 And on the eighth day they held a solemn assembly: for they kept the dedication of the altar seven days, and the feast seven days. 10 And on the three and twentieth day of the seventh month he sent the people away unto their tents, joyful and glad of heart for the goodness that Jehovah had showed unto David, and to Solomon, and to Israel his people.

Here we have the information that explains the need for the tremendous number of animals sacrificed. The whole nation of Israel, perhaps a million or more, all the way from Hamath to the brook of Egypt attended this celebration; and they had to be fed for almost a month (twenty-three days).

On the three and twentieth day of the seventh month (v. 10). "The seventh month was September/October. The dedication did not take place till ***after*** the work was completed (v. 1) in the eighth month (Oct./Nov.) of Solomon's eleventh year (960 BC). So the temple was not dedicated till eleven months had passed, that is, in 959 BC, at the time of the annual feast of the tabernacles (cf 7:8-10)."[3] From this it is evident that Solomon delayed the dedication almost a year in order to make it coincide with the annual feast of tabernacles which the whole nation was required to attend, thus assuring the largest possible assembly.

God's Response to Solomon's Prayer

Verses 11-18, Thus Solomon finished the house of Jehovah, and the king's house: and all that came into Solomon's heart to make in the house of Jehovah, and in his own house, he prosperously effected. 12 And Jehovah appeared to Solomon by night, and said unto him, I have heard thy prayer, and have chosen this place to myself for a house of sacrifice. 13 If I shut up the heavens so that there is no rain, or if I command the locust to devour the land, or if I send pestilence among my people; 14 if my people who are called by name, shall humble themselves, and pray, and seek my face, and turn from their wicked ways; then will I hear from heaven, and will forgive their sin, and will heal their land. 15 Now mine eyes shall be open, and mine ears attent, unto the prayer that is made in this place. 16 For now have I chosen and hallowed this house, that my name may be there for ever; and mine eyes and my heart shall be there perpetually. 17 And as for thee, if thou wilt walk before me as David thy father walked, and do according to all that I have commanded thee, and wilt keep my statutes and mine ordinances; 18 then will I establish the throne of thy kingdom, according as I covenanted with

---

[3] WYC, p. 395.

David thy father, saying, there shall not fail thee a son to be ruler in Israel.

Thus Solomon finished ... all that came into Solomon's heart (v. 11). These are the ominous words in the paragraph. Solomon did not do everything according to God's word, but according to everything he imagined, being guided, only in the most general sense, by the pattern that David had given him for the temple. Nevertheless, before giving Solomon the stern warning that he deserved, God announced his favorable response to Solomon's prayer. In a word, it merely stated that God would do the things Solomon had prayed for. Then came the warning.

Jehovah appeared to Solomon by night (v. 12). There is nothing here to indicate that this was some kind of a dazzling personal appearance. The very fact of its having been at night supports the presumption that God appeared unto him in a dream, as he had appeared the first time at Gibeon.

God's Warning to King Solomon

Verses 19-22, But if ye turn away and forsake my statutes and my commandments which I have set before you, and shall go and serve other gods, and worship them; 20 then will I pluck them up by the roots out of my land which I have given them; and this house, which I have hallowed for my name, will I cast out of my sight, and I will make it a proverb and a byword among all peoples. 21 And

this house, which is so high, everyone that passeth by it shall be astonished, and shall say, Why hath Jehovah done this unto this land? 22 And they shall answer, Because they forsook Jehovah, the God of their fathers, who brought them forth out of the land of Egypt, and laid hold on other gods, and worshipped them, and served them: therefore hath he brought all this evil upon them.

This heavenly warning Solomon ignored and continued to do exactly as he pleased without regard to anything except his conceited opinions; and when he became old, his many pagan wives turned his heart away from the Lord; and he built pagan temples for every one of them. This needs no further comment, except to note that the removal of Israel from Palestine and the destruction of their temple indeed took place, exactly as God had warned.

XXX

CHAPTER 8

Concluding Summary of Solomon's Reign

Regarding His Extensive Building Program

Verses 1-6, And it came to pass at the end of twenty years, wherein Solomon had built the house of Jehovah, and his own house, 2 that the cities which Huram had given to Solomon, Solomon built them, and caused the children of Israel to dwell in them. 3 And Solomon went to Hamath-Zobah, and prevailed against it. 4 And he built Tadmore in the wilderness, and all the store-cities which he built in Hamath. 5 Also he built Beth-horon the upper, and Beth-horon the nether, fortified cities with walls, gates, and bars; 6 and Baalath, and all the store-cities that Solomon had, and the cities for the horsemen, and all that Solomon desired to build for his pleasure in Jerusalem, and in Lebanon, and in all the land of his dominion.

The 20th Century Christian, as a general rule, could have little or no interest in Solomon's building program, which, in the matter of his huge horse business, to say nothing of anything else, was a violation of God's word.

And all that Solomon desired to build for his pleasure in Jerusalem ... Lebanon ... in all ... his dominion (v.6). Again we have the Chronicler's word that Solomon recognized no other limitation except his own undisciplined desires. Read our comment under 7:11, above. The Chronicler has mercifully spared us the details concerning these multiple pleasure-houses

Solomon built all over Palestine.

Solomon's Merciless Enslavement of the Residual Canaanites

Verses 7-10, As for all the people that were left of the Hittites, and the Amorites, and the Perizzites, and the Hivites, and the Jebusites, that were not of Israel; 8 of their children that were left after them in the land, whom the children of Israel consumed not, of them did Solomon raise a levy of bondservants unto this day. 9 But of the children of Israel did Solomon make no servants for his work; but they were men of war, and chief of his captains, and rulers of his chariots and his horsemen. 10 And these were the chief officers of king Solomon, even two hundred and fifty, that bare rule over the people.

Solomon raised a levy of bondservants (v. 8). These descendants of the original Canaanites whom Israel had displaced, were first conscripted and enslaved for building the temple and the king's house, some 153,600 of them (2C 2:1-2); but the significance of this mention of them is that, after the completion of Solomon's building program, they were permanently enslaved. No doubt these were used as waiters and servants of that vast concourse of people who attended the feast of the dedication.

It is not hard to understand why the Israelites considered this an ideal arrangement indeed, and why, even down to the times of Christ, the Jews desired absolutely nothing, either in heaven or on earth, except the restoration of that godless slave-state of king Solomon, to which restoration their expected Messiah was vainly supposed by them to devote his entire resources! The reason they rejected Christ was their realization that he would never cooperate in such a restoration.

The Removal of Pharaoh's Daughter from the Holy Places

Verse 11. And Solomon brought up the daughter of Pharaoh out of the city of David unto the house he had built for her; and he said, My wife shall not dwell in the house of David king of Israel, because the places are holy, whereunto the ark of Jehovah hath come.

Solomon had married the daughter of Pharaoh quite early in his reign (1K 3:1), and the action mentioned here evidently took place at an early time in Solomon's reign when he still retained some sensitivity to the implications of the word of God. "This daughter of Pharaoh was the daughter of Hor-Psibkhannu, the last Pharaoh of the weak Twenty-First Dynasty. Her idolatries eventually led to the apostasy of Israel (1K 11:1ff)"[1]

Solomon's Offering the Commanded Sacrifices

Verses 12-13, Then Solomon offered burnt-offerings unto Jehovah on the altar of Jehovah which he

---

1 WYC, p. 398.

had built before the porch, 13 even as the duty of every day required, offering according to the commandment of Moses, on the sabbaths, and on the new moons, and on the set feasts, three times in the year, even in the feast of unleavened bread, and in the feast of weeks, and in the feast of tabernacles.

There are some uncertainties here. There seems to be an implied disapproval of Solomon's actions in offering all these sacrifices, which certainly were offered upon an unauthorized altar; and the word ***even*** in v. 13 most certainly suggests that what Solomon did here was sinful in usurping ritualistic functions that pertained to the priests. Francisco, however, insists that, "Solomon was directing the activities and was not personally involved."[2] We accept this opinion as accurate, because we cannot possibly imagine that this pleasure-mad monarch would have had the self-discipline required for doing what is stated in these verses.

Of course, the specific mention of all these sacrifices which are elaborately spelled out in the Pentateuch is further proof of its Mosaic authorship, and of king Solomon's thorough acquaintance with it a full half millennium before modern radical critics would date it if they could.

---

2 BBC, Vol. 3, p. 374.

Solomon Confirmed David's Instructions for the Levites

Verses 14-15, And he appointed, according to the ordinance of David his father, the courses of the priests to their service, and the Levites to their offices, to praise, and to minister before the priests, as the duty of every day required; the doorkeepers also by their courses at every gate: for so had David the man of God commanded. 15 And they departed not from the commandment of the king unto the priests and Levites concerning any matter, or concerning the treasure.

David's commandments regarding the duties of the priests and the Levites, in many particulars, were derived from instructions in the Pentateuch, but that does not apply to his innovative introduction of all kinds of mechanical instruments of music.

Conclusion of Work on the Temple

Verse 16, Now all the works of Solomon were prepared unto the day of the foundation of the house of Jehovah, and until it was finished. So the house of Jehovah was completed.

Solomon's Navy

Verses 17-18, Then went Solomon to Ezion-geber, and to Eloth, on the seashore in the land of Edom. 18 And Huram sent him by the hands of his servants ships, and servants that had knowledge of the sea; and they came with

the servants of Solomon to Ophir, and fetched from thence four hundred and fifty talents of gold, and brought them to king Solomon.

Ezion-geber, and Eloth (v.17). "These two places were near each other at the northern extremity of the Gulf of Aqabah."[3]

Four hundred and fifty talents of gold (v. 18). One can always count on the nit-pickers to contrast this with the statement in Kings that the amount was four hundred and twenty talents. Maybe sea-port taxes, sailors' wages, and other expenses were deducted in the King's account! Such variations are unimportant.

XXX

---

[3] ICC, Chronicles, p. 355.

CHAPTER 9

Conclusion of the Reign of Solomon

a. Visit of the queen of Sheba:

Verses 1-8, And when the queen of Sheba heard of the fame of Solomon, she came to prove Solomon with hard questions at Jerusalem, with a very great train, and camels that bare spices, and gold in abundance, and precious stones: and when she was come to Solomon, she communed with him of all that was in her heart. 2 And Solomon told her all her questions; and there was not anything hid from Solomon which he told her not. 3 And when the queen of Sheba had seen the wisdom of Solomon, and the house that he had built, 4 and the food of his table, and the sitting of his servants, and the attendance of his ministers, and their apparel, his cupbearers also, and their apparel, and his ascent by which he went up into the house of Jehovah; there was no more spirit in her. 5 And she said to the king, It was a true report which I heard in mine own land of thine acts and of thy wisdom. 6 Howbeit I believed not their words, until I came, and mine eyes have seen it; and, behold, the half of the greatness of thy wisdom was not told me: thou exceedest the fame that I heard. 7 Happy are thy men, and happy are these thy servants, that stand continually before thee, and hear thy wisdom. 8 Blessed be Jehovah thy God, who delighteth in thee, to set thee on his throne, to be king for Jehovah thy God: because thy God loved Israel, to establish them for ever, therefore made he thee king over them, to do justice and righteousness.

We have thoroughly discussed this visit of the queen of Sheba to Solomon in our ***Commentary on First Kings***, pp. 129-137; and there is little that we wish to add here. To summarize: (1) Sheba was most likely that Ethiopia over which Haile Selassie was the ruler during this century. (2) Solomon evidently was Haile Selassie's ancestor through this Ethiopian queen.

b. The queen and Solomon exchange gifts:

Verses 9-12, And she gave the king a hundred and twenty talents of gold, and spices in great abundance, and precious stones: neither was there any such spice as the queen of Sheba gave to king Solomon. 10 And the servants also of Huram, and the servants of Solomon, that brought gold from Ophir, brought algum trees and precious stones. 11 And the king made of the algum trees terraces for the house of Jehovah, and for the king's house, and harps and psalteries for the singers: and there was none such seen before in the land of Judah. 12 And king Solomon gave to the queen of Sheba all her desire, whatsoever she asked, besides that which she had brought to the king. So she turned and went to her own land, she and her servants.

c. Solomon multiplies unto himself silver and gold:

Verses 13-16, Now the weight of gold that came to Solomon in one year was six hundred and threescore and six talents of gold, 14 besides that which the merchants and traders brought: and all the kings of Arabia and the governors of the country brought gold and silver to

Solomon. 15 And king Solomon made two hundred bucklers of beaten gold; six hundred shekels of beaten gold went to one buckler. 16 And he made three hundred shields of beaten gold; three hundred shekels of gold went to one shield: and the king put them in the house of the forest of Lebanon.

And the kings ... and the governors ... brought gold and silver to Solomon (14). These 'gifts' must not be understood as voluntary in any sense of the word. Solomon's power which he had inherited from David gave him the means of extorting every possible penny out of the whole region. Solomon's conduct, as the Chronicler has outlined it here, is an anthology of Solomon's gross disobedience of all of God's commandments. God had specifically warned Israel's kings not to, "multiply unto themselves silver and gold," (Deuteronomy 17:16-17); and it would have been impossible for anyone to violate that commandment with any more contempt than did Solomon.

Also the Decalogue had specifically forbidden God's people to make images or likenesses of anything either in heaven or upon earth; but look at what Solomon did in the matter of those images of lions on his throne.

d. Regarding that gold-plated, idolatrous throne:

Verses 17-21, Moreover the king made a great throne of ivory, and overlaid it with pure gold. 18 And there were six steps to the throne, with a footstool of gold,

which were fastened to the throne, and stays on either side by the place of the seat, and two lions standing beside the stays. 19 And twelve lions stood there on the one side and on the other upon the six steps: there was not the like made in any kingdom. 20 And all king Solomon's drinking vessels were of gold, and all the vessels of the house of the forest of Lebanon were of pure gold: silver was nothing accounted of in the days of Solomon. 21 For the king had ships that went to Tarshish with the servants of Huram; once every three years came the ships of Tarshish, bringing gold, and silver, and ivory, and apes, and peacocks.

In addition to all of the wealth brought to Solomon by his commercial ventures, "the governors of the country" (the provincial authorities in Israel, v. 14) were also subject to oppressive taxation, to such an extent that the northern tribes demanded an easement of the burden when Solomon's son succeeded him. And what did Solomon do with all that wealth? He blew all of it in ostentatious decorations of his personal effects, "a footstool of gold"! What earthly benefit was there in a thing like that? It ministered to only one thing, Solomon's colossal, conceited pride!

One thing is absolutely a mystery to this writer. How could any scholar ever have written a paragraph like the following?

> These verses are closely paralleled in 1Kings x, the source upon which the writer relied. There was no reason to deviate from the source for it fitted quite well into his scheme for the

glorification of King Solomon![1]

Contrary to this allegation, which is frequently parroted by critical scholars, a more eloquent or convincing condemnation of Solomon's sinful conceit and violation of God's word, than that which we find right here, could not possibly have been written.

e. Solomon's riches and his alleged wisdom,

Verses 22-28, So king Solomon exceeded all the kings of the earth in riches and wisdom. 23 And all the kings of the earth sought the presence of Solomon, to hear his wisdom, which God had put in his heart. 24 And they brought every man his tribute, vessels of silver, and vessels of gold, and raiment, armor, and spices, horses and mules, a rate year by year. 25 And Solomon had four thousand stalls for horses and chariots, and twelve thousand horsemen, that he bestowed in the chariot cities, and with the king at Jerusalem. 26 And he ruled over all the kings from the River even unto the land of the Philistines, and to the border of Egypt. 27 And the king made silver to be in Jerusalem as stones, and cedars made he to be as the sycamore-trees that are in the lowland, for abundance. 28 And they brought horses for Solomon out of Egypt, and out of all lands.

Solomon exceeded all the kings ... in riches and wisdom (v. 22). Solomon's wisdom was unrelated to what we know as ***true widsom,*** that kind of wisdom is

---

1 AnBi, *2 Chronicles,* p. 56.

defined in God's word: "The fear of Jehovah is the begining of wisdom; a good understanding have all they that do his commandments" (Psalm 111:10). The meaning of the word ***wisdom,*** as it was used by the Chronicler, was evidently something else. As the term was used by his self-seeking flatterers, it meant little or nothing; and it could be that the Chronicler here was using it in exactly the same way. One thing is certain; namely, that Solomon neither feared God nor honored his commandments.

The passage that we have so often cited in Deuteronomy 17:16-17 specifically forbade Israel's kings to multiply unto themselves (1) wives, (2) silver and gold and (3) horses. Solomon wantonly violated all these commandments in the most extravagant manner.

A rate year by year (v. 24). These words identify all those 'gifts' that came to Solomon by those rulers throughout the world of that era, as 'taxes,' or 'tribute,' imposed, not occasionally, but continually ***year by year***. This also explains why they, "sought the presence of Solomon to hear his wisdom." Their fulsome compliments paid to Solomon were nothing but the flattery of vassal underlings seeking to make a good impression on the conceited Solomon, whom they unwillingly served as his vassals.

f. Death of Solomon and the accession of Rehoboam:

Verses 29-31, Now the rest of the acts of Solomon, first and last, are they not written in the history of Nathan the prophet, and in the prophecy of Ahijah the Shilonite,

and in the visions of Iddo the seer concerning Jeroboam the son of Nebat? 30 And Solomon reigned in Jerusalem over all Israel forty years. 31 And Solomon slept with his fathers, and he was buried in the city of David his father: and Rehoboam his son reigned in his stead.

The important thing here is the Chronicler's mention of several of his sources. See our ***Introduction*** to this volume for a more complete list of these. We reject as worthless the allegation of some critics that the Chronicler invented or composed much of his material; for it is quite evident that he followed all of his sources very accurately, a fact indicated by the truth that he was careful in the use of 1 Kings, a source that we know he used.

As often noted, ***the only reason*** for the critic's rejection of much of the material in Chronicles is the havoc that it plays with a number of their favorite fairy tales, such as (1) the gradual evolution of Israel's conception of the person and nature of God, (2) the discovery of that alleged Deuteronomic document in the reign of Josiah, and (3) the late dating of the Mosaic Pentateuch.

The death of Solomon and the accession of his harem-bred son Rehoboam marked the end of the united kingdom and the beginning of a long chain of tragic events that would result in the destruction of Jerusalem and the temple, and the Babylonian captivity of the People of God.

XXX

II. FROM THE REIGN OF SOLOMON THROUGH THE CAPTIVITY TO CYRUS' DECREE
(Chapters 10-36)

I. REHOBOAM (922-915 BC)

Israel Demands an Easement of Excessive Taxes

Verses 1-5, ***And Rehoboam went to Shechem; for all Israel were come to Shechem to make him king. 2 And it came to pass when Jeroboam the son of Nebat heard of it (for he was in Egypt, whither he had fled from the presence of king Solomon), that Jeroboam returned out of Egypt. 3 And they went and called him; and Jeroboam and all Israel came and spoke to Rehoboam, saying, 4 Thy father made our yoke grievous: now therefore make thou the grievous service of thy father, and his heavy yoke which he put upon us lighter, and we will serve thee. 5 And he said unto them, Come again unto me after three days. And the people departed.***

Rehoboam Seeks Advice of Two Groups, the Old Counsellors, and his Contemporaries

Verses 6-11, ***And king Rehoboam took counsel from the old men, that had stood before Solomon his father while he yet lived, saying, What counsel give ye to me to return answer to this people? 7 And they spake unto him, saying, If thou be kind to this people, and please them, and speak good words to them, then they will be thy servants for ever. 8 But he forsook the counsel of the old men which they had given him, and took counsel with the young men that had grown up with him, and stood before him. 9 And***

what counsel give ye, that we may return answer to this people, who have spoken to me, saying, Make the yoke that thy father did put upon us lighter? 10 And the young men that were grown up with him spake unto him, saying, Thus shalt thou say unto the people that spake unto thee, saying, Thy father made our yoke heavy, but make thou it lighter unto us; thou shalt say unto them, My little finger is thicker than my father's loins. 11 And now whereas my father did lade you with a heavy yoke, I will add to your yoke: my father chastised you with whips, but I will chastise you with scorpions.

The young men that had grown up with him (v. 8). This whole chapter is virtually identical with 1K 12:1-20; and in both accounts, mention is made of Rehoboam's associates, referring to them in these words. This is the only hint in the Bible that Solomon had any other sons besides Rehoboam. Evidently these were other children brought up in Solomon's godless harem.

Rehoboam Follows the Advise of His Harem Associates

Verses 12-15, So Jeroboam and all the people came to Rehoboam the third day, as the king bade, saying, Come to me again the third day. 13 And the king answered them roughly; and king Rehoboam forsook the counsel of the old men, 14 and spake to them after the counsel of the young men, saying, My father made your yoke heavy, but I will add thereto: my father chastised you with whips, but I will chastise you with scorpions. 15 So the king hearkened not

unto the people; but it was brought about of God, that Jehovah might establish his word, which he spake by Abijah the Shilonite to Jeroboam the son of Nebat.

My father chastised you with whips (v. 14). This is a somewhat sour note in that sweet symphony of ***The Glory of Solomon.*** Furthermore, right here is the contradiction of the opinions of many that Solomon did not enslave any Israelites, but only the foreigners. If Solomon had been whipping only the descendants of the Canaanites, there is hardly any possibility that Jeroboam and the other Israelites would have been at all concerned about it.

See our ***Commentary on First Kings,*** pp. 151-158, for further comment on the events of this chapter.

Northern Israel Rebels Against Rehoboam

Verses 16-19, And when all Israel saw that the king hearkened not unto them, the people answered the king, saying, What portion have we in David? neither have we inheritance in the son of Jesse: every man to your tents, O Israel: now see to thine own house, David. So all Israel departed unto their tents. 17 But as for the children of Israel that dwelt in the cities of Judah, Rehoboam reigned over them. 18 Then king Rehoboam sent Hadoram, who was over the men subject to task-work; and the children of Israel stoned him to death with stones. And king Rehoboam made speed to get him up to his chariot, to flee to Jerusalem. 19 So Israel rebelled against the house of David to this day.

Hadoram ... over the men subject to task-work (v. 18). This is merely the Chronicler's polite word for, "Hadoram ... the slave-driver," the most hated man in Solomon's kingdom, the same as Adoram in the First Kings narrative. Rehoboam could not possibly have made a more serious mistake than asking Hadoram to accompany him in his negotiations with Israel. Not only did they stone Hadoram, but they would also have stoned Rehoboam if he had not escaped. Thus Rehoboam lost the greater part of his kingdom by one idiotic acceptance of the foolish advice of his harem-born associates.

xxx

CHAPTER 11

The First Three Years of Rehoboam's Reign

Rehoboam Prepares for War

Verses 1-4, And when Rehoboam was come to Jerusalem, he assembled the house of Judah and Benjamin, a hundred and fourscore thousand chosen men, that were warriors, to fight against Israel, to bring the kingdom again to Rehoboam. 2 But the word of Jehovah came to Shemaiah the man of God, saying, 3 Speak unto Rehoboam the son of Solomon, king of Judah, and unto all Israel in Judah and Benjamin, saying, 4 Thus saith Jehovah, Ye shall not go up, nor fight against your brethren: return every man to his house; for this thing is of me. So they hearkened unto the words of Jehovah, and refrained from going against Jeroboam.

It was impossible for Rehoboam to recover from the stupid blunder he had already made. If he had proceeded against Jeroboam, the strong probability is that Jeroboam would have defeated him and brought an even greater disaster upon Rehoboam and Jerusalem. See the parallel account in First Kings 12:21-24.

Rehoboam's Building Program

The Chronicler accepted the renunciation of Northern Israel regarding their having "no inheritance in the son of Jesse" (10:16), and proceeded to ignore the northern kingdom altogether, except where their history involved Judah. He turned his attention to recording the progression of the southern kingdom's rulers, in some instances, giving a more complete report than we found in Kings. Examples of this are in this chapter.

Verses 5-12, And Rehoboam dwelt in Jerusalem, and built cities for defence in Judah. 6 He built Bethlehem, and Elam, and Tekoa, 7 and Beth-zur, and Soco, and Adullum, 8 and Gath, and Mareshah, and Ziph, 9 and Adoraim, and Lachish, and Azekah, 10 and Zorah, and Aijalon and Hebron, which are in Judah and in Benjamin, fortified cities. 11 And he fortified the strongholds, and put captains in them, and stores of victuals, and oil and wine. 12 And in every city he put shields and spears, and made them exceeding strong. And Judah and Benjamin belonged to him.

These verses and through v. 17, below, are parallel to 1K 12:25-33, where one will find most of our comments. These preparations which Rehoboam made against possible invasion of the greatly weakened southern Israel were a prophecy of the beleaguered nation's future history. A divided Israel would be unable to dominate the Mid-east as did David and Solomon.

The True Worshippers of God Migrate to Jerusalem

Verses 13-17, And the priests and the Levites that were in all Israel resorted to him out of all their border. 14 For the Levites left their suburbs and their possession, and came to Judah and Jerusalem: for Jeroboam and his sons

cast them off, that they should not execute the priest's office unto Jehovah; 15 and he appointed him priests for the high places, and for the he-goats, and for the calves which he had made. 16 And after them, out of all the tribes of Israel, such as set their hearts to seek Jehovah, the God of Israel, came to Jerusalem to sacrifice unto Jehovah, the God of their fathers. 17 So they strengthened the kingdom of Judah, and made Rehoboam the son of Solomon strong, three years; for they walked three years in the way of David and Solomon.

There is important new information here. Jeroboam's "casting off" of the Levites, his images of the he-goats, and the fact of the Levites losing their possessions in order to live in Judah are not mentioned in Kings. Thus the Chronicler makes it clear enough that there was absolutely nothing whatever honorable or legitimate in the sinful worship Jeroboam installed in Israel. "The priests and Levites who were deposed could still have kept their lands, but they relinquished them in order to live in Judah where they could carry on their calling. They were accompanied by laymen who shared their disillusionment."[1]

Moses told us what this worship of the he-goats was like, when he forbade it to Israel. "They shall no more sacrifice their sacrifices unto the goats, after which they play the harlot" (Leviticus 17:7). There can be little doubt that the golden calves set up by Jeroboam were also used in the same licentious

---

1 BBC, Vol. 3, p. 378.

manner.

They strengthened ... Judah ... three years (v. 17). These are ominous words, for they indicate a drastic change afterwards. The change came in the fourth year, for in the fifth year, Rehoboam and all Israel forsook the God of Israel; and God's punishment quickly fell upon them in the invasion of Shishak, recorded in the next chapter.

Rehoboam's Sixty Concubines and Eighteen Wives

Verses 18-23, And Rehoboam took him a wife, Mahalath the daughter of Jerimoth the son of David, and of Abihail the daughter of Eliab the son of Jesse; 19 and she bare him sons: Jeush, and Shemariah, and Zaham. 20 And after her he took Maacah the daughter of Absalom; and she bare him Abijah, and Attai, and Zizi, and Shelomith. 21 And Rehoboam loved Maacah the daughter of Absalom above all his wives and his concubines (for he took eighteen wives and threescore concubines), and begat twenty and eight sons and threescore daughters. 22 And Rehoboam appointed Abijah the son of Maacah to be chief, even the prince among his brethren; for he was minded to make him king. 23 And he dealt wisely, and dispersed of all his sons throughout all the lands of Judah and Benjamin, unto every fortified city: and he gave them victuals in abundance. And he sought for them many wives.

There is no parallel passage with this in Kings; and we are thankful for this intimate glimpse of what life must have been like in the harems of Jewish kings. One may only imagine the intrigues, jealousies, outright hatreds, and bitter rivalries that resulted from a large compound filled with a total of seventy-eight women competing with each other for their husband's affections, and secretly hating the king for his partiality, first to one, and then to another.

There was no spiritual compatibility whatever with such an arrangement as that revealed here; and by the Chronicler's placement of this paragraph just prior to the mention of Rehoboam's shameful apostasy, he might indeed have considered this as contributory to that apostasy. Indeed, it could hardly have been otherwise.

XXX

CHAPTER 12

Rehoboam's Apostasy, Invasion of Shishak, Death of Rehoboam

God's Punishment Of Israel by Shishak

Verses 1-8, And it came to pass when the kingdom of Rehoboam was established, and he was strong, that he forsook the law of Jehovah, and all Israel with him. 2 And it came to pass in the fifth year of king Rehoboam, that Shishak king of Egypt came up against Jerusalem, because they had trespassed against Jehovah, 3 with twelve hundred chariots and threescore thousand horsemen. And the people were without number that came with him out of Egypt: the Lubim, the Sukkiim, and the Ethiopians. 4 And he took the fortified cities that pertained to Judah, and came unto Jerusalem. 5 Now Shemaiah the prophet came to Rehoboam, and to the princes of Judah, that were gathered together to Jerusalem because of Shishak, and said unto them, Thus saith Jehovah, Ye have forsaken me, therefore have I also left you in the hands of Shishak. 6 Then the princes of Israel and the king humbled themselves; and they said, Jehovah is righteous. 7 And when Jehovah saw that they humbled themselves, the word of Jehovah came to Shemaiah, saying, They have humbled themselves; I will not destroy them; but I will grant them some deliverance, and my wrath shall not be poured out upon Jerusalem by the hand of Shishak. 8 Nevertheless they shall be his servants, that they may know my service, and the service of the kingdoms of the countries.

Because they had trespassed against Jehovah (v. 2). The aggressive war of Shishak against Jerusalem is here stated to have been brought about by God himself because of Israel's rebellion against God's law. It is the conviction of this writer that God still rules in the kingdoms of men, and that no nation that turns its back upon God's teachings can escape the eventual and certain judgment against them by Almighty God.

We live in a generation that appears no longer to believe this, despite the fact that all of the great leaders of America's past believed it, as attested by George Washington's kneeling in the snows at Valley Forge, a fact beautifully memorialized by Ward's famous bronze plaque attached to the old Sub Treasury building of the United States across from the New York Stock Exchange building. Nevertheless, it still stands in the Eternal Word, "God rules in the kingdom of men and giveth it to whomsoever he will" (Daniel 4:25). In the words of Rudyard Kipling,

> ***"LORD GOD OF HOSTS, BE WITH US YET,***
> ***LEST WE FORGET, LEST WE FORGET."***

That they may know my service and the service of the kingdoms of the countries (v. 8). This meant that Israel might find out the difference between serving God and serving Shishak! These verses are not parallel to Kings, but Shishak's invasion is mentioned in 1K 14:25-26.

Shishak Robs the Sacred Treasures of Israel

Verses 9-12, So Shishak king of Egypt came up against Jerusalem, and took away the treasures of the house of Jehovah, and the treasures of the king's house; he took all away; he took away also the shields of gold that Solomon had made. 10 And king Rehoboam made in their stead shields of brass, and committed them to the hands of the captain of the guard, that kept the door of the king's house. 11 And it was so, that as oft as the king entered into the house of Jehovah, the guard came and bare them, and brought them back into the guard-chamber. 12 And when he humbled himself the wrath of Jehovah turned from him, so as not to destroy him altogether: moreover there was in Judah good things found.

Much of 1 Kings 14 is parallel with what we have here. Oddly enough, neither in Kings nor in Chronicles is it stated that Shishak captured Jerusalem; but either he actually did this, or Rehoboam was able to buy him off with ***all the treasures*** both of the temple and of the king's house.

And king Rehoboam made in their stead shields of brass (v. 10). See our somewhat extensive comment on this in ***I Kings*** pp, 185-186.

Conclusion of Rehoboam's Evil Reign

Verses 13-16, So king Rehoboam strengthened himself in Jerusalem, and reigned: for Rehoboam was forty and one years old when he began to reign, and he reigned

seventeen years in Jerusalem, the city which Jehovah had chosen out of all the tribes of Israel, to put his name there: and his mother's name was Naamah the Ammonitess. 14 And he did that which was evil, because he set not his heart to seek Jehovah.

15 Now the acts of Rehoboam, first and last, are they not written in the histories of Shemaiah the prophet and of Iddo the seer, after the manner of genealogies? And there were wars between Rehoboam and Jeroboam continually. 16 And Rehoboam slept with his fathers, and was buried in the city of David: and Abijah his son reigned in his stead.

And he did that which was evil (v. 14). The Chronicler did not dwell unnecessarily upon the details of Rehoboam's wickedness, but it was very great indeed. His wickedness exceeded anything that his fathers had done before him. The sodomites were brought into the land; the high places were built; and Israel even sinned beyond that of the ancient Canaanites who preceded Israel in Palestine. A fuller account of all this is in 1K 14:21-24.

God had forbidden the Israelites to intermarry with foreigners; but Rehoboam's mother was an Ammonitess.

XXX

CHAPTER 13

Savage Civil War Between Northern and Southern Israel

II. ABIJAH (915-913 BC)

Vast Armies Confront Each Other

Verses 1-3, In the eighteenth year of king Jeroboam began Abijah to reign over Judah. 2 Three years reigned he in Jerusalem: and his mother's name was Micaiah the daughter of Uriel of Gibeah. And there was war between Abijah and Jeroboam, 3 And Abijah joined battle with an army of valiant men of war, even four hundred thousand chosen men: and Jeroboam set the battle in array against him with eight hundred thousand chosen men, who were mighty men of valor.

There are a number of variations here as compared with 1K 15:1-8, for different spellings of the king's name and the names of his mother and of her father; and we have no good explanation of this. As frequently noted, many people in that day were known by more than one name. His mother's name, as given here, is that of a man.

For some, these tremendously large numbers of the troops on each side of the conflict are also considered to be a problem. One common understanding of it is the very great possibility that the word ***thousand*** was from a technical word that really meant a military unit that could have been much smaller than a literal thousand. We accept the numbers as given here, because they are far more trustworthy than 20th century guesses by critical scholars.

The big point in this paragraph is that Jeroboam's army outnumbered Abijah's two to one.

Abijah's Address Before the Army of Jeroboam

Verses 4-12, ***And Abijah stood up upon mount Zemaraim, which is in the hill country of Ephraim, and said, Hear me, O Jeroboam and all Israel: 5 Ought ye not to know that Jehovah, the God of Israel, gave the kingdom over Israel to David for ever, even to him and his sons by a covenant of salt? 6 Yet Jeroboam the son of Nebat, the servant of Solomon the son of David, rose up, and rebelled against his lord. 7 And there were gathered unto him worthless men, base fellows, that strengthened themselves against Rehoboam the son of Solomon, when Rehoboam was young and tender-hearted, and could not withstand him. 8 And now ye think to withstand the kingdom of Jehovah in the hand of the sons of David; and ye are a great multitude, and there are with you the golden calves which Jeroboam made you for gods. 9 Have ye not driven out the priests of Jehovah, the sons of Aaron, and the Levites, and made you priests after the manner of other lands? so that whosoever cometh to consecrate himself with a young bullock and seven rams, the same may be a priest of them that are no gods. 10 But as for me, Jehovah is our God, and we have not forsaken him; and we have priests ministering unto Jehovah, the sons of Aaron, and the Levites in their work: 11 And they burn unto Jehovah every morning and every evening burnt-offerings and sweet incense: the showbread also set they in order upon the pure***

table; and the candlestick of gold with the lamps thereof, to burn every evening; for we keep the charge of Jehovah our God; but ye have forsaken him. 12 And, behold, God is with us at our head, and his priests with the trumpets of alarm to sound an alarm against you. O children of Israel, fight ye not against Jehovah, the God of your fathers; for ye shall not prosper.

Upon mount Zemaraim in the land of Ephraim (v. 4). By penetrating that far into Israel's territory, Abijah had made a very stupid move, giving Jeroboam the opportunity to surround him and cut him off from retreat. Perhaps God allowed him to do this in order that Judah could not claim a victory that was solely due to God's intervention.

When Jeroboam was young and tender-hearted (v. 7). This was a falsehood, for the Chroincler tells us that Rehoboam was forty-one years old when he began to reign (2C 12:13). The falsehood here was not that of the Chronicler but of Abijah. The Chronicler accurately reported the speech as it was recorded in the commentary of the prophet Iddo.

There can be no doubt that whatever portion of Jeroboam's vast army was in hearing distance of this address by Abijah was thoroughly demoralized and intimidated by it. What Abijah said here was known to be true by everyone in Israel.

The great significance of the passage is its reference to the sacred religious regalia that God through Moses had ordained in the Pentateuch for the tabernacle, and which had been incorporated by

Solomon into the temple. It should be remembered that all of this knowledge of the Pentateuch and its contents was common public information centuries before the discovery of that alleged document in the reign of Josiah.

Abijah was an evil king (1K 15:3); but the speech he made here was loaded with significant truth. It is of special interest that Abijah knew nothing of the critical canard that those golden calves were in any manner symbols of Jehovah. They were indeed ***no gods,*** as Abijah said; and everything pertaining to the true worship of Jehovah, even its priesthood, had been thrown out of the country by Jeroboam. Note also that Jeroboam's army had brought along their golden calves into the battle.

The Battle, Jeroboam's Defeat, and Abijah's death

Verses 13-22, But Jeroboam caused an ambushment to come about behind them; so they were before Judah, and the ambushment was behind them; 14 and when Judah looked back, behold, the battle was before and behind them; and they cried unto Jehovah, and the priests sounded with the trumpets. 15 Then the men of Judah gave a shout; and as the men of Judah shouted, it came to pass, that God smote Jeroboam and all Israel before Abijah and Judah. 16 And the children of Israel fled before Judah; and God delivered them into their hand. 17 And Abijah and his people slew them with a great slaughter: so there fell down slain of Israel five hundred thousand men. 18 Thus the children of Israel were brought

under at that time, and the children of Judah prevailed, because they relied upon Jehovah, the God of their fathers. 19 And Abijah pursued after Jeroboam, and took cities from him, Bethel with the towns thereof, and Ephron with the towns thereof. 20 Neither did Jeroboam recover strength again in the days of Abijah: and Jehovah smote him, and he died. 21 But Abijah waxed mighty, and took unto himself fourteen wives, and begat twenty and two sons, and sixteen daughters. 22 And the rest of the acts of Abijah, and his ways, and his sayings, are written in the commentary of the prophet Iddo.

Regarding the huge numbers of the troops engaged in this battle, Curtis (Madsen) characterized them as 'Midrash,'[1] which is a critcal code-word for 'false.' However the same writers admitted that, "The number of Jeroboam's warriors is exactly the same as the number credited to Israel in the census taken by Joab."[2] To this writer it appears to be an altogether gratuitous and unfounded allegation that, "These numbers are utterly unhistorical."[3] Oh yes, there are unexplained discrepancies here; but, so what? one may read conflicting biographies of John F. Kennedy! The Chronicler was merely quoting the public records, in this case, the commentary of the prophet Iddo; and there is no dependable authority today for setting aside as "unhistorical" any of this material. ***This IS the history***,

---

1 ICC, Chronicles, p. 374

2 Ibid.

3 Ibid.

as it has come down to us. It is of no importance that some do not believe it. Neither do they believe that God created heaven and earth.

A little reflection will support the proposition so eloquently propounded in this chapter that Judah's victory was of God. They were fighting two tribes against ten! They were surrounded! Jeroboam was a conceited, mad killer determined to take the whole world if he had been able to do so. Why did he fail? This chapter has the correct answer.

Furthermore, Abijah was not the reason for God's intervention upon behalf of Judah. He was an evil king. "He walked in all the sins of his father, which he had done before him; and his heart was not perfect with Jehovah ... Nevertheless for David's sake ... God gave him a lamp in Jerusalem, to set up his son after him" (1K 15:3-4). This was vitally related to God's purpose of eventually bringing in the Messiah to provide an opportunity for all mankind to be saved. It was that fundamental truth that required the intervention of God himself in the events of this chapter.

XXX

CHAPTER 14

Asa's War With Zerah the Ethiopian

III. ASA (913-873 BC)

The Death of Abijah and the Accession of Asa

Verses 1-8, So Abijah slept with his fathers, and they buried him in the city of David; and Asa his son reigned in his stead. In his days the land was quiet ten years. 2 And Asa did that which was good and right in the eyes of Jehovah his God: 3 for he took away the foreign altars, and the high places, and brake down the pillars, and hewed down the Asherim, 4 and commanded Judah to seek Jehovah, the God of their fathers, and to do the law and the commandment. 5 Also he took away out of all the cities of Judah the high places and the sun-images: and the kingdom was quiet before him. 6 And he built fortified cities in Judah; for the land was quiet, and he had no war in those years, because Jehovah had given him rest. 7 For he said unto Judah, Let us build these cities, and make about them walls, and towers, gates, and bars; the land is yet before us, because we have sought Jehovah our God; we have sought him, and he hath given us rest on every side. So they built and prospered. 8 And Asa had an army that bare bucklers and spears, out of Judah three hundred thousand; and out of Benjamin, that bare shields and drew bows two hundred and fourscore thousand: all these were mighty men of war.

In his days, the land was quiet ten years (v. 1). This was most likely due in large part to the tremendous victory that God had given Abijah over Jeroboam. Judah had rest, "Until the invasion of Zerah in 896 BC; and this was God's reward for Asa's reforms."[1]

The Chronicler gave much more space to Asa than was given in Kings; but this was not due to the Chronicler's having derived all of this, "from his Midrashic source,"[2] a false allegation common enough among critics. Greater and greater respect among competent scholars for Chronicles tends more and more to the acceptance of the asbsolute historicity of every word in it.

He took away ... the foreign altars ... the high places ... brake down the pillars ... hewed down the Asherim (v. 3). Kings also records other reforms of Asa, but these are supplementary, not contradictory. Some scholars have fallen into the error of supposing that the high places, "In earlier years, had been acceptable secondary places for worshipping Jehovah";[3] but this cannot possibly be true. God had specifically forbidden all of these pagan things in Deuteronomy 16:21-22, and had sternly demanded their destruction (Deuteronomy 7:5, 12:3).

We reject the ridiculous emendation by which the RSV translated ***pillars*** in this passage (v. 5) as ***incense altars***. They were no such thing. The very height of them would have made them useless as altars of incense; those that Solomon put in the temple were 35

---

1 WYC, p. 402.

2 ICC, ***Chronicles***, p. 380.

3 NLBC, p. 503.

cubits high! "They were probably the symbols of the male element in nature ... they and the sacred trees of the Asherah were associated with sexual practices repugnant to the worshippers of God."[4] P. C. Barker backs up this opinion in the Pulpit Commentary.[5]

While serving as a chaplain in Japan and Korea during the Korean war, this writer saw some of those 'pillars' associated with pagan worship. They were carved wooden models of the human penis six to eight feet in height; and he still has photographs of them. They were carried in a procession by young virgins in an annual parade.

Three hundred thousand ... two hundred and fourscore thousand (v. 8). Payne thought that, "These figures must have included the whole popularion";[6] and Ellison rejected the mention of Zerah's million man army in v. 9 with the comment that, "A million probably means no more than an exceedingly large number."[7] Such comments must be rejected, because they are merely scholarly devices for saying, "Of course, this is not true." Regarding the numbers in v. 8, Canon F. C. Cook observed that, "They correspond well with the numbers given in 13:19. In ten years of peace, the army had grown from 400,000 to 580,000, as should have been expected in a time of peace and prosperity."[8]

---

4 Ibid.

5 PC, Vol 6b, p. 168.

6 WYC, p. 402.

7 NBCR, p. 388.

8 AB, *Chronicles,* p. 390.

And, as regards that million man army mentioned in v. 9, below, Cook pointed out that, "This is the largest collected army of which we read in Scripture; but it does not exceed the known numbers of other Oriental armies of ancient times. Darius Codomannus brought into the field of Abela a force of 1,040,000; and Xerxes crossed the Hellespont with more than a million combatants."[9]

Any thoughtful person may see prejudice and bias in the fact than any statement by any pagan writer whomsover, regardless of how preposterous it may be, is received as gospel truth, while a malicious skepticism is pointed at every line of the sacred scriptures. The army of Zerah mentioned in the next verse, below, just as certainly had a million men in it as did the army of Zerxes, a fact that is implicit in Asa's prayer in which he recognized that his own force of only 580,000 was as nothing compared with it.

Asa and Judah Overcome Zerah's Mighty Force

Verses 9-15, And there came out against them Zerah the Ethiopian with an army of a thousand thousand, and three hundred chariots; and he came unto Mareshah. 10 Then Asa went out to meet him, and they set the battle in array in the valley of Zephathah at Mareshah. 11 And Asa cried unto his God, and said, Jehovah, there is none beside thee to help, between the mighty and him that hath no strength; help us, O Jehovah our God; for we rely on

---

[9] Ibid.

thee, and in thy name are we come against this multitude, O Jehovah, thou art our God; let not man prevail against thee. 12 So Jehovah smote the Ethiopians before Asa, and before Judah, and the Ethiopians fled. 13 And Asa and the people that were with him pursued them unto Gerar: and there fell of the Ethiopians so many that they could not recover themselves; for they were destroyed before Jehovah, and before his host; and they carried away very much booty. 14 And they smote all the cities round about Gerar; for the fear of Jehovah came upon them: and they despoiled all the cities; for there was much spoil in them. 15 They smote also the tents of cattle, and carried away sheep in abundance, and camels, and returned to Jerusalem.

They set the battle in array ... at Mareshah (vv. 9-10). "This place was in the valley that marks the entrance into the hills, half way between Gaza and Jerusalem. This was one of the cities that Rehoboam had fortified in anticipation of just such an attack."[10]

Some scholars have tried to make it out that this was an invasion of Arabians, but Payne is doubtless correct. He identified Zerah as, "Osorkon I, the second Pharaoh of the Twenty-second Dynasty in Egypt, who attempted to duplicate the the invasion and pillage of his predecessor Sheshonk (Shishak)."[11] The truth of this identification is corroborated by the historical truth that, "It was ***Egypt (not Arabia)*** that never recovered from this blow for more than three centuries; not until

---

10 WYC, p. 402.

11 WYC, p.402,

609 BC, did Egypt again venture into Palestine with hostile intentions."[12]

Also when Judah defeated the enemy, they fled to Gerar, "A town to the south of Gaza,"[13] which was in the direction of Egypt, not Arabia.

They smote also the tents of the cattle (v. 15). "These were the tents associated with cattle, wherein the owners of the cattle lived."[14] The RSV makes it more understandable, "They smote the tents of those who had cattle."

XXX

---

12 AB, op. cit., p. 390.

13 WYC, p. 402.

14 BBC, Vol. 3, p. 382.

CHAPTER 15

Asa's Faithful Efforts to Bring Israel Back to God

Azariah's Admonition For Israel

Verses 1-7, And the Spirit of God came upon Azariah the son of Obed: 2 and he went out to meet Asa, and said unto him, Hear ye me, Asa, and all Judah and Benjamin: for Jehovah is with you while ye are with him; and if ye seek him he will be found of you; but if ye forsake him, he will forsake you. 3 Now for a long season Israel was without the true God, and without a teaching priest, and without law: 4 but when in their distress they turned unto Jehovah, the God of Israel, and sought him, he was found of them. 5 And in those times there was no peace to him that went out, nor to him that came in; but great vexations were upon all the inhabitants of the lands. 6 And they were broken in pieces, nation against nation, and city against city; for God did vex them with all adversity. 7 But be ye strong, and let not your hands be slack; for your work shall be rewarded.

Azariah's purpose here is clear enough, namely, the encouragement of God's people to be constant in their faithfulness to their God, for it was their lack of faithfulness which had so frequently resulted in manifold sorrows for the Chosen People.

Verses 3-6 are interpreted in various ways. Cook believed that, "They refer to the many apostasies of God's people in the times of the Judges."[1] Curtis

---

[1] AB, *Chronicles,* p. 391.

(Madsen) applied the words to, "The Northern Kingdom";[2] and Keil stated that, "We must take the words in a general sense, applying then exclusively neither to the past nor to the future, because the truth uttered here has force at all times."[3]

Without the true God, without a teaching priest, and without law (v.3). There were many times in Israel's history when these conditions prevailed. "It was not that Israel did not have instruction; Israel would not receive it."[4]

Asa's Continuing Program of Religious Reform

Verses 8-15 And when Asa heard these words, and the prophecy of Obed the prophet, he took courage and put away the abominations out of all the land of Judah and Benjamin, and out of the cities which he had taken from the hill-country of Ephraim; and he renewed the altar of Jehovah, that was before the porch of Jehovah. 9 And he gathered all Judah and Benjamin, and them that sojourned with them out of Ephraim, and Mansasseh, and out of Simeon: for they fell to him out of Israel in abundance, when they saw that Jehovah his God was with him. 10 So they gathered themselves together at Jerusalem in the third month in the fifteenth year of the reign of Asa. 11 And they sacrificed to Jehovah in that day, of the spoil which they had brought, seven hundred oxen, and seven thousand

---

[2] ICC, *Chronicles*, p. 384.

[3] CFK, Vol. 3b, p. 361.

[4] BBC, Vol. 3, p. 383.

sheep. 12 And they entered into the covenant to seek Jehovah, the God of their fathers, with all their heart and with all their soul; 13 and that whosoever would not seek Jehovah, the God of Israel, should be put to death, whether small or great, whether man or woman. 14 And they sware unto Jehovah with a loud voice, and with shouting, and with trumpets, and with cornets. 15 And all Judah rejoiced at the oath; for they had sworn with all their heart, and sought him with their whole desire; and he was found of them: and Jehovah gave them rest round about.

And the prophecy of Obed (v. 8). "Some versions have, 'the prophecy of Azariah the son of Obed,' which may be the true reading."[5]

In the third month of the fifteen year of Asa (v. 10). "This was June (Sivan), on the sixth day of which the Feast of Weeks (Pentecost) was observed. The great sacrifices on this occasion included some of the booty they had taken in the war with Zerah";[6] and if the conjecture that Zerah came against Asa in his eleventh year is correct, this would indicate that the war lasted four years. However, a great deal of the chronology of all of these Hebrew kings is very uncertain.

And they entered into the covenant (v. 12). The original covenant bewteen God and his people is recorded in Exodus 24:3-8; it was renewed again at Schechem (Joshua 8:30-35); this was a third ratification; and still another took place in the times of Nehemiah

---

[5] AB, op. cit., p. 391.

[6] PC. Vol. 6b, p. 182.

(Nehemiah 10:20).

Whosoever would not seek Jehovah ... should be put to death (v. 23). This was part of the original covenant (Deuteronomy 17:2-8); and thus we have another testimonial to the prior existence of the Pentateuch, long centuries before the times of Josiah. The account here is a true record of what occurred in the reign of Asa (913-873 BC). [7]

More About Asa's Reforms

Verses 16-19, And also Maacah, the mother of Asa the king, he removed from being the queen (mother), because she had made an abominable image for an Asherah and Asa cut down her image and made dust of it, and burnt it at the brook Kidron. 17 But the high places were not taken away out of Israel: nevertheless the heart of Asa was perfect all his days. 18 And he brought into the house of God the things that his father had dedicated, and that he himself had dedicated, silver, and gold, and vessels. 19 And there was no more war unto the five and thirtieth year of the reign of Asa.

The unceasing war against Chronicles by the radical critics focuses upon two things in this paragraph.

(1) "In verse 17 we read that the high places were not taken away, but in verse 8 that they were!"[8] This is typical of the type of unprincipled and dishonest

---

[7] AnBi. *Chronicles*, p. 91.

[8] IB, Vol. 3, p. 485.

efforts of unbelievers to discredit Chronicles. Note that verse 8 does not even mention the high places! Furthermore, the abominations which Asa put away were those "in the cities"; and many of them continued to be observed in the rural areas. "Even Asa's best efforts were not sufficient to eradicate pagan practices entirely."[9]

(2) The other attack is directed against an alleged 'contradiction' between 1 Kings 15:16, which says, "There was war between Asa and Baasha king of Israel all their days," and the word here in v. 19 that, "There was no more war unto the five and thirtieth year of the reign of Asa." Cook suggested that a corrupted text is responsible for this;[10] but Barker has an even better explanation: "What this says, actually, is that a state of war was chronic between Asa and Baasha."[11] Of course, this savage hatred between the two Israels continued without intermission as long as the Northern Israel existed.

The mother of Asa ... had made an abominable image for an Asherah (v. 16). This was some kind of a pillar, called here an image; and we have been encouraged by some to think of it as an incense altar (See the RSV). However, the word ***abominable***, as used here, is also rendered ***unspeakable, horrible,*** etc. by translators. These words are much too strong for anything innocent.

---

[9] AnBi, op. cit., p. 89.

[10] AB, op. cit., p. 392.

[11] PC, Col. 6b, p. 184.

The Douay Version tranlsates this passage like it is: "Maacah the mother of Asa made in a grove an idol of Priapus." This was an image of the human phallus, which in all probability was the usual form these pillars took. Curtis (Madsen) accepted this meaning of this passage, writing that, "This understanding of it is as good as any, and it is generally accepted."[12] "In Greek and Roman mythology, this was the god of male procreative power."[13]

XXX

---

[12] ICC, ***Chronicles,*** p. 386.

[13] As defined in Britannica World Language Dictionary.

CHAPTER 16

Conclusion of the Reign of Asa; His Rebuke by the Prophet

Baasha King of Israel Begins to Fortify Ramah

***Verses 1-6,** In the sixth and thirtieth year of the reign of Asa, Baasha king of Israel went up against Judah, and built Ramah, that he might not suffer any one to come unto or go in to Asa king of Judah. 2 Then Asa brought out silver and gold out of the treasures of the house of Jehovah and of the king's house, and sent to Benhadad king of Syria, that dwelt at Damascus, saying, 3 There is a league between me and thee, as there was between my father and thy father, behold, I have sent thee silver and gold; go, break thy league with Baasha king of Israel, that he may depart from me. 4 Then Benhadad hearkened unto king Asa, and sent the captains of his armies against the cities of Israel; and they smote Ijon, and Dan, and Abel-maim, and all the store-cities of Napthtali. 5 And it came to pass when Baasha heard thereof, that he left off building Ramah, and let the work cease. 6 Then Asa the king took all Judah; and they carried away the stones of Ramah, and the timber thereof, wherewith Baasha had builded; and he built therewith Geba and Mizpah.*

David was "a man after God's own heart"; yet he was guilty of many sins; and likewise Asa, although his heart was "perfect toward Jehovah," yet, like all mortals, he was guilty of sin; and the Chronicler in this chapter cites two events in which king Asa did wrong in the sight of God. The first of these was his seeking aid of Benhadad the king of Syria instead of seeking it of the

Lord.

Baasha ... built Ramah (v. 1). That is, ***he began to do so,*** because the invasion of Benhadad compelled him to abandon the project. It is not hard to see what was in the mind of Baasha. The popularity of Asa's reign, and the general knowledge that God was blessing him had led many in Baasha's northern kingdom to go to Jerusalem for the legitimate worship of God. All of the northern kings vigorously opposed this, because they considered it a threat to the continuity of Northern Israel; and Baasha, by fortifying Ramah, had in mind to prohibit such excursions to Jerusalem, which, of course, occurred three times annually on the occasions of the three set feasts: Passover, Pentecost and Tabernacles.

Asa brought out silver and gold (v. 2). It apparently never entered the mind of Asa that, "If silver and gold could buy the help of Syria, a ***little more*** silver and gold could cancel it and deliver their help to someone else."

One may only wonder at Asa's actions here. God had delivered him from a far greater threat in that war with Zerah. Northern Israel was nothing compared with the tremendous strength of Egypt; and perhaps that was the reason that Asa might have felt that he did not need God in this instance, feeling that he was able to take care of this threat without God's help. Such a feeling on the part of any mortal is never justified. All men need God's help continually, in small matters as well as large ones; and it is always sinful for men to trust in themselves instead of seeking God's help.

God's Prophet Rebuked Asa, and Asa was Angry

Verses 7-10, And at that time Hanani the seer came to Asa king of Judah, and said unto him, Because thou hast relied on the king of Syria, and hast not relied on Jehovah thy God, therefore is the host of the king of Syria escaped out of thy hand. 8 Were not the Ethiopians and the Lubim a huge host, with chariots and horsemen exceeding many? yet, because thou didst rely on Jehovah, he delivered them into thy hand. 9 For the eyes of Jehovah run to and fro throughout the whole earth, to show himself strong in the behalf of them whose heart is perfect before him. Herein thou hast done foolishly; for from henceforth thou shalt have wars. 10 Then Asa was wroth with the seer, and put him in the prison-house; for he was in a rage with him because of this thing. And Asa oppressed some of the people at the same time.

One thing that the Chronicler most certainly had in mind here was to show the colossal failure of the whole institution of the monarchy. Even a good king like Asa could not remain uncorrupted while wielding the scepter of unchallenged power. The constant pressure of the flattering sycophants that surround every ruler, and the constantlly nourished and promoted conceit of any natural man have the power eventually to break down the strongest heart.

Also, it may have been his way of establishing the principle that all men are sinners. The Sinless One did not appear till the Christ was cradled in the manger at Bethlehem.

The Death of Asa

Verses 11-14. And, behold, the acts of Asa, first and last, lo, they are written in the book of the kings of Judah and Israel. 12 And in the thirty and ninth year of his reign, Asa was diseased in his feet; his disease was exceeding great: yet in his disease he sought not to Jehovah, but to the physicians. 13 And Asa slept with his fathers, and died in the one and fortieth year of his reign. 14 And they buried him in his own sepulchres, which he had hewn out for himself in the city of David, and laid him in the bed which was filled with sweet odors and divers kinds of spices prepared by the perfumers' art: and they made a very great burning for him.

And they made a very great burning for him (v. 14). "This is a reference to the burning of spices,"[1] an ancient custom designed to fill the atmosphere with sweet odors accompanying a funeral procession. The Romans used large quantities of incense for this purpose. We have discussed this custom rather extensively under the title, ***The Triumph Metaphor,*** in Vol. 7 (***Corinthians***) of our NT Commentaries, pp. 324, 325.

xxx

---

[1] PC, Vol. 6b, p. 195.

CHAPTER 17

God Favors the Reign of Jehoshaphat

IV. JEHOSHAPHAT (873-849 BC)

Jehoshaphat Succeeds His Father Asa

Verses 1-6, And Jehoshaphat his son reigned in his stead, and strengthened himself against Israel. 2 And he placed forces in all the fortified cities of Judah, and set garrisons in the land of Judah, and in the cities of Ephraim which Asa his father had taken. 3 And Jehovah was with Jehoshaphat, because he walked in the first ways of David his father, and sought not unto the Baalim, 4 but sought to the God of his father, and walked in his commandments, and not after the doings of Israel. 5 Therefore Jehovah established the kingdom in his hand; and all Judah brought to Jehoshaphat tribute; and he had riches and honor in abundance. 6 And his heart was lifted up in the ways of Jehovah: and furthermore he took away the high places and the Asherim out of Judah.

So far, so good. Jehoshaphat, like some others of the kings of Judah, began very well, receiving as their reward the blessing of the Lord and the prosperity of the people; but his alliance with Ahab (described in chapter 18) would cast a dark shadow over what is written here.

(He) walked not after the doings of Israel (4). The contempt in which the author of Chronicles held the Northern Israel appears in a clause like this. The outstanding feature of Chronicles is the omission, wherever possible, of practically the entire history of their kings. This reminds us of the book of Numbers, in which the whole history of the apostate Israel records only a few events for the whole period. Why? It was because of the fact that what any nation does, after they have rejected God, is of minor importance.

With the apostasy of the Northern Israel and their rejection of God's choice of the house of David, the history of the redemption of mankind dramatically shifted to what happened in Jerusalem.

The Law of Jehovah, the Torah, (Genesis, Exodus, Leviticus, Numbers, and Deuteronomy) Taught by the Princes to All Judah

Verses 7-9, Also in the third year of his reign he sent his princes, even Ben-hail, and Obadiah, and Zechariah, and Nethanel, and Micaiah, to teach in the cities of Judah; 8 and with them the Levites, even Shemaiah, and Nethaniah, and Zebadiah, and Asahel, and Sheminamoth, and Jehonathan, and Adonijah, and Tobijah, and Tob-adonijah the Levites; and with them Elishama, and Jehoram the priests. 9 And they taught in Judah HAVING THE BOOK OF THE LAW OF JEHOVAH WITH THEM; and they went about through all the cities of Judah, and taught among the people.

Because of the clause which we have capitalized, this is one of the most important passages in Chronicles. Right here is the reason radical critics have extended themselves so unreaonably in their efforts to discredit

Chronicles. Here is dependable, historical proof of the continued existence of the Torah from the days of Moses throughout the history of Israel. As Keil stated it, "The book of the law of Jehovah is the Pentateuch, not merely a collection of Mosaic laws, since in Jehoshaphat's time the Mosaic Book of the Law (the Pentateuch) had been long in existence."[1] We shall not take the space to repeat the vociferous denials of critics, except to cite one knee-jerk remark that characterizes all of them, "Such action was not taken in Jehoshaphat's time."[2] What is the basis of such a blatant denial of what God's word states as a fact? even giving the very names of the royal princes who did the teaching. ***THERE IS NONE***. No matter what unbelievers say, this chapter ***IS*** the historical record of what happened in the reign of Jehoshaphat; and those who live two and one half millenniums afterwards have nothing of value by which they may challenge it. Then why do men deny it? The false theories they have invented are here contradicted, ***forcing*** them either to give up their false theories, or to deny the sacred scriptures that contradict them.

The Prosperity of Judah Under Jehoshaphat

Verses 10-13, And the fear of Jehovah fell upon all the kingdoms of the lands that were round about Judah, so that they made no war against Jehoshaphat. 11 And some

---

1 CFK, Vol 3b, p. 374.

2 IB, Vol. 3, p. 488.

of the Philistines brought Jehoshaphat presents, and silver for tribute; and the Arabians also brought him flocks, seven thousand and seven hundred rams, and seven thousand and seven hundred he-goats. 12 And Jehoshaphat waxed great exceedingly; and he built in Judah, castles and cities of store. 13 And he had many works in the cities of Judah; and men of war, mighty men of valor in Jerusalem.

All of this peace and prosperity were directly due to the respect which Jehoshaphat had shown to the Law of God and to his efforts to teach that word to all the people. It is no problem that much of the material here is omitted in Kings, because the primary focus there was political; whereas, in Chronicles the focus is upon the spiritual and religious significance of the same history.

Numbering of Jehoshaphat's Mighty Men of War

Verses 14-19, And this was the numbering of them according to their fathers' houses: of Judah, the captains of thousands: Adnah the captain, and with him mighty men of valor three hundred thousand; 15 and next to him Jehohanan the captain, and with him two hundred and fourscore thousand; 16 and next to him Amasiah the son of Zichri, who willingly offered himself unto Jehovah, and with him two hundred thousand mighty men of valor. 17 And of Benjamin: Eliada a mighty man of valor, and with him two hundred thousand armed with bow and shield; 18 and next to him Jehozabad, and with him a hundred and fourscore thousand ready prepared for war. 19 These were they that waited on the king, besides those whom the king

put in fortified cities throughout all Judah.

This represented a standing army of 1,160,000 men, besides the garrisons in the fortified cities; and this goes a long way to explaining why the Arabians and the Philistines brought tribute to Jehoshaphat. In ancient times, as in our own day, peace frequently depended upon the strength of those who desired it.

We should ignore the screams of "exaggeration"[3] which mark the writings of radical critics. Pagan rulers of that era reported even larger armies than this; and until the critics can prove that those were exaggerated reports, they should let these alone. Besides that, we have already noted that the very word from which ***thousand*** is translated is disputed as to its exact meaning.

xxx

---

[3] Ibid.

CHAPTER 18

Jehoshaphat's Unholy Alliance With the Wicked Ahab

Jehoshaphat Accepts Ahab's Invitation to Aid in War to Recover Ramoth-gilead from Syria

Verses 1-3, Now Jehoshaphat had riches and honor in abundance; and he joined affinity with Ahab. 2 And after certain years he went down to Ahab to Samaria. And Ahab killed sheep and oxen for him in abundance, and for the people that were with him, and moved him to go up with him to Ramoth-gilead. 3 And Ahab king of Israel said unto Jehoshaphat king of Judah, Wilt thou go with me to Ramoth-gilead? And he answered him, I am as thou art, and my people as thy people; and we will be with thee in the war.

The False Prophets of Ahab Fail to Convince Jehoshaphat

Verses 4-6, And Jehoshaphat said unto the king of Israel, Inquire first, I pray thee, for the word of Jehovah. 5 Then the king of Israel gathered the prophets together, four hundred men, and said unto them, Shall we go to Ramoth-gilead to battle, or shall I forbear? And they said, Go up; for God will deliver IT[1] into the hand of the king. 6 But Jehoshaphat said, Is there not here a prophet of Jehovah besides, that we may inquire of him?

---

[1] See the KJV, where this word is in italics, because it is not in the Hebrew.

Jehoshaphat's asking here for ***a prophet of Jehovah*** dramatically states that the four hundred prophets of Ahab were not prophets of Jehovah. Ahab's god was Baal; and ***his prophets*** were automatically ***prophets of Baal,*** not of Jehovah (1 Kings 22:53).

Ahab Reluctantly Sends for Micaiah

Verses 7-8, ***And the king of Israel said unto Jehoshaphat, There is yet one man by whom we may inquire of Jehovah; but I hate him; for he never prophesieth good concerning me, but always evil: the same is Micaiah the son of Imla. And Jehoshaphat said, Let not the king say so, 8 Then the king of Israel called an officer, and said, Fetch quickly Micaiah the son of Imla.***[2]

The False Priests Put on Their Act

Verses 9-11, ***Now the king of Israel and Jehoshaphat the king of Judah sat each on his throne, arrayed in their robes, and they were sitting in an open place at the entrance of the gate of Samaria; and all the prophts were prophesying before them. 10 And Zedekiah the son of Chenaanah made him horns of iron and said, Thus saith Jehovah, With these shalt thou push the Syrians until they be consumed. 11 And all the prophets prophesied so, saying, Go up to Ramoth-gilead, and prosper; for Jehovah will deliver it into the hand of the king.***

---

[2] Apparently Micaiah was already a prisoner of Ahab.

Micaiah Prophesies Defeat and the Death of Ahab

Verses 12-22, And the messenger that went to call Micaiah spake to him, saying, Behold, the words of the prophets declare good to the king with one mouth: let thy word therefore, I pray thee, be like one of theirs, and speak thou good. 13 And Micaiah said, As Jehovah liveth, what my God saith, that will I speak. 14 And when he was come to the king, the king said unto him, Micaiah, shall we go to Ramoth-gilead to battle, or shall I forbear. And he said, Go ye up, and prosper; and they shall be delivered into your hand.[3] *15 And the king said unto him, How many times shall I adjure thee that thou speak unto me nothing but the truth in the name of Jehovah?*[4] *16 And he said, I saw all Israel scattered upon the mountains, as sheep that have no shepherd: and Jehovah said, These have no master; let them return every man to his house in peace. 17 And the king of Israel said to Jehoshaphat, Did I not tell thee that he would not prophesy good concerning me, but evil? 18 And Micaiah said, Therefore hear ye the word of Jehovah: I saw Jehovah sitting upon his throne, and all the host of heaven standing on his right hand and on his left. 19 And Jehovah said, Who shall entice Ahab king of Israel, that he may go up and fall at Ramoth-gilead? And one spake, saying after this manner, and another saying after that manner. 20 And there came forth a spirit, and stood before Jehovah, and said, I will entice him. And Jehovah said*

---

[3] Not a prophecy, but merely Micaiah's "good wishes."

[4] These last five words Micaiah had omitted.

unto him, Wherewith? 21 And he said, I will go forth, and I will be a lying spirit in the mouth of all his prophets. And he said, Thou shalt entice him, and shalt prevail also: go forth, and do so. 22 Now therefore, behold, Jehovah hath put a lying spirit in the mouth of these thy prophets; and Jehovah hath spoken evil concerning thee.

The False Prophet Smites Micaiah

Verses 23-27, Then Zedekiah the son of Chenaanah came near, and smote Micaiah upon the cheek, and said, Which way went the Spirit of Jehovah from me to speak unto thee? 24 And Micaiah said, Behold, thou shalt see on that day, when thou shalt go to an inner chamber to hide thyself. 25 And the king of Israel said, Take ye Micaiah, and carry him back unto Amon the governor of the city, and to Joash the king's son; 26 and say, Thus saith the king, Put this fellow in the prison, and feed him with bread of affliction and with water of affliction,[5] *until I return in peace. 27 And Micaiah said, If thou return at all in peace, Jehovah hath not spoken by me. And he said, Hear, ye people, all of you!*

Ahab Was Mortally Wounded at Ramoth-gilead

Verses 28-34, So the king of Israel and Jehoshaphat the king of Judah went up to Ramoth-gilead. 29 And the king of Israel said unto Jehoshaphat, I will disguise myself, and go into the battle; but put thou on thy

---

[5] Myers in Anchor Bible translated this: "Meager rations of bread and water."

robes. So the king of Israel disguised himself; and they went into the battle. 30 Now the king of Syria had commanded the captains of his chariots, saying, Fight neither with small nor great, save only with the king of Israel. 31 And it came to pass, when the captains of the chariots saw Jehoshaphat, that they said, It is the king of Israel. Therefore they turned about to fight against him: but Jehoshaphat cried out, and Jehovah helped him; and God moved them to depart from him. 32 And it came to pass, when the captains of the chariots saw that it was not the king of Israel, that they turned back from pursuing him. 33 And a certain man drew his bow at a venture, and smote the king of Israel between the joints of the armor: wherefore he said to the driver of the chariot, Turn thy hand, and carry me out of the host; for I am sore wounded. 34 And the battle increased that day: howbeit the king of Israel stayed himself up in his chariot against the Syrians until even; and about the time of the going down of the sun he died.

This entire chapter is parallel to chapter 22 of First Kings, where we have written twenty-three pages of comments (pp. 283-305 in that commentary); and it is not necessary to add anything here. The variations are unimportant.

XXX

CHAPTER 19

Rebuked by the Prophet, Jehoshaphat Does Better

Jehu the Seer Rebukes Jehoshaphat

Verses 1-3, And Jehoshaphat the king of Judah returned to his house in peace in Jerusalem. 2 And Jehu the son of Hanani the seer went out to meet him, and said to king Jehoshaphat, Shouldest thou help the wicked, and love them that hate Jehovah? for this thing wrath is upon thee from before Jehovah. 3 Nevertheless there are good things found in thee, in that thou hast put away the Asheroth out of the land, and hast set thy heart to seek God.

In the appraisal of Jehoshaphat's reign, it was, in a general sense, approved, despite the serious, even sinful, mistakes, one of which was that marriage with the daughter of Ahab which he arranged for his heir and successor to the throne.

Also, note that nothing is said here about the removal of the high places, despite the fact that 17:6 states that he took away the high places, indicating that the citizens had, in the meanwhile, rebuilt them. This was done many times in the history of Judah.

Jehoshaphat Again Stresses the Law of God

Verses 4-7, And Jehoshaphat dwelt in Jerusalem: and he went out again among the people from Beersheba to the hill-country of Ephraim, and brought them back unto Jehovah, the God of their fathers. 5 And he set judges in

the land throughout all the fortified cities of Judah, city by city, 6 and said to the judges, Consider what ye do: for ye judge not for man, but for Jehovah; and he is with you in the judgment. 7 Now therefore let the fear of Jehovah be upon you; take heed and do it: for there is no iniquity with Jehovah our God, nor respect of persons, nor taking of bribes.

By his placement of this paragraph, the Chronicler intends for us to understand that Jehoshaphat had been sternly warned by the Lord at Ramoth-gilead, and that, for the time present at least, he did an about-face, attempting to bring all the people back to the proper worship and obedience of God. It is highly commendable that the king himself set a good example in this.

It must have come as a severe shock to him that his evil friend Ahab had received a mortal blow from the God he despised, and that only the intervention of God had saved Jehoshaphat himself from a similar fate.

His Righteous Instructions for Priests, Levites

Verses 8-11, Moreover in Jerusalem did Jehoshaphat set of the Levites and the priests, and of the heads of the fathers' houses of Israel, for the judgment of Jehovah, and for controversies. And they returned to Jerusalem. 9 And he charged them, saying, Thus shall ye do in the fear of Jehovah, faithfully, and with a perfect heart. 10 And whensoever any controversy shall come to you from your brethren that dwell in their cities, between

blood and blood, between law and commandment, statutes, and ordinances, ye shall warn them that they be not guilty towards Jehovah, and so wrath come upon you and upon your brethren: this do, and ye shall not be guilty. 11 And, behold, Amariah the chief priest in all matters of Jehovah; and Zebadiah the son of Ishmael, the ruler of the house of Judah, in all the king's matters: also the Levites shall be officers before you. Deal courageously, and Jehovah be with the good.

This chapter makes it clear that too close association with evil people is a fearful danger to Christian people. It is not that we should not love "all men," even as our Father in heaven; but cooperative alliances with wicked partners can easily prove to be an unqualified disaster, as was Jehoshaphat's alliance with Ahab. The danger comes from all directions. The evil partner himself is a threat, as when Ahab disguised himself, almost causing the death of Jehoshaphat; furthermore, the wrath of God can be incurred through our cooperative aid of wicked men.

This careful reorganization of the judiciary and the discrimination between religious matters and the king's matters was an evident improvement over previous practices in Jerusalem.

xxx

CHAPTER 20

God Delivered Jehoshaphat and Israel From an Invasion

A Coalition of Enemies Came Against Israel

Verses 1-4, And it came to pass after this, that the children of Moab, and the children of Ammon, and with them some of the Ammonites, came against Jehoshaphat to battle. 2 Then there came some and told Jehoshaphat, saying, There cometh a great multitude against thee from beyond the sea from Syria; and, behold, they are in Hazazon-tamor, (the same is Engedi), 3 And Jehoshaphat feared, and set himself to seek Jehovah; and he proclaimed a fast throughout all Judah. 4 And Judah gathered themselves together, to seek help of Jehovah: even out of all the cities of Judah they came to seek Jehovah.

The great significance of this is found in the faith of all the people of Judah who joined their king in the fervent plea for the help of the Lord.

And with some of the Ammonites (v. 1). This is an accurate rendition of the Hebrew as attested by the marginal reference; but it sounds awkward, so the RSV has changed it to read, ***Some of the Meunites;*** but based upon a various reading,[1] which has "certain of the Ammonites," this writer views the change in the RSV to be unnecessary. The meaning is clear enough as it is. "The whole strength of the Moabites was mobilized, but only certain of the Ammonites." Later in the chapter, it is revealed that the Edomites (those of mount Seir)

---

[1] CRB, p. 769

were also a part of this coalition against Israel.

Jehoshaphat Leads the Whole Nation in Prayer

Verses 5-13, And Jehoshaphat stood in the assembly of Judah and Jerusalem, in the house of Jehovah before the new court; 6 and he said, O Jehovah, the God of our fathers, art thou God in heaven? and art not thou ruler over all the kingdoms of the nations? and in thy hand is power and might, so that none is able to withstand thee. 7 Didst not thou, O our God, drive out the inhabitants of this land before thy people Israel, and give it to the seed of Abraham thy friend for ever? 8 And they dwelt therein, and have built thee a sanctuary therein for thy name, saying, 9 If evil come upon us, the sword, judgment, or pestilence, or famine, we will stand before this house, and before thee (for thy name is in this house), and cry unto thee in our affliction, and thou wilt hear and save. 10 And now, behold, the children of Moab and Ammon and mount Seir, whom thou wouldest not let Israel invade, when they came out of the land of Egypt, but they turned aside from them, and destroyed them not; 11 behold, how they reward us, to come to cast us out of thy possession, which thou hast given us to inherit. 12 O our God, wilt thou not judge them? for we have no might against this great company that cometh against us; neither know we what to do: but our eyes are upon thee. 13 And all Judah stood before Jehovah, with their little ones, their wives, and their children.

Although Jehoshaphat did not quote ***ver batim*** from Solomon's dedicatory prayer, some of the thought here clearly reflects the sentiments Solomon expressed in that prayer. This was not Jehoshaphat's prayer alone, but a great assembly from all Judah were silent participants in it. The king was leading prayer for all of them.

The Prophetic Answer to Jehoshaphat's Prayer

Verses 14-19, Then upon Jehaziel the son of Zechariah, the son of Benaiah, the son of Jeiel, the son of Mattaniah, the Levite, of the sons of Asaph, came the spirit of Jehovah in the midst of the assembly; 15 and he said, Hearken ye, all Judah, and ye inhabitants of Jerusalem, and thou king Jehoshaphat: Thus saith Jehovah unto to you, Fear not ye, neither be dismayed by reason of this great multitude; for the battle is not yours, but God's. 16 Tomorrow go ye down against them: behold, they come up by the ascent of Ziz; and ye shall find them at the end of the valley, before the wilderness of Jeruel. 17 Ye shall not need to fight in this battle: set yourselves, stand ye still, and see the salvation of Jehovah with you, O Judah and Jerusalem; fear not, nor be dismayed: tomorrow go out against them; for Jehovah is with you. 18 And Jehoshaphat bowed his head with his face to the ground; and all Judah and the inhabitants of Jerusalem fell down before Jehovah, worshipping Jehovah. 19 And the Levites, of the children of the Kohathites and the children of the Korahites, stood up to praise Jehovah the God of Israel, with an exceeding loud voice.

Here we have the picture of a worshipping,

praying Israel as the background of a most remarkable deliverance of God's people from the ravages of a hostile invasion. There cannot be any doubt that many such deliverances of God's people were similarly preceded by this same kind of a spiritual awakening of God's people, and by their most fervent prayers and supplications.

There was one exceedingly unfortunate result of these many divine deliverances of Israel. Long after the nation as a whole had lost all faith in God and were indulging themselves in the most shameful immoralities, when they were threatened, as here, they pleaded for God's deliverance; and the frequencey of those rescues led eventually to a conviction in Israel that, regardless of their gross sins and immoralities, God would always rescue them, solely upon the basis of who they were, namely, the seed of Abraham the friend of God.

Even after Israel rejected the Messiah, God's Only Begotten Son, and during the siege of Jerusalem by the Romans, the last High Priest, comforted and encouraged the people with his declaration that they had nothing to fear, "Because," he said, "The Messiah has not yet come." They truly believed that no matter what they did, God would still bless them at the expense of the whole Gentile world, whom they hated, supposing that when the Messiah came he would either kill all the Gentiles or subject them to Jewish rule, as in the days of their beloved Solomon.

The events of this chapter reveal that, at this time, there still remained an effective reservoir of faith among the Chosen People.

The Enemies of Israel Destroy Each Other

Verses 20-23, And they rose early in the morning, and went forth into the wilderness of Tekoa: and as they went forth, Jehoshaphat stood and said, Hear me, O Judah, and ye inhabitants of Jerusalem; believe in Jehovah your God, and so shall ye be established; believe his prophets, so shall ye prosper. 21 And when he had taken counsel with the people, he appointed them that should sing unto Jehovah, and give praise in holy array, as they went out before the army, and say, Give thanks unto Jehovah; for his lovingkindness endureth for ever. 22 And when they began to sing and to praise, Jehovah set liers-in-wait against the children of Ammon, Moab, and mount Seir, that were come up against Judah; and they were smitten. 23 For the children of Ammon and Moab stood up against the inhabitants of mount Seir, utterly to slay and destroy them: and when they had made an end of the inhabitants of Seir, every one helped to destroy another.

What happened here reminds one of the victory of Gideon over the Midianites in Judges 7th chapter, in which the invading forces destroyed themselves.

God's People Have Only to Recover the Spoil
Left by the Fallen Armies

Verses 24-30, And when Judah came to the watch-tower of the wilderness, they looked upon the multitude; and, behold, they were dead bodies fallen to the earth, and

there were none that escaped. 25 And when Jehoshaphat and his people came to take the spoil of them, they found them in abundance both riches, and dead bodies[2], and precious jewels, which they stripped off for themselves, more than they could carry away: and they were three days in taking the spoil, it was so much. 26 And on the fourth day they assembled themselves in the valley of Beracah; for there they blessed Jehovah: therefore the name of that place was called The Valley of Beracah[3] unto this day. 27 Then they returned every man of Judah and Jerusalem, and Jehoshaphat in the fore-front of them, to go again to Jerusalem with joy; for Jehovah had made them to rejoice over their enemies. 28 And they came to Jerusalem with psalteries and harps and trumpets unto the house of Jehovah. 29 And the fear of God was on all the kingdoms of the countries, when they heard that Jehovah fought against the enemies of Israel. 30 So the realm of Jehoshaphat was quiet; for his God gave him rest round about.

"On the main road between Hebron and Jerusalem, near Tekoa, there is even today a valley that bears a form of the ancient name ***Beracah,***"[4] the same being a very strong evidence of the historicity of this event.

---

[2] Marginal note reads "and garments." See RSV.

[3] Beracah means ***blesssing.*** E. W. G. Masterman in ***ISBE,*** p. 439.

[4] Ibid.

Summary of the Reign of Jehoshaphat

Verses 31-34, And Jehoshaphat reigned over Judah: he was thirty and five years old when he began to reign; and he reigned twenty and five years in Jerusalem: and his mother's name was Azubah the daughter of Shilhi. 32 And he walked in the way of Asa his father, and turned not aside from it, doing that which was right in the eyes of Jehovah. 33 Howbeit the high places were not taken away; neither as yet had the people set their hearts unto the God of their fathers. 34 Now the rest of the acts of Jehoshaphat, first and last, behold, they are written in the history of Jehu the son of Hanani, which is inserted in the book of the kings of Israel.

The last line here indicates that everything the Chronicler has written was taken from the authentic records of the Jewish people. See our introduction to Chronicles for a list of those records which are quoted in Chronicles.

Although, in the general sense, Jehoshaphat did that which was right in the eyes of Jehovah, there were nevertheless some failures on his part. His failure to remove the high places (which had been removed, of course, but had been rebuilt by the people, again and a again), and his alliance with Ahaziah (mentioned in the final paragraph here) were two examples. A third, which we should mention, was his choice of a wife for his son and heir Jehoram. Jehoshaphat evidently hoped to promote peace between Israel and Judah by arranging for the marriage of Jehoram to the daughter of Jezebel and Ahab. This might not have been considered a sin by some, but it was an unqualified disaster, nevertheless; and it resulted in great sorrows for God's people.

Jehoshaphat Rejects Partnership With Ahaziah

Verses 35-37, And after this did Jehoshaphat king of Judah join himself with Ahaziah the king of Israel; the same did very wickedly: 36 and he joined himself with him to make ships to go to Tarshish; and they made ships in Ezion-geber. 37 Then Eliezer the son of Dodavahu of Mareshah prophesied against Jehoshaphat, saying, Because thou hast joined thyself with Ahaziah, Jehovah hath destroyed thy works. And the ships were broken, so they were not able to go to Tarshish.

First Kings 22:49-50 is parallel with these three verses. The account in Kings speaks of Ahaziah's attempt to continue as a partner with Jehoshaphat in that ship-building venture; but it is to the great credit of Jehoshaphat that, acting upon the warning of the prophet, he refused to allow it.

XXX

CHAPTER 21

Jehoram, Wicked Son-in-law of Ahab, Rules Judah

V. JEHORAM (949-942 BC)

"This chapter is a commentary on the man who married the daughter of Ahab and Jezebel, and who walked in their ways (v. 6). It describes his viciousness and his apostasy (vv. 1-11), and God's condemnation of him through the prophet Elijah, and the failures both national and personal that overwhelmed him as a result (vv. 12-20)."[1]

His evil wife was Athaliah who in time also became a ruler of Judah. She attempted to destroy completely the house of David and almost, but not quite, succeeded in doing so. She was, in many respects, a carbon copy of her evil mother Jezebel. Athaliah was never accepted by Judah, and her name was never included in the list of Judah's legitimate rulers.

Death of Jehoshaphat and Succession of Jehoram

Verses 1-3, And Jehoshaphat slept with his fathers, and was buried with his fathers in the city of David: and Jehoram his son reigned in his stead. 2 And he had brethren, the sons of Jehoshaphat: Azariah, and Jehiel, and Zechariah, and Azariah, and Michael, and Shephaliah; all these were the sons of Jehoshaphat king of Israel. 3 And their father gave them great gifts, of silver, and of gold, and

---

[1] WYC, p. 406.

of precious things, with fortified cities in Judah: but the kingdom gave he to Jehoram, because he was the first-born.

Azariah ... Azariah (v. 2). "These names are written differently in the Hebrew: ***Azarjah*** and ***Azarjahu.***"[2] It is not clear why the translators rendered the two names alike. On the strange identification of Jehoshaphat as ***king of Israel*** (v. 2), this designation was correct, because Judah was indeed the true Israel; and those northern tribes who called themselves Israel were no longer part of God's true Israel.

Jehoram's Vicious Murder of All His Brothers

Verses 4-7, Now when Jehoram was risen up over the kingdom of his father, and had strengthened himslf, he slew all his brethren with the sword, and divers also of the princes of Israel. 5 Jehoram was thirty and two years old when he began to reign; and he reigned eight years in Jerusalem. 6 And he walked in the way of the kings of Israel, as did the house of Ahab; for he had the daughter of Ahab to wife: and he did that which was evil in the sight of Jehovah. 7 Howbeit Jehovah would not destroy the house of David, because of the covenant that he had made with David, and as he promised to give a lamp to him and to his children alway.

Jehovah would not destroy the house of David (v. 7). The very mention of such a thing in this paragraph

---

[2] CFK, 3b, p. 395.

is a mark of the diabolical threat that existed at this moment in the history of the Chosen People. In these events, Satan was moving swiftly and methodically toward that very goal: the total destruction of the house of David. And when Jehoram's evil mother Athaliah was finally able to seize power for herself, she all but accomplished it.

We cannot leave this without mentioning the disaster that always results from contracting a marriage with an evil partner. Jehoshaphat is credited with being a good king; but he was incredibly stupid in arranging a marriage for his first-born son and presumptive heir to the throne of Judah with the wicked Jezebel II, whose name was Athaliah.

Jehoram Promptly Lost Edom and Libnah

Verses 8-10, In his days Edom revolted from under the hand of Judah, and made a king over themselves. 9 Then Jehoram passed over with his captains, and all his chariots with him; and he rose up by night, and smote the Edomites that compassed him about, and the captains of the chariots. 10 So Edom revolted from under the hand of Judah unto this day: then did Libnah revolt at the same time from under his hand, because he had forsaken Jehovah, the God of his fathers.

"What appears to have happened here is that Jehoram and his army went to teach the Edomites a lesson, but found out that the Edomites had surrounded him and his chariots."[3] The consequent loss of two subject peoples, the Edomites from east of Jordan, and those of Libnah from the area of the Philistines, was directly due to the wickedness of Jehoram and were the result of the judgment of God upon him.

Part of this chapter is parallel to 2K 8:17-24, and our comments on some of these events are found in the ***Commentary on Second Kings.***

That Writing From Elijah Regarding Jehoram

Verses 11-15, Moreover he made high places in the montains of Judah, and made the inhabitants of Jerusalem to play the harlot, and led Judah astray. 12 And there came a writing to him from Elijah the prophet, saying, Thus saith Jehovah, the God of David thy father, Because thou hast not walked in the ways of Jehoshaphat thy father, nor in the ways of Asa king of Judah, 13 but hast walked in the ways of the kings of Israel, and hast made Judah and the inhabitants of Jerusalem to play the harlot, like as the house of Ahab did, and also hast slain thy brethren of thy father's house, who were better than thyself: 14 behold, Jehovah will smite with a great plague thy people, and thy children, and thy wives, and all thy substance; 15 and thou shalt have great sickness by disease of thy bowels, until thy bowels fall out by reason of thy sickness, day by day.

Some scholars have argued that Elijah was already deceased at the times of Jehoram and that he

---

[3] NLBC, p. 5o8.

could not have written the letter mentioned here; but this criticism is groundless for two reasons: (1) Elijah might indeed still have been living, a rather attractive argument for this having been cited by Myers.[4] That Elijah did indeed write this 'document' and that it was sent during Elijah's lifetime was flatly declared by Josephus.[5] William Whiston, who translated the works of Josephus, however, insisted that Elijah had died four years previously to the times indicated here, and that the simplest explanation is that some copier inadvertantly substituted the name Elijah for that of Elisha.[6] (2) The passage does not indicate that the "document"[7] (as the word is translated by Myers) was written druing Elijah's lifetime. Furthermore, the Chronicler gives five other examples of prophets predicting disaster to kings before the event (12:5, 16:7, 19:2, 24:20, and 26:16).[8] In this light, we find no difficulty whatever in what is written here.

The Fulfilment of Elijah's Prophecy

Verses 16-17, And Jehovah stirred up against Jehoram the spirit of the Philistines, and of the Arabians that are beside the Ethiopians: 17 and they came up against Judah, and brake into it, and carried away all the

---

4 AnBi, *Chronicles*, p. 121.

5 JOSA, p. 284.

6 Ibid.

7 AnBi, op. cit., p. 121.

8 Ibid., p. 122.

substance that was in the king's house, and his sons also, and his wives; so that there was never a son left him, save Jehoahaz, the youngest of his sons.

It was retribution in kind for this evil ruler. He who had murdered all of his fathers sons except himself experienced the same deprivation. His wives also were carried away. It was a pity that they did not take his mother Athaliah also. His terrible sickness would fulfil Elijah's prophecy, and that came at once.

Prophecy of Sickness and Death Fulfilled

Verses 18-20, And after all this Jehovah smote him in his bowels with an incurable disease. 19 And it came to pass, in process of time, at the end of two years, that his bowels fell out by reason of his sickness, and he died of sore diseases. And his people made no burning for him, like the burning of his fathers. 20 Thirty and two years old was he when he began to reign, and he reigned in Jerusalem eight years: and he departed without being desired; and they buried him in the city of David, but not in the sepulchres of the kings.

Despite those titles, power, and pelf
The wretch concentred all in self,
Living shall forfeit fair renown.
And, doubly dying, shall go down
To the vile dust from which he sprung,
Unwept, unhonored, and unsung.

---Sir Walter Scott, ***The Lay of the Last Minstrel.***

XXX

CHAPTER 22
The Brief Evil Reign of Ahaziah

VI. AHAZIAH (842 BC)

Ahaziah Made King of Judah

Verses 1-3, And the inhabitants of Jerusalem made Ahaziah his youngest son king in his stead; for the band of men that came with the Arabians to the camp had slain all the eldest. So Ahaziah the son of Jehoram king of Judah reigned. 2 Forty and two years old was Ahaziah when he began to reign; and he reigned one year in Jerusalem: and his mother's name was Athaliah the daughter of Omri. 3 He also walked in the ways of the house of Ahab; for his mother was his counsellor to do wickedly.

Ahaziah his youngest son (v. 1). The youngest son of Jehoram is called Jehoahaz in the previous chapter (21:17); "But Jehoahaz and Azariah are equivalent names."[1] There was nothing unusual about variations in Hebrew names. "Bathsheba was also known as Bathshua; and her father was called Amiel or Eliam. Either spelling of such duplicate names gave the same meanings in Hebrew."[2]

Forty and two years old was Ahaziah when he began to reign (v. 2). Ahaziah's father was only forty-two years old when he died (21:5), so we should follow later renditions which read, "Twenty and two years" instead

---

1 AB, ***Chronicles,*** p. 402.

2 A. L. Breslich in ***ISBE,*** p. 416.

of "Forty and two."

Athaliah the daughter of Omri (v. 2). She was actually the daughter of Ahab and a granddaughter of Omri; but such a loose usage of the terms ***son*** or ***daughter*** is quite common in the OT.

Circumstances Leading to the Death of Ahaziah

Verses 4-6, And he did that which was evil in the sight of Jehovah, as did the house of Ahab, for they were his counsellors after the death of his father, to his destruction. 5 He walked also after their counsel, and went with Jehoram the king of Israel to war against Hazael king of Syria at Ramoth-gilead: and the Syrians wounded Joram. 6 And he returned to be healed in Jezreel of the wounds which they had given him at Ramoth, when he fought against Hazael king of Syria. And Ahaziah the son of Jehoram king of Judah went down to see Jehoram the son of Ahab in Jezreel, because he was sick.

Joram king of Israel ... Jehoram king of Israel (vv. 5,6). This is another example of alternate names for the same person.

This paragraph reveals that the king of Judah was at that time totally dominated by his mother's family, namely, the house of Ahab; and by Ahaziah's leaving his capital city to visit his sick relative in Jezreel, it gave Jehu the opportunity to exterminate both royal houses, both that of Jehoram king of Israel and that of Ahaziah king of Judah.

The first nine verses here are parallel with 2K

8:24b-29, and 9:21, 27-28). See our comments under those verses.

Ahab's House Destroyed; the Death of Ahaziah

Verses 7-9, Now the destruction of Ahaziah was of God, in that he went unto Joram: for when he was come, he went out with Jehoran against Jehu the son of Nimshi, whom Jehovah had anointed to cut off the house of Ahab. 8 And it came to pass when Jehu was executing judgment upon the house of Ahab, that he found the princes of Judah, and the sons of the brethren of Ahaziah, ministering to Ahaziah, and slew them. 9 And he sought Ahaziah, and they caught him (now he was hiding in Samaria), and they brought him to Jehu, and slew him; and they buried him, for they said, He is the son of Jehoshaphat, who sought Jehovah with all his heart. And the house of Ahaziah had no power to hold the kingdom.

The destruction of Ahaziah was of God (v. 7). This means that it was due to God's providential arrangements that Ahaziah was found in close companionship with Ahab at the very moment when God's appointed exterminator of the house of Ahab appeared and included Ahaziah in the slaughter, quite properly enough; because by Jehoshaphat's foolish marriage of Ahaziah to Athaliah, Ahab's daughter, he had made his son Ahaziah definitely a part of '***the house of Ahab.***'

The house of Ahaziah had no power to hold the kingdom (v. 9). This was the power vacuum that enabled the evil Athaliah to seize the throne and to proceed with her intention of destroying the last vestiges of the house of David, a purpose which, in the providence of God, was thwarted.

God Saved Joash Alive From the Wrath of Athaliah

Verses 10-12, Now when Athaliah the mother of Ahaziah saw that her son was dead, she arose and destroyed all the seed royal of the house of Judah. 11 But Jehoshabeath, the daughter of the king, took Joash the son of Ahaziah, and stole him away from among the king's sons that were slain, and put him and his nurse in the bed-chamber. So Jehoshabeath, the daughter of king Jehoram, the wife of Jehoiada the priest (for she was the sister of Ahaziah), hid him from Athaliah, so that she slew him not. 12 And he was with them in the house of God six years: and Athaliah reigned in the land.

Our comments on the narration in these three verses are found in the parallel account in 2K 11:1-3.

xxx

CHAPTER 23

Six Year Reign of Athaliah Ends in Her Execution

VII. JOASH (837-800 BC)

Jehoiada's Plan to Crown Joash and Execute Athaliah

Verses 1-7 ***And in the seventh year, Jehoiada strengthened himself, and took the captains of hundreds, Azariah the son of Jeroham, and Ishmael the son of Jehohanan, and Azariah the son of Obed, and Maaseiah the son of Adaiah, and Elishaphat the son of Zichri, into covenant with him. 2 And they went about in Judah and gathered the Levites out of all the cities of Judah, and the heads of the fathers' houses of Israel, and they came to Jerusalem. 3 And all the assembly made a covenant with the king in the house of God. And he said unto them, Behold, the king's son shall reign, as Jehovah hath spoken concerning the sons of David. 4 This is the thing that ye shall do: a third part of you that come in on the sabbath, of the priests and of the Levites, shall be porters of the thresholds; 5 and a third part shall be at the king's house; and a third part at the gate of the foundation: and all the people shall be in the courts of the house of Jehovah. 6 But let none come into the house of Jehovah, save the priests, and they that minister of the Levites: they shall come in, for they are holy: but all the people shall keep the charge of Jehovah. 7 And the Levites shall compass the king round about, every man with his weapons in his hand; and whosoever cometh into the house, let him be slain: and be ye with the king when he cometh in, and when he goeth out.***

Long Live the King

Verses 8-15, So the Levites and all Judah did according to all that Jehoiada the priest commanded: and took every man his men, those that were to come in on the sabbath, with those that were to go out on the sabbath; for Jehoiada the priest dismissed not the courses. 9 And Jehoiada the priest delivered to the captains of hundreds, the spears, and bucklers, and shields, that had been king David's, which were in the house of God. 10 And he set all the people, every man with his weapon in his hand, from the right side of the house to the left side of the house, by the king round about. 11 Then they brought out the king's son, and put the crown upon him, and gave him the testimony, and made him king: and Jehoiada and his sons anointed him; and they said, Long live the king!

The Execution of Athaliah

Verses 12-15, And when Athaliah heard the noise of the people running and praising the king, she came to the people into the house of Jehovah: 13 and she looked, and, behold, the king stood by the pillar at the entrance, and the captains and the trumpets by the king; and all the people of the land rejoiced, and blew trumpets; the singers also played on instruments of music, and led the singing of praise. Then Athaliah rent her clothes, and said, Treason! treason! 14 And Jehoiada the priest brought out the captains of hundreds that were set over the host, and said unto them, Have her forth between the ranks; and whoso followeth her, let him be slain with the sword: for the priest

said, Let her not be slain in the house of Jehovah. 15 So they made way for her; and she went to the entrance of the horse gate to the king's house, and they slew her there.

Joash Established as King of Judah

Verses 16-21, And Jehoiada made a covenant between himself, and all the people, and the king, that they should be Jehovah's people. 17 And all the people went to the house of Baal, and brake it down, and brake his altars and his images in pieces, and slew Mattan the priest of Baal before the altars. 18 And Jehoiada appointed the officers of the house of Jehovah under the hand of the priests the Levites, whom David had distributed in the house of Jehovah, to offer the burnt-offerings of Jehovah, as it is written in the law of Moses, with rejoicing and with singing, according to the order of David. 19 And he set the porters at the gates of the house of Jehovah, that none that was unclean in anything should enter in. 20 And he took the captains of hundreds, and the nobles, and the governors of all the people, and all the people of the land, and brought down the king from the house of Jehovah: and they came through the upper gate unto the king's house, and set the king upon the throne of the kingdom. 21 So all the people of the land rejoiced, and the city was quiet. And Athaliah they had slain with the sword.

This whole chapter, along with the last three verses of the previous chapter, is parallel with 2 Kings eleventh chapter. In our ***Commentary on Second Kings***, we have written ten pages of comments on these events and do not wish to add anything here. See pages 139-148 of our commentary on that volume. There are a few unimportant variations, but the narratives are essentially identical.

xxx

CHAPTER 24

End of the Reign of Joash

Verses 1-3, ***Joash was seven years old when he began to reign; and he reigned forty years in Jerusalem: and his mother's name was Zibiah, of Beersheba. 2 And Joash did that which was right in the eyes of Jehovah all the days of Jehoiada the priest. 3 And Jehoiada took for him two wives; and he begat sons and daughters.***

These three verses are parallel with 2K 12:1-4. See our comments there.

Joash Made Extensive Repairs and Reconstruction of the Temple, Which Had Been Robbed and Plundered by Athaliah

Verses 4-7, ***And it came to pass after this, that Joash minded to restore the house of Jehovah. 5 And he gathered together the priests and the Levites, and said unto them, Go out into the cities of Judah, and gather of all Israel money to repair the house of your God from year to year; and see that ye hasten the matter. Howbeit the Levites hastened it not. 6 And the king called for Jehoiada the chief, and said unto him, Why hast thou not required of the Levites to bring in out of Judah and out of Jerusalem the tax of Moses the servant of Jehovah, and of the assembly of Israel, and for the tent of the testimony. 7 For the sons of Athaliah, that wicked woman, had broken up the house of God; and also all the dedicated things of the house of Jehovah did they bestow upon the Baalim.***

A Collection Box Installed at the Temple Gate

Verses 8-14, So the king commanded, and they made a chest, and set it without at the gate of Jehovah. 9 And they made a proclamation through Judah and Jerusalem, to bring in for Jehovah the tax that Moses the servant of God laid upon Israel in the wilderness. 10 And all the princes and all the people rejoiced, and brought in, and cast into the chest, until they had made an end. 11 And it was so, that at what time the chest was brought unto the king's officers by the hand of the Levites, and when they saw that there was much money, the king's scribe and the chief priest's officer came and emptied the chest, and took it, and carried it to its place again. Thus they did day by day, and gathered money in abundance. 12 And the king and Jehoiada gave it to such as did the work of the service of the house of Jehovah; and they hired masons and carpenters to restore the house of Jehovah, and also such as wrought iron and brass to repair the house of Jehovah. 13 So the workmen wrought, and the work of repairing went forward in their hands, and they set up the house of God in its state, and strengthened it. 14 And when they had made an end, they brought the rest of the money before the king and Jehoiada, whereof were made vessels for the house of Jehovah, even vessels wherewith to minister and to offer, and spoons, and vessels of gold and silver. And they offered burnt-offerings in the house of Jehovah continually all the days of Jehoiada.

This chapter in verses 5-14 is parallel with Second Kings 12:5-16; and most of our comments on these paragraphs will be found in our Commentary on Second Kings.

We wish to stress, however, the repeated references to the teachings of Moses, thus sustaining the unimpeachable witness of Chronicles to the continual existence of the Pentateuch from the days of Moses throughout the history of Israel.

The following verses 15-22 appear only here and are not in Kings.

The Shameful Apostasy of Joash

Verses 15-19,** **But Jehoiada waxed old and was full of days, and he died; a hundred and thirty years old was he when he died. 16 And they buried him in the city of David among the kings, because he had done good in Israel, and toward God and his house. 17 Now after the death of Jehoiada came the princes of Judah, and made obeisance to the king. Then the king hearkened unto them. 18 And they forsook the house of Jehovah, the God of their fathers, and served the Asherim and the idols: and wrath came upon Judah and Jerusalem for this their guiltiness. 19 Yet he sent prophets to them, to bring them again unto Jehovah; and they testified against them: but they would not give ear.

Joash's Heartless Murder of Zechariah

Verses 20-22, And the Spirit of God came upon Zechariah the son of Jehoiada the priest; and he stood above the people, and said unto them, Thus saith God, Why

transgress ye the commandments of Jehovah, so that ye cannot prosper? because ye have forsaken Jehovah, he hath forsaken you. 21 And they conspired against him, and stoned him with stones at the commandment of the king in the court of the house of Jehovah. 22 Thus Joash the king remembered not the kindness which Jehoiada his father had done to him, but slew his son. And when he died, he said, Jehovah look upon it and require it.

These two paragraphs reveal that Joash, at heart, was a true descendant of his evil ancester Ahab. As long as Jehoiada was available as a wise and able counsellor, Joash did very well; but as soon as Jehoiada was dead, the princes of Judah seduced him with their flattery and induced him to reopen the high places with their licentious worship of the pagan idols.

Jehoiada's son Zechariah, under the influence of the Spirit of God, pronounced a severe warning; but the king's response was to honor the conspiracy of the evil princes and order the man of God stoned to death within the court of the temple itself.

Zechariah's prayer that God would see their terrible crime and pronounce a judgment against them was honored immediately.

God's Summary Punishment of Judah and Jerusalem

Verses 23-24, ***And it came to pass at the end of the year, that the army of the Syrians came up against him: and they came to Judah and Jerusalem, and destroyed all the princes of the people from among the people, and sent***

all the spoil of them unto the king of Damascus. 24 For the army of the Syrians came with a small company; and Jehovah delivered a very great host into their hand, because they had forsaken Jehovah, the God of their fathers. So they executed Judgment upon Joash.

It was especially appropriate that the Syrians killed all the princes, the very people who had seduced Joash to accept idolatry. Significantly, this judgment fell upon Joash and his kingdom within less than a year following the heartless murder of Zechariah. But God was not finished with his judgment against Joash. The next paragraph gives the conclusion of it.

Joash's Illness and Murder by His Own Servants

Verses 25-27, And when they were departed from him (for they left him very sick), his own servants conspired against him for the blood of the sons[1] of Jehoiada the priest, and slew him on his bed, and he died; and they buried him in the city of David, but they buried him not in the sepulchre of the kings. 26 And these are they that conspired against him: Zabad the son of Shemeath the Ammonitess, and Jehozabad the son of Shimrith the Moabitess. 27 Now concerning his sons, and the greatness of the burdens laid upon him, and the rebuilding of the house of God, behold, they are written in

---

[1] Some versions read *son* here. We do not know, however, whether Joash's murder of Zechariah was extended to other sons of Jehoiada or not, Either *son* or *sons* might be correct.

the commentary of the book of the kings. And Amaziah his son reigned in his stead.

Verses 23-27 here are parallel with Second Kings 12:18-22; and we have written additional comments on these verses in that commentary.

XXX

CHAPTER 25

The Tragic Record of Amaziah's Reign in Judah

VIII. AMAZIAH (800-783 BC)

We have already written about a dozen pages in 2 Kings fourteenth chapter regarding the reign of Amaziah, taking due note of the additional information provided in this chapter. We shall do little here except print the chapter.

Amaziah Slays the Murderers of His Father

Verses 1-4, Amaziah was twenty and five years old when he began to reign; and he reigned twenty and nine years in Jerusalem. 2 And he did that which was right in the eyes of Jehovah, but not with a perfect heart. 3 And it came to pass when the kingdom was established unto him, that he slew his servants who had killed the king his father. 4 But he put not their children to death, according to that which is written in the law in the book of Moses, as Jehovah commanded, saying, The fathers shall not die for the children, neither shall the children die for the fathers; but every man shall die for his own sin.

He did that which was right in the eyes of Jehovah (v. 2). The qualifying clause, "not with a perfect heart" is in effect an admission that his reign was evil. His doing right in God's sight apparently applies only to his sparing the children of his servants whom he executed for the death of his father.

The commandment of God through Moses, mentioned in verse four, is found in Deuteronomy 24:16. See our comments in the Commentary on 2 Kings 14 for the very great significance of this reference.

Amaziah's Sinful Preparations for War Against Edom

Verses 5-13, Moreover Amaziah gathered Judah together, and ordered them according to their fathers' houses, under captains of thousands and captains of hundreds, even all Judah and Benjamin: and he numbered them from twenty years old and upward, and found them three hundred thousand chosen men, able to go forth to war, that could handle spear and shield. 6 He hired also a hundred thousand mighty men of valor out of Israel for a hundred talents of silver. 7 But there came a man of God to him, saying, O king, let not the army of Israel go with thee; for Jehovah is not with Israel, to wit, with all the children of Ephraim. 8 But if thou wilt go, do valiantly, be strong for the battle: God will cast thee down before the enemy; for God hath power to help, and to cast down. 9 And Amaziah said to the man of God, But what shall we do for the hundred talents which I have given to the army of Israel? And the man of God answered, Jehovah is able to give thee much more than this. 10 Then Amaziah separated them, to wit, the army that was come to him out of Ephraim to go home again: wherefore their anger was greatly kindled against Judah, and they returned home in fierce anger. 11 And Amaziah took courage, and led forth his people, and went to the Valley of Salt, and smote of the children of Seir ten thousand. 12 And other ten thousamd

did the children of Judah carry away alive, and brought them unto the top of the rock, and cast them down from the top of the rock, so that they were all broken in pieces. 13 But the men of the army whom Amaziah sent back, that they should not go with him to battle, fell upon the cities of Judah, from Samaria even unto Beth-horon, and smote of them three thousand, and took much spoil.

Jehovah is not with Israel, to wit, the children of Ephraim (v. 7). The man of God here made it plain that the rebellion of the northern tribes against the Davidic dynasty had forfeited their further identity as "God's Chosen People." This is the reason that the Chronicler completely ignored, in as much as it was possible, the entire Northern Israel, focussing his attention completely upon the fortunes of Judah.

The top of the rock (v. 12). "This was the height of Petra, the Edomite capital, near where the battle was fought."[1]

Other scriptures which relate the horrible cruelties of the Edomite wars with Israel are 1K 11:15, Ezekiel 25:12, and Obadiah 14. The Edomites were descendants of Esau, Jacob's twin brother; and there is no more terrible an example of brother hating brother in human history.

---

[1] AB, *Chronicles,* p. 408.

Amaziah's Sinful Worship of Edomite Gods

Verses 14-16, Now it came to pass, after Amaziah was come from the slaughter of the Edomites, that he brought the gods of the children of Seir, and bowed down himself before them, and burned incense unto them. 15 Wherefore the anger of Jehovah was kindled against Amaziah, and he sent unto him a prophet, who said unto him, Why hast thou sought after the gods of the people, which have not delivered their own people out of thy hand? 16 And it came to pass as he talked with him, that the king said unto him, Have we made thee of the king's counsel? forbear; why shouldest thou be smitten? Then the prophet forbare, and said, I know that God hath determined to destroy thee, because thou hast done this, and hast not hearkened unto my counsel.

Ellison noted that, "Amaziah held the debased view that Jehovah was the supreme God, but yet was only one god among many gods."[2] His purpose in carrying away the gods of Edom (of whom we know nothing) was perhaps that of depriving the Edomites of any support they might have been supposed to give Edom. Amaziah's worshipping them and burning incense to them was a cardinal violation of the Law of Moses and the Decalogue, "Thou shalt not bow down thyself unto them (images)" (Exodus 20:5).

Amaziah's victory over Edom had apparently completely turned his head. His subsequent behavior

2 NBCR, p. 390.

was that of a fool.

Amaziah Decides to Declare War Against Northern Israel

Verses 17-19, Then Amaziah king of Judah took advice, and sent to Joash, the son of Jehoahaz, king of Israel, saying, Come, let us look one another in the face. 18 And Joash king of Israel sent to Amaziah king of Judah, saying, The thistle that was in Lebanon sent to the cedar that was in Lebanon, saying, Give thy daughter to my son to wife; and there passed by a wild beast that was in Lebanon, and trod down the thistle. 19 Thou sayest, Lo, thou hast smitten Edom; and thy heart lifteth thee up to boast: abide now at home; why shouldest thou meddle to thy hurt, that thou shouldest fall, even thou, and Judah with thee?

And Amaziah ... took advice (v. 17). Moffatt renders this, "Let himself be counselled." The previous paragraph reveals that Amaziah rejected the word of God's prophet; and therefore the counsel which he received here was not of God but of Satan.

Let us look one another in the face (v. 17). This was both intended and understood to be a declaration of war. Joash properly understood the arrogant and egotistical intentions of Amaziah and warned him of the fate that would overtake him; but Amaziah would not hearken to any sound advice.

Amaziah Defeated, Captured, and Jerusalem Plundered

Verses 20-24, ***But Amaziah would not hear; for it was of God, that he might deliver them into the hand of their enemies, because they had sought after the gods of Edom. 21 So Joash king of Israel went up; and he and Amaziah king of Judah looked one another in the face at Beth-shemesh, which belongeth to Judah. 22 And Judah was put to the worse before Israel; and they fled every man to his tent. 23 And Joash king of Israel took Amaziah king of Judah, the son of Joash, the son of Jehoahaz, at Beth-shemesh, and brought him to Jerusalem, and brake down the wall of Jerusalem from the gate of Ephraim to the corner gate, four hundred cubits. 24 And he took all the gold and silver, and all the vessels that were found in the house of God with Obed-edom, and the treasures of the king's house, and the hostages also, and returned to Samaria.***

See our discussion in the parallel account in Kings. This was a catastrophic defeat and humiliation for the arrogant Amaziah. He was left on the throne, purely by the contemptuous mercy and forbearance of the king of Israel, who might indeed have killed him.

Conspiracy Against Amaziah, and His Murder

Verses 25-28, ***And Amaziah the son of Joash king of Judah lived after the death of Joash son of Jehoahaz king of Israel fifteen years. 26 Now the rest of the acts of Amaziah, first and last, behold, are they not written in the***

book of the kings of Judah and Israel? 27 Now from the time that Amaziah did turn away from following Jehovah they made a conspiracy against him in Jerusalem; and he fled to Lachish; but they sent after him to Lachish, and slew him there. 28 And they brought him upon horses, and buried him with his fathers in the city of Judah.

XXX

CHAPTER 26

The Reign of Uzziah (Azariah in Kings) Over Judah

IX. UZZIAH (783-742 BC)

Uzziah Succeeds Amaziah as King

Verses 1-5, ***And all the people of Judah took Uzziah, who was sixteen years old, and made him king in the room of his father Amaziah. 2 He built Eloth, and restored it to Judah, after that the king slept with his fathers. 3 Sixteen years old was Uzziah when he began to reign; and he reigned fifty and two years in Jerusalem; and his mother's name was Jechiliah, of Jerusalem. 4 And he did that which was right in the eyes of Jehovah, according to all that his father Amaziah had done. 5 And he set himself to seek God in the days of Zechariah, who had understanding in the vision of God: and as long as he sought Jehovah, God made him to prosper.***

Sixteen years old was Uzziah when he began to reign (v. 3). The youth of Uzziah probably accounts for the fact that the conspirators against Amaziah waited so long to murder him; for they had surely determined to do so as soon as he worshipped the gods of Edom, an event that took place when Uzziah was an infant.

He did that which was right in the eyes of Jehovah (v. 4). As in the case of his father, this only means that he began well. Later in the chapter, we learn of the corruption that fell upon him.

His was a long and powerful reign indeed. "He successfully defended Judah against the belligerent

Ammonites, Philistines and Arabians, developed a strong standing army, and rebuilt the nation's fortifications. He even reopened the Red Sea port of Eloth, and promoted commerce."[1] Eloth is the same as Ezion-geber.

The Record of Uzziah's Mighty Achievements

Verses 6-15, And he went forth and warred against the Philistines, and brake down the wall of Gath, and the wall of Jabneh, and the wall of Ashdod; and he built cities in the country of Ashdod, and among the Philistines. 7 And God helped him against the Philistines, and against the Ammonites that dwelt in Gur-baal, and the Meunim. 8 And the Ammonites gave tribute to Uzziah: and his name spread abroad, even to the entrance of Egypt; for he waxed exceeding strong. 9 Moreover Uzziah built towers in Jerusalem at the corner gate, and at the valley gate, and at the turning of the wall, and fortified them. 10 And he built towers in the wilderness, and hewed out many cisterns, for he had much cattle; in the lowland also, and in the plain: and he had husbandmen and vinedressers in the mountains and in the fruitful fields; for he loved husbandry. 11 Moreover Uzziah had an army of fighting men, that went out to war by bands, according to the number of their reckoning by Jeiel the scribe and Maaseiah the officer, under the hand of Hananiah, one of the king's captains. 12 The whole numbr of the heads of the fathers' houses, even the mighty men of valor, was two thousand

---

[1] EOTB, p. 350.

and six hundred. 13 And under their hand was an army, three hundred thousand and seven thousand and five hundred, that made war with mighty power, to help the king against the enemy. 14 And Uzziah prepared for them, even for all the host, shields, and spears, and helmets, and coats of mail, and bows, and stones for slinging. 15 And he made in Jerusalem engines, invented by skilful men, to be upon the towers and upon the battlements, wherewith to shoot arrows and great stones. And his name spread far abroad; for he was marvelously helped, till he was strong.

The Presumption, Sin, and Punishment of Uzziah

Verses 16-23, But when he was strong, his heart was lifted up, so that he did corruptly; and he trespassed against Jehovah his God; for he went into the temple of Jehovah to burn incense upon the altar of incense. 17 And Azariah the priest went in after him, and with him fourscore priests of Jehovah, that were valiant men: 18 and they withstood Uzziah the king, and said unto him, It pertaineth not unto thee, Uzziah, to burn incense unto Jehovah, but to the priests the sons of Aaron, that are consecrated to burn incense: go out of the sanctuary; for thou hast trespassed; neither shall it be for thine honor from Jehovah God. 19 Then Uzziah was wroth; and he had a censer in his hand to burn incense; and while he was wroth with the priests, the leprosy brake forth in his forehead before the priests in the house of Jehovah, beside the altar of incense. 20 And Azariah the chief priest, and all the priests, looked upon him, and, behold, he was leprous in his forehead, and they thrust him out quickly

from thence; yea, himself hasted also to go out, because Jehovah had smitten him. 21 And Uzziah the king was a leper unto the day of his death, and dwelt in a separate house, being a leper; for he was cut off from the house of Jehovah: and Jothan his son was over the king's house, judging the people of the land. 22 Now the rest of the acts of Uzziah, first and last, did Isaiah the prophet, the son of Amoz, write. 23 So Uzziah slept with his fathers; and they buried him with his fathers, in the field of burial which belonged to the kings; for they said, He is a leper; and Jotham his son reigned in his stead.

This writer has dilgently studied the Bible, and the commentraries that men have written concerning it, for the greater part of a long lifetime; and the most unbelievable, the most ridiculous, and the most fradulent comments we have encountered regarding God's word are such as the following from Jacob M. Meyers:

> The misfortune that befell the king, his leprosy, was due directly to his violation of the priestly prerogatives set up by the ***P Code***.[2]

This explanation offered here in Anchor Bible harmonizes completely with what many modern liberal and radical scholars teach; but there are some Gargantuan reasons why their position regarding that imaginary ***P Code*** must be rejected by believers. Throughout our commentaries we have continually stressed the weak and precarious grounds which

---

[2] AnBi, ***Chronicles***, p. 153.

underlie the speculation that postulates any such code. Throughout the Holy Bible, it is referred to again and again as the Law of God given through Moses; and ***that*** is what Uzziah violated. The Bible verse that teaches this is not in Deuteronomy but in Exodus 29:29. If it had been only a man-made prerogative, fraudulently invented and imposed upon God's people by unscrupulous priests, which Uzziah violated, ***GOD WOULD NOT HAVE PUNISHED HIM BY STRIKING HIM WITH LEPROSY!*** If the ***P Code*** inventors want us to believe their fairy tale, let them explain why God smote Uzziah with leprosy.

Oh yes, their defence is merely to deny what is written here; but this circumstantially reported episode is obviously that of nearly a hundred eye-witnesses! The king himself renounced his authority on account of it; and it was officially attested and proved by his burial, not in the tombs of the kings, but in a field nearby. All the critics on earth cannot get rid of what is written here.

Furthermore, the allegation, made to back up their speculations, that David, Solomon, and Ahaz indeed sometimes offered incense in the temple, while true enough, is not relevant. In a million years their violations of God's word could not justify Uzziah's doing so. Throughout the Samuels, the Kings, and the Chronicles, the sins of David and Solomon read like a complete anthology of human wickedness. We challenge the liberal and radical commentators to name one sin of any description that either Solomon or David, or both of them, did not commit.

What Uzziah actually violated here was the divine instructions of God himself through Moses in the Pentateuch (Exodus 29:29). Saul lost his kingship for failing to respect those very restrictons; and that was centuries prior to the allleged date of the imaginary ***P Code.***

And speaking of the P Code, Where is it? Who has ever seen it? And just what was in it? It is our opinion that no genuine scholar has any right to appeal to imaginary documents.

xxx

CHAPTER 27

The Reign of Jotham the son of Uzziah

X. JOTHAM (750-735 BC)

Verses 1-9, Jotham was twenty and five years old when he began to reign; and he reigned sixteen years in Jerusalem: and his mother's name was Jerushah the daughter of Zadok. 2 And he did that which was right in the eyes of Jehovah, according to all that his father Uzziah had done: howbeit he entered not into the temple of Jehovah. And the people did yet corruptly. 3 He built the upper gate of the house of Jehovah, and on the wall of Ophel he built much. 4 Moreover he built cities in the hill-country of Judah, and in the forests he built castles and towers. 5 He fought also with the king of the children of Ammon, and prevailed against them. And the children of Ammon gave him the same year a hundred talents of silver, and ten thousand measures of wheat, and ten thousand of barley. So much did the children of Ammon render unto him, in the second year also, and in the third. 6 So Jotham became mighty, because he ordered his ways before Jehovah his God. 7 Now the rest of the acts of Jotham, and all his wars, and his ways, behold, they are written in the book of the kings of Israel and Judah. 8 He was five and twenty years old when he began to reign, and reigned sixteen years in Jerusalem. 9 And Jotham slept with his fathers, and they buried him in the city of David; and Ahaz his son reigned in his stead

The people did yet corruptly (v. 2). 2 Kings 15:35 has the information that the high places were not removed; thus God's people continued their idolatrous worship in the high places.

The wall of Ophel (v. 3). "This wall was part of the old Jebusite city, a very important part of Jerusalem, also called 'the City of David.'"[1] Jotham's fortifying this part of Jerusalem, "Indicated that he feared an external attack, probably from Assyria and Samaria. This faithless trust which Judah at that time put in fortifications was rebuked by the prophets (Hosea 8:14, and Isaiah 2:15)."[2]

Ten thousand measures of wheat (v. 5). Curtis (Madsen) estimates this amount of wheat as 120,331 bushels.[3] Ammon had been subject to Uzziah, Jotham's father, but they rebelled against Jotham who put down their insurrection and exacted heavy toll for three years.

None of the commentaries available to us carries any extensive comment on Jotham's reign.

XXX

---

1 NBCR, p. 391.

2 AB, ***Chronicles,*** p. 411.

3 ICC, ***Chronicles***, p. 454.

CHAPTER 28
The Wicked Reign of Ahaz Brings Awful Punishment Upon Judah

XI. AHAZ (735-715 BC)

A Summary of the Wickedness of Ahaz

Verses 1-4, Ahaz was twenty years old when he began to reign; and he reigned sixteen years in Jerusalem: 2 and he did not that which was right in the eyes of Jehovah, like David his father; but he walked in the ways of the kings of Israel, and made also molten images for the Baalim. 3 Moreover he burnt incense in the valley of the sons of Hinnom, and burnt his children in the fire, according to the abominations of the nations whom Jehovah cast out before the children of Israel. 4 And he sacrificed and burnt incense in the high places, and on the hills, and under every green tree.

Pages 197-207 in our commentary on Second Kings are devoted to a discussion of the reign of Ahaz; and the only section of this chapter which is not mentioned there is found in vv. 8-15. These verses provide a remarakbly interesting insight into the problems of those times.

It will suffice here to note that Ahaz was by far the most wicked of the kings of Judah up to this point in their history. He even sacrificed his son to Molech, closed the temple, and worshipped pagan gods.

God Delivered Judah Into the Hands of Damascus and Samaria

Verses 5:7, Wherefore Jehovah his God delivered him into the hand of the king of Syria; and they smote him, and carried away of his a great multitude of captives, and brought them to Damascus. And he also delivered him into the hand of the king of Israel, who smote him with a great slaughter. 6 For Pekah the son of Remaliah slew in Judah a hundred and twenty thousand in one day, all of them valiant men; because they had forsaken Jehovah, the God of their fathers. 7 And Zichri, a mighty man of Ephraim, slew Maaseiah the king's son, and Azrikam the ruler of the house, and Elkanah that was next to the king.

This disaster that fell upon Judah was wrought by a coalition of Rezin king of Syria (Damascus) and Pekah the king of Israel. They almost succeeded in capturing Ahaz, but they could not actually overcome him. However, they carried away two hundred thousand captives and much spoil.

The Prophet Obed Intercedes for the Captives

Verses 8-15, And the children of Israel carried away captive of their brethren two hundred thousand, women, sons, and daughters, and also took away much spoil from them, and brought the spoil to Samaria. 9 But a prophet of Jehovah was there, whose name was Obed: and he went out to meet the host that came to Samaria, and

said unto them, because Jehovah, the God of your fathers, was wroth with Judah, he hath delivered them into your hand, and ye have slain them in a rage which hath reached up into heaven. 10 And now ye purpose to keep under the children of Judah and Jerusalem for bondmen and bondwomen unto you: but are there not even with you trespasses of your own against Jehovah your God? 11 Now hear me therefore and send back the captives, that ye have taken captive of your brethren; for the fierce wrath of Jehovah is upon you. 12 Then certain of the heads of the children of Ephraim, Azariah the son of Johanan, Berechiah the son of Meshillemoth, and Jehizkiah the son of Shallum, and Amasa the son of Hadlai, stood up against them that came from the war, 13 and said unto them, Ye shall not bring in the captives hither: for ye purpose that which will bring upon us a trespass against Jehovah, to add unto our sins, and to our trespass; for our trespass is great, and there is fierce wrath against Israel. 14 So the armed men left the captives and the spoil before the princes and all the assembly. 15 And the men that have been mentioned by name rose up, and took the captives, and with the spoil clothed all that were naked among them, and arrayed them, and shod them, and gave them to eat and to drink, and anointed them, and carried all the feeble of them upon asses, and brought them to Jericho, the city of palm-trees, unto their brethren: then they returned to Samaria.

But a prophet of Jehovah was there ... Obed (v. 9). God never stopped his pleading with the northern tribes through his holy prophets, despite the fact that within a decade, or a little less time, the Northern Israel would be destroyed and many of them transported as captives by Assyria in 722 BC. The reign of Ahaz (735-715 BC)[1] would not close till after the fall of Samaria. "Thus this change of heart by some of the men of Ephraim came at at a time when it was already too late."[2] This act of mercy on their part must therefore be viewed, not as any fundamental change in the apostate Israel, but as an act of God's mercy upon Judah, even in his judgment against them. Significantly, "Nothing is known of this prophet Obed, except what is written here."[3] There may have been many such prophets whom God sent in his futile efforts to win back from their rebellion the northern kingdom.

Certain of the heads of the children of Ephraim (v. 12). Here the word ***Ephraim*** is used, as frequently in the OT, for all of northern Israel.

The radical critics' hatred of Chronicles is typically expressed by Curtis (Madsen) who called this passage (vv. 8-15), "A good example of Midrash."[4] The meaning of such a comment is simply that, "There's not a word of truth in it." This writer is happy to reject out of hand such unbelieving, unsupported, and inaccurate comments. It is refreshing indeed to find that today, long after the fulminations of the ICC, many great scholars, even liberal critics, give a much more favorable view of this passage. Myers, for example,

---

1 AnBi, ***Chronicles***, p. 258.

2 NBCR, p. 391.

3 AB, ***Chronicles***, p. 412.

4 ICC, ***Chronicles***, p.458.

treated this paragraph as authentic, and as being supported by the sources available to the Chronicler.[5] There are no legitimate grounds for denying anything in Chronicles.

Ahaz Makes Judah a Vassal of Assyria in His Appeal to Them for Help

Verses 16-21, At that time did king Ahaz send unto the kings of Assyria to help him. 17 For again the Edomites had come and smitten Judah, and carried away captives. 18 The Philistines also had invaded the cities of the lowland, and of the South of Judah, and had taken Beth-shemesh, and Aijalon, and Gederoth, and Soco with the towns thereof, and Timnah with the towns thereof, and Gimzo with the towns thereof: and they dwelt there. 19 For Jehovah brought Judah low because of Ahaz king of Israel; for he had dealt wantonly in Judah, and trespassed sore against Jeghovah. 20 And Tilgath-pilneser king of Assyria came unto him and distressed him, but strengthened him not. 21 For Ahaz took away a portion out of the house of Jehovah, and out of the house of the king and of the princes, and gave it unto the king of Assyria, but it helped him not.

Ahaz king of Israel (v. 19). In the view of the Chronicler, Judah was the only real Israel left, after the apostasy of the northern tribes, and thus in this line he referred to Ahaz as king of Israel, meaning the king of

---

[5] AnBi, op. cit., p. 162.

Judah, the only real Israel.

See our comments in Second Kings upon this disastrous maneuver of Ahaz in seeking aid from Assyria and, in doing so, making himself, in effect, a vassal of that ambitious and cruel monolithic empire.

Further Wickedness of Ahaz, His Death, and Succession of Hezekiah

Verses 22-27, And in the time of his distress did he transgress yet more against Jehovah, this same Ahaz. 23 For he sacrificed unto the gods of Damascus, which smote him; amd he said, Because the gods of the kings of Assyria helped them, therefore will I sacrifice to them, that they may help me. But they were the ruin of him, and of all Israel. 24 And Ahaz gathered together the vessels of the house of God, and cut in pieces the vessels of the house of God, and shut up the doors of the house of Jehovah; and he made him altars in every corner of Jeusalem. 25 And in every city of Judah he made high places to burn incense to other gods, and provoked to anger Jehovah, the God of his fathers. 26 Now the rest of his acts, and all his ways, first and last, behold, they are written in the book of the kings of Judah and Israel. 27 And Ahaz slept with his fathers, and they buried him in the city, even in Jerusalem, for they brought him not into the sepulchres of the kings of Israel: and Hezekiah his son reigned in his stead.

We have commented extensively upon the wickedness of Ahaz in Second Kings; and there is no need to elaborate the discussion here.

His great failure was his adoption of the theological ideas that prevailed thoughout the ancient world, namely, that each country had its gods, and that their victories or defeats were due to the will of such pagan deities. In God's delivernce of Israel from Egypt, he had established most conclusively the principle that there is only one true and Almighty God, that the pagan deities are not merely powerless, but that they are actually nonentities, and finally that God's People would prosper or suffer in direct proportion to their fidelity, or lack of it, to the One True and Only God.

The long time sins and apostasies of the Chosen People had all but completely erased from their hearts those basic truths; and the final result of that shameful development would be rapidly revealed in the defeat and deportation, first, of Northern Israel to Assyria (722 BC), and later, in the defeat and captivity of Judah in Babylon (586 BC).

XXX

CHAPTER 29
Beginning of the Reign of Hezekiah

XII. HEZEKIAH (715-687 BC)

Hezekiah's Move to Restore the True Worship

Verses 1-11, Hezekiah began to reign when he was five and twenty years old; and he reigned nine and twenty years in Jerusalem; and his mother's name was Abijah, the daughter of Zechariah. 2 And he did that which was right in the eyes of Jehovah, according to all that David his father had done. 3 He in the first year of his reign, in the first month, opened the doors of the house of Jehovah, and repaired them. 4 And he brought in the priests and the Levites, and gathered them together in the broad place on the east, 5 and said unto them, Hear me, ye Levites; now sanctify yourselves, and sanctify the house of Jehovah, the God of your fathers, and carry forth the filthiness out of the holy place. 6 For our fathers have trespassed, and done that which was evil in the sight of Jehovah our God, and have forsaken him, and have turned away their faces from the habitation of Jehovah, and turned their back. 7 Also they have shut up the doors of the porch, and have put out the lamps, and have not burned incense nor offered burnt-offerings in the holy place unto the God of Israel. 8 Wherefore the wrath of Jehovah was upon Judah and Jerusalem, and he hath deliverd them to be tossed to and fro, to be an astonishment, and a hissing, as ye see with your eyes. 9 For, lo, our fathers are fallen by the sword, and our sons and our daughters and our wives are in captivity for this. 10 Now it is in my heart to make a

covenant with Jehovah, the God of Israel, that his fierce anger may turn away from us. 11 My sons, be not now negligent; for Jehovah hath chosen you to stand before him, to minister unto him, and that ye should be his ministers, and burn incense.

Practically all of this chapter is without parallel in Kings. It supplements the record of Hezekiah's extensive reforms that are mentioned there. We see here that his work was not merely negative, in such things as destroying the high places and cutting down the Asherim. He also did many positive things toward pointing Israel back to the true worship of God.

Carry forth the filthiness out of the holy place (v. 5). "This was the accumulated dirt from years of neglect."[1]

They have not burned incense nor offered burnt-offerings in the holy place unto the God of Israel (v. 7). But does not 2K 16:14-16 state that Ahaz himself made offerings on that special altar? Yes, indeed; but there is no contradiction here. The Chronicler is merely telling us (and those Levites) that those sacrifices that Ahaz offered on an Assyrian altar, were, in no sense, offered ***unto the God of Israel,*** but were actually sacrifices to Assyrian gods.[2] Note the underlined words in this paragraph.

Jehovah hath chosen you (the Levites) to stand

---

1 NBCR, p. 391.

2 Ibid.

before him (v. 11). Here again we find an acute consciousness of the Law of God through Moses in the Pentateuch, especially in Exodus, Leviticus and Numbers, where the choice of the Levites and the sons of Aaron was first revealed. It is the proliferation of dozens of such references as these in Chronicles that sends the radical critics into frantic screams of "Midrash"!

This single chapter is a complete contradiction of the critical denials of it with abundant proof of the existence of the whole Pentateuch in the reign of Hezekiah, generations prior to Josiah and that fairy tale about the ***P Code.***

It is the conviction of this writer that the author of whatever ***source*** was quoted by the Chronicler here (see our introduction for a list of these) had a complete copy of the Law of Moses (the whole Pentateuch) before him when he wrote down the events related in this chapter.

Undeniable Reflections of the Pentateuch in this Chapter

(1) ***The wrath of Jehòvah was upon Judah (v. 8).*** "This word (wrath) is used in Deuteronomy 28:25,"[3] where Moses had predicted this very disaster that befell Judah.

(2) ***For Jehovah hath chosen you (v. 11).*** This is stated in Numbers 3:6, 8:6, and in Deuteronomy 10:8.

(3) ***They brought seven bullocks, and seven rams,***

---

[3] ICC, *Chronicles*, p. 464.

and seven lambs, and seven he-goats for a sin-offering for the kingdom (v. 21). The use of these animals for that purpose was authorized in Leviticus 1:3f, 14:20, and 16:24. "Seven victims were offered because seven was a sacred number."[4]

(4) The use of seven victims instead of one in certain sacrifices was authorized in Numbers 28:11ff.

(5) ***The priests received the blood and sprinkled it upon the altar (v. 22).*** The ritual for this action is found in the law of Moses in Exodus 29:16, and in Leviticus 1:5, 11.

(6) ***The king and the assembly laid their hands upon them (the sacrifices) (v. 23).*** This ceremony is described in Leviticus 1:4.

(7) ***And they made a sin-offering with their blood upon the altar (v. 24)*** In Leviticus 4:25, 34 is found the description of exactly how this was done.

(8) ***Come near, ... and bring thank-offerings into the house of Jehovah (v. 31)*** "The thanksgiving here was for the joy over the renewal of the worship of Jehovah."[5] Instructions for the offerings and ceremonies for such an occasion are found in Leviticus 7:12ff.

(9) ***The burnt-offerings ... with the fat of the peace-offerings, and with the drink-offerings for every burnt-offering ... so the service for the house of Jehovah was set in order (v. 35).*** "The drink offerings were of wine and probably poured like the blood at the base of the altar."[6]

---

[4] Ibid., p. 467.
[5] Ibid., p. 469.
[6] Ibid., p. 470.

Very complete and detailed instructions for these sacrifices, including the drink-offerings, are found in Numbers 15:1-15.

Note here that Hezekiah followed instructions for the services of the house of Jehovah, instructions that are detailed in the Mosaic writings of the Pentateuch.

Before leaving this analysis, we must ask, "How do the critics attempt to get rid of such proof as this? Curtis has this succint statement of their ***only*** answer.

> It must be remembered that the writer was drawing largely upon his imagination, and evidently cared little about accuracy of detail.[7]

To such so-called scholarship as this, we wish to say ***NO***! It is the evil radical critics, seeking to destroy faith in the word of God, who are drawing upon ***their*** imagination. The ***real*** biblical Midrash is that imaginary ***P Code,*** that alleged ***discovery*** in the reign of Josiah, the ***Jehovist,*** the ***Elohist***, the ***Deuteronomist,*** and the ***Second, Third***, or ***Twentieth ISAIAH,*** and all the rest of those fraudulent, imaginary, ephemeral and constantly changing "documents" invented by evil men and imposed upon believers under the guise of their being scholarly. And may it be said again that until all of those ***alleged documents*** (or any single one of them, for that matter) can be produced and scientifically evaluated, the truly intelligent person may safely reject them.

---

[7] ICC, op. cit., p. 466.

Within Sixteen Days the Levites Cleanse the Temple

Verses 12-19, Then the Levites arose, Mahath, the son of Amasai, of the sons of the Kohathites; and of the sons of Merari, Kish the son of Abdi, and Azariah the son of Jehallelel; and of the Gershonites, Joah the son of Zimmah, and Eden the son of Joah; 13 and of the sons of Elizaphan, Shemri and Jeuel; and of the sons of Asaph, Zechariah and Mattaniah; 14 and of the sons of Heman, Jehuel and Shimei; and of the sons of Jeduthun, Shemaiah and Uzziel. 15 And they gathered their brethren, and sanctified themselves, and went in, according to the commandment of the king by the words of Jehovah, to cleanse the house of Jehovah. 16 And the priests went in unto the inner part of the house of Jehovah, to cleanse it, and brought out all the uncleanness that they found in the temple of Jehovah into the court of the house of Jehovah. And the Levites took it to carry it out abroad to the brook Kidron. 17 Now they began on the first day of the first month to sanctify, and on the eighth day of the month came they to the porch of Jehovah; and they sanctified the house of Jehovah in eight days: and on the sixteenth day of the first month they made an end. 18 Then they went in to Hezekiah the king within the palace, and said, We have cleansed all the house of Jehovah, and the altar of burnt-offering, with all the vessels thereof, and the table of showbread, with all the vessels thereof. 19 Moreover all the vessels which king Ahaz in his reign did cast away when he trespassed, have we prepared and sanctified; and, behold, they are before the altar of Jehovah.

Sin-Offerings Were Made for All Israel

Verses 20-24, Then Hezekiah the king arose early, and gathered the princes of the city, and went up to the house of Jehovah. 21 And they brought seven bullocks, and seven rams, and seven lambs, and seven he-goats, for a sin-offering for the kingdom, and for the sanctuary of Jehovah. And he commanded the priests the sons of Aaron to offer them on the altar of Jehovah. 22 So they killed the bullocks, and the priests received the blood, and sprinkled it on the altar: and they killed the rams, and sprinkled the blood upon the altar: they killed also the lambs, and sprinkled the blood upon the altar. 23 And they brought near the he-goats for the sin offering before the king and the assembly; and they laid their hands upon them; 24 and the priests killed them, and they made a sin-offering with their blood upon the altar, to make atonement for all Israel; for the king commanded that the burnt-offering and the sin-offering should be made for all Israel.

See our discussion above regarding the many reflections of the Pentateuch in this chapter, especially in this paragraph.

Musical Accompaniment of these Impressive Ceremonies

Verses 25-30, And he set the Levites in the house of Jehovah with cymbals, with psalteries, and with harps, according to the commandment of David, and of Gad the king's seer, and Nathan the prophet; for the commandment was of Jehovah by his prophets. 26 And the Levites stood

with the instruments of David, and the priests with the trumpets. 27 And Hezekiah commanded to offer the burnt-offering upon the altar. And when the burnt-offering began, the song of Jehovah began also, and the trumpets, and the instruments of David king of Israel. 28 And all the assembly worshipped, and the singers sang, and the trumpeters sounded; and all this continued till the burnt-offering was finished. 29 And when they had made an end of offering, the king and all that were present with him bowed themselves and worshipped. 30 Moreover Hezekiah the king and the princes commanded the Levites to sing praises unto Jehovah with the words of David, and of Asaph the seer. And they sang praises with gladness, and bowed their heads and worshipped.

For the commandment was of Jehovah by his prophets (v. 25). This is the passage in the OT which is supposed to justify the use of mechanical instruments of music in the ancient worship of the Jews; but it should be observed that "the commandment" which is here said to have come from God is not specifically identified in this key sentence; and the Syriac and Arabic versions in this place do not support what is written here. Both those versions make "the commandment" which came of God through his prophets applicable exclusively to the order that the Levites should praise God; "And the Hebrew text certainly supports such a rendition."[8] Note that there is a distinction made in this very passage between ***the instruments of David*** (v. 26) and ***the song of***

---

[8] AC, Vol. 3, p. 690.

Jehovah (v. 27).

The importance of this is emphasized by the apparent contradiction which the ASV and other current versions make in this passage with the prophet Amos. The passage has no bearing whatever upon the question of the use of such instruments in Christian worship; but an investigation of it is important because the word of God does not contradict itself; and if this passage stands as it appears here, what about the passages in Amos? This writer holds the passages in Amos to be correct, and this one to be mistranslated here. See our Excursus on this subject at the end of Psalms II.

The position which we have taken on this is very strongly supported by the fact that the Othodox Hebrew religion has never allowed instruments of music in their worship; and, presumably, they know the Hebrew a lot better than modern critics.

In the words of David, and of Asaph the seer (v. 30). This indicates that what we know as ***The Psalms*** were sung as hymns on this occasion.

All Israel Brings Abundant Thank-offerings to Jehovah

Verses 31-36, Then Hezekiah answered and said, Now ye have consecrated yourselves unto Jehovah; come near and bring sacrifices and thank-offerings into the house of Jehovah. And the assembly brought in sacrifices and thank-offerings; and as many as were of a willing heart brought burnt-offerings. 32 And the number of the burnt-offerings which the assembly brought was threescore and ten bullocks, a hundred rams, and two hundred lambs; all

these were for a burnt-offering unto Jehovah. 33 And the consecrated things were six hundred oxen and three thousand sheep. 34 But the priests were too few, so that they could not flay all the burnt-offerings; wherefore their brethren the Levites did help them, till the work was ended, and until the priests had sanctified themselves; for the Levites were more upright in heart to sanctify themslves than the priests. 35 And also the burnt-offerings were in abundance, with the fat of the peace-offerings, and with the drink-offerings for every burnt-offering. So the service of the house of Jehovah was set in order. 36 And Hezekiah rejoiced, and all the people, because of that which God had prepared for the people: for this thing was done suddenly.

The Levites were more upright ... than the priests (v. 34). That this opinion of the Levites might be, "A reflection of the Chronicler's personal bias,"[9] is unacceptable. The truth of what he said had already been demonstrated before all Israel in the subserviency of the priest Urijah to king Ahaz (2K 16:16).

For the thing was done suddenly (v. 36). "This change from apostasy to loyalty to Jehovah took place almost immediately upon Hezekiah's accession to the throne. It was the result of a common impulse both of the king and of the people, apparently without any preparation (or delay)."[10]

XXX

---

[9] ICC, op. cit., p. 469.

[10] Ibid., p. 470.

CHAPTER 30

Hezekiah Leads Israel in Observance of Passover

Invitation Sent to All Israel to Come to Jeruslaem for the Passover

***Verses 1-9,** And Hezekiah sent to all Israel and Judah, and wrote letters to Ephraim and Manasseh, that they should come to the house of Jehovah at Jerusalem, to keep the passover unto Jehovah, the God of Israel. 2 For the king had taken counsel, and his princes, and all the assembly in Jerusalem, to keep the passover in the second month. 3 For they could not keep it at that time, because the priests had not sanctified themslves in sufficient number, neither had the people gathered themslves together at Jerusalem. 4 And the thing was right in the eyes of the king and of all the assembly. 5 So they established a decree to make proclamation throughout all Israel, from Beersheba even to Dan, that they should come to keep the passover unto Jehovah, the God of Israel, at Jeruslaem: for they had not kept it in great numbers in such sort as it is written. 6 So the posts went out with letters from the king and his princes throughout all Israel and Judah, according to the commandment of the king, saying, Ye children of Israel, turn again unto Jehovah, the God of Abraham, Isaac, and Israel, that he may return to the remnant that are escaped out of the hand of the kings of Assyria. 7 And be not ye like your fathers, and like your brethren, who trespassed against Jehovah, the God of their fathers, so that he gave them up to desolation, as ye see. 8 Now be ye not stiff-necked as your fathers were; but yield yourselves unto Jehovah, and enter into his sanctuary, which he hath*

sanctified for ever, and serve Jehovah your God, that his fierce anger may turn away from you. 9 For if ye turn again unto Jehovah, your brethren and your children shall find compassion before them that led them captive, and shall come again unto this land: for Jehovah your God is gracious and merciful, and will not turn away his face from you, if ye return unto him.

This wonderful invitation from Hezekiah is a remarkable testimony. It came following the fall of the Northern Israel to Assyria in 722 BC, a disaster that Hezekiah attributed to their forsaking the true worship of God in Jerusalem. This is proof that long before the times of Josiah God had commanded the centralization of his worship in Jerusalem. Note also the significant words ***as it is written (v. 5)***. The Book of the Law (the Pentateuch) was appealed to by Hezekiah in these words. It is also significant that Hezekiah admits here that the passover had indeed been kept previously but by small numbers of people (v. 5).

The king had taken counsel ... to keep the passover in the second month (v. 2). The divine instructions for the passover required its observance in the first month (Exodus 12:1-3); but the urgency of Hezekiah in his efforts to rally all Israel to a rebirth of their loyalty to God prompted this technical violation. Note also that not even the priests of Judah and Jerusalem had bothered to sanctify themslves for the legal passover a month earlier.

Some Spurn the King's Invitation, But Many Accepted

Verses 10-12, So the posts passed from city to city through the country of Ephraim and Manasseh, even unto Zebulun: but they laughed them to scorn, and mocked them. 11 Nevertheless certain men of Ashur and Manasseh and Zebulun humbled themselves, and came to Jerusalem. 12 Also upon Judah came the hand of God to give them one heart, to do the commandment of the king and of the princes by the word of Jehovah.

The remnant of the northern tribes that had been left in the land by the kings of Assyria had, in the principal part, degenerated into paganism and were naturally resentful that Judah had been spared, because they were fully aware that Judah's sins against God were just as extensive as their own. They did not realize that God had humbled and destroyed their kingdom as an example of what would also eventually happen to Judah. It was not merely northern Israel that needed to return to God, but all Israel. Hezekiah did his best to bring the people back to God; and, for awhile, he succeeded; but as soon as his son Manasseh came to the throne, his reformation was quickly repudiated.

Israel Again Kept the Passover

Verses 13-22, And there assembled at Jerusalem much people to keep the feast of unleavened bread in the second month, a very great assembly. 14 And they arose and took away the altars that were in Jerusalem, and all

the altars for incense took they away, and cast them into the brook Kidron. 15 Then they killed the passover on the fourteenth day of the second month: and the priests and the Levites were ashamed, and sanctified themselves, and brought burnt-offerings into the house of Jehovah. 16 And they stood in their place after their order, according to the Law of Moses the man of God: the priests sprinkled the blood which they received of the Levites. 17 For there were many in the assembly that had not sanctified themselves: therefore the Levites had the charge of killing the passovers for every one that was not clean, to sanctify them unto Jehovah. 18 For a multitude of the people, even many of Ephraim and Manasseh, Issachar and Zebulun, had not cleansed themsleves, yet did they eat the passover otherwise than it is written. For Hezekiah had prayed for them, saying, The good Jehovah pardon every one 19 that setteth his heart to seek God, Jehovah, the God of his fathers, though he be not cleansed according to the purification of the sanctuary. 20 And Jehovah hearkened to Hezekiah, and healed the people. 21 And the children of Israel that were at Jerusalem kept the feast of unleavened bread seven days with great gladness; and the Levites and the priests praised Jehovah day by day, singing with loud instruments unto Jehovah. 22 And Hezekiah spake comfortably unto all the Levites that had good understanding in the service of Jehovah. So they did eat throughout the feast for the seven days, offering sacrifices of peace-offerings, and making confession to Jehovah, the God of their fathers.

They killed the passover on the fourteenth day of the second month (v. 15). Even in this Hezekiah followed closely the instructions of Moses in the Pentateuch (Numbers 9:11).

The good Jehovah pardon (v. 19). The RSV very properly has ***the good Lord*** here which is a far better translation. "This expression is found only here in the OT, but it has now become proverbial."[1]

This celebration of the passover two long generations prior to Josiah is an acute embarrassment to the radical critics and their fairy tale regarding that ***P Document*** discovered in the temple during Joisah's reign; and their knee-jerk response to everything in God's word that contradicts their false allegations was clearly stated by Jacob M. Meyers who wrote that, "They hold that the Chronicler transferred to Hezekiah ... the religious celebrations of Josiah, notably this one."[2] Such a false allegation as that one, however, is only a rather timid and somewhat clever way of calling the Chronicler's report here a lie. We believe the lie is that of the radical critics, not that of the Chronicler.

We are very thankful that present-day scholars are turning away from the gross errors advocated by the ICC. Jacob M. Meyers in Anchor Bible makes the truthful observation that:

THERE IS NO REASON TO BELIEVE THAT THE CHRONICLER INVENTED THE STORY.[3]

It is distressing to this writer that commentators who claim to be Christians will pose a snide question

---

1 BBC, Vol. 3, p. 410.

2 AnBi, ***Chronicles,*** p. 176.

3 Ibid.

regarding this passover, asking, "Is this alleged event fact or fiction"?[4] and leave the question unanswered. More and more great scholars of the present day are beginning to see the truth regarding the accuracy of what we find in the Bible (all of it).

They Decide to Celebrate Another Seven Days

Verses 23-27, And the whole assembly took counsel to keep other seven days; and they kept other seven days with gladness. 24 For Hezekiah king of Judah did give to the assembly for offerings a thousand bullocks and seven thousand sheep; and the princes gave to the assembly a thousand bullocks and ten thousand sheep; and a great number of priests sanctified themselves. 25 And all the assembly of Judah, with the priests and the Levites, and all the assembly that came out of Israel, and the sojourners that came out of the land of Israel, and that dwelt in Judah, rejoiced. 26 So there was great joy in Jerusalem; for since the time of Solomon the son of David king of Israel there was not the like in Jerusalem. 27 Then the priests the Levites arose and blessed the people: and their voice was heard, and their prayer came up to his holy habitation, even unto heaven.

This additional week of feasting and celebration was made possible by the generous contributions of the king and the princes.

Their voice was heard ... even unto heaven (v. 27).

---

[4] IB, Vol. 3, p. 524.

Hezekiah's respect for the temple had not blinded him to the sublime fact that "God dwelleth not in temples made with hands," and that his throne is in the heaven of heavens.

One may wonder why this observance of the passover was not reported in Kings, but the reason is not far to seek. Kings carries an abbreviated report of both the Northern and Southern Israels, whereas the Chronicles focusses attention upon the Southern Kingdom only; and this passover celebration pertained particularly to Judah and Jerusalem. Furthermore, all of the information that has come down to us from that remote period is fragmentary. No important arguments can be logically founded upon what this or that source does not contain.

XXX

CHAPTER 31

The Prosperity of Israel Under Hezekiah

The People Destroy the Pillars, the Asherim and the High Places

Verse 1, Now when this was all finished, all Israel that were present went out to the cities of Judah, and brake in pieces the pillars, and hewed down the Asherim, and brake down the high places and the altars out of all Judah, Ephraim also and Manasseh, until they had destroyed them all. Then all the children of Israel returned, every man to his possession, in their own cities.

The Magnificent Generosity of the Israelites

Verses 2-10, And Hezekiah appointed the courses of the priests and the Levites after their courses, every man according to his service, both the priests and the Levites, for burnt-offerings and for peace-offerings, to minister, and to give thanks, and to praise in the gates of the camp of Jehovah. 3 He appointed also the king's portion of his substance for the burnt-offerings, to wit, for the morning and evening burnt-offerings, and the burnt-offerings for the sabbaths, and for the new moons, and for the set feasts, as it is written in the law of Jehovah. 4 Moreover he commanded the people that dwelt in Jerusalem to give the portion of the priests and the Levites, that they might give themselves to the law of Jehovah. 5 And as soon as the commandment came abroad, the children of Israel gave in abundnce the first-fruits of grain, and new wine, and oil, and honey, and of all the increase of the field; and the tithe

of all things brought they in abundantly. 6 And the children of Israel and Judah, that dwelt in the cities of Judah, they also brought in the tithe of oxen and sheep, and the tithe of dedicated things which were consecrated unto Jehovah their God, and laid them by heaps. 7 In the third month they began to lay the foundation of the heaps, and finished them in the seventh month. 8 And when Hezekiah and the princes came and saw the heaps, they blessed Jehovah, and his people Israel. 9 Then Hezekiah and the princes questioned the priests and the Levites concerning the heaps. 10 And Azariah the chief priest, of the house of Zadok, answered him and said, Since the people began to bring the oblations into the house of Jehovah, we have eaten and had enough, and have left plenty: for Jehovah hath blessed his people; and that which is left is this great store.

"This paragraph pictures Hezekiah, not only as a second Solomon, but as a second David."[1] There was a wholesale reordering of the the religious life and personnel of Israel. The freedom provided by these events gave the Levites time to devote themselves to the Law of Jehovah, thus making it absolutely certain that during the times of Josiah, less than seventy-five years later, there would be countless persons left in Israel who were thoroughly familiar with the entire Mosaic covenant and the precious "Book of Moses" that attended it. This effectively refutes the notion that a reprobate priesthood could have gotten away with

---

[1] NLBC, p. 517.

forging any kind of a brand new religious constitution of Israel so soon afterwards. It is ***this mountain fact*** that leads the radical critics to write that, "The Chronicler writes (in these chapters) much that is quite unhistorical."[2] Where is the proof that any of this material is unhistorical? The only thing on earth that contradicts any of what is written here is that favorite fairy tale of unbelievers frequently referred to as the ***D Document.*** To allow that to be true is to allow that ***an HISTORICAL REPORT (CHRONICLES)*** can be nullified ***by an imaginary***, fraudulent, and absolutely ***UNHISTORICAL REPORT.*** This writer cannot subscribe to any such proposition, nor can he accept the allegation that any scientifically minded scholar could be persuaded to do so.

Preparations for Storing and Distributing the 'Heaps'

Verses 11-19, Then Hezekiah commanded to prepare chambers in the house of Jehovah; and they prepared them; 12 and they brought in the oblations and the tithes and the dedicated things faithfully. And over them Conaniah the Levite was ruler, and Shemei his brother was second; 13 and Jehiel, and Azaziah, and Nahath, and Asahel, and Jerimoth, and Jozabad, and Eliel, and Ismachiah, and Mahath, and Benaiah, were overseers under the hand of Conaniah and Shimei his brother, by the appointment of Hezekiah the king, and Azaziah the ruler of the house of God. 14 And Kore the son

---

[2] ASP, p. 321.

of Imnah the Levite, the porter at the east gate, was over the freewill-offerings of God, to distribute the oblations of Jehovah, and the most holy things. 15 And under him was Eden, and Menianim, and Jeshua, and Shemaiah, Amariah, and Shecaniah, in the cities of the priests, in their office of trust, to give to their brethren by courses, as well to the great as to the small: 16 besides them that were reckoned by genealogy of males, from three years old and upward, even every one that entered into the house of Jehovah, as the duty of every day required, for their service in their offices according to their courses; 17 and them that were reckoned by genealogy of the priests by their fathers' houses, and the Levites from twenty years old and upward, in their offices by their courses; 18 and them that were reckoned by genealogy of all their little ones, their wives, and their sons, and their daughters, through all the congregation: for in their office of trust they sanctified themsleves in holiness. 19 Also for the sons of Aaron the priests, that were in the fields of the suburbs of their cities, in every city, there were men that were mentioned by name, to give portions to all the males among the priests, and to all that were reckoned by genealogy among the Levites.

The historicity and accuracy of this account is evident in the very nature of it, there being no earthly explanation of such a paragraph as this otherwise. Only those blinded by some false theory could view this as anything other than historical material. The mention of all these names could not be a forgery, because the Jews knew too much about their genealogies (even down to and including the times of Jesus Christ) to have allowed such a thing. This account was written by the Chronicler about the time of the end of the Babylonian captivity; and the author followed very closely the records before his eyes. Furthermore, in instances where we are able to find parallel accounts in other scriptures, we are impressed with the fact that the Chronicler's accounts are ***always*** reconcilable with the parallels.

Summary of Hezekiah's Devotion to the Lord

Verses 20-21, And thus did Hezekiah throughout all Judah; and he wrought that which was good and right and faithful before Jehovah his God. 21 And in every work that he began in the service of the house of God, and in the law, and in the commandments, to seek his God, he did it with all his heart, and prospered.

XXX

CHAPTER 32

The Invasion of Judah by Sennacherib, Hezekiah's Sickness; the Embassy from Babylon, Conclusion of Hezekiah's Reign

See our Commentary on Isaiah (pp. 329-361) for a discussion of Sennacherib's invasion and the other events mentioned in this chapter. Also, the same material has been discussed in our Commentary on Second Kings chapters 18-20. There is no need whatever for any further discussion of the historical events of this chapter. Montgomery referred to these several accounts as "parallel and duplicates."[1] Rawlinson wrote that, "Isaiah wrote the history of Hezekiah for this chapter, from which the account in 2 Kings is almost certainly taken."[2] Derek Kidner also agreed with this, noting that, "Except for Hezekiah's psalm (only in Isaiah) and for that prophet's omission of 2K 18:14-16, much of the material in this part of Chronicles coincides almost word for word with Second Kings chapters 18-20."[3]

Hezekiah Prepares For the Invasion

Verses 1-8, After these things, and this faithfulness, Sennacherib king of Assyria came, and entered into Judah, and encamped against the fortified cities, and thought to win these for himself. 2 And when Hezekiah saw that

---

1 ICC, Kings, pp. 482, 486.

2 PC, Vol. 10b, p. 1.

3 NBCR, p. 610.

Sennacherib was come, and that he was purposed to fight against Jerusalem, 3 he took counsel with his princes and his mighty men to stop the waters of the fountains which were without the city; and they helped him. 4 So there was gathered much people together, and they stopped all the fountains, and the brook that flowed through the midst of the land, saying, Why should the kings of Assyria come, and find much water? 5 And he took courage, and built up all the wall that was broken down, and raised it up to the towers, and the other wall without, and strengthened Millo in the city of David, and made weapons and shields in abundance. 6 And he set captains of war over the people, and gathered them together to him in the broad place at the gate of the city, and spake comfortably to them, saying, 7 Be strong and of good courage, be not afraid nor dismayed for the king of Assyria, nor for all the multitude that is with him; for there is a greater with us than with him: 8 with him is an arm of flesh; but with us is Jehovah our God to help us, and to fight our battles. And the people rested themselves upon the words of Hezekiah king of Judah.

Sennacherib Seeks to Intimidate Jeruslaem

Verses 9-15, After this did Sennacherib king of Assyria send his servants to Jerusalem (now he was before Lachish, and all his power was with him), unto Hezekiah king of Judah, and unto all Judah that were at Jerusalem, saying, 10 Thus saith Sennacherib king of Assyria, Whereon do ye trust, that ye abide the siege in Jerusalem? 11 Doth not Hezekiah persuade you, to give you over to die by famine and by thirst, saying, Jehovah our God will deliver us out of the hand of the king of Assyria? 12 Hath not the same Hezekiah taken away his high places and his altars, and commanded Judah and Jerusalem, saying, Ye shall worship before one altar, and upon it shall ye burn incense? 13 Know ye not what I and my fathers have done unto all the peoples of the lands? Were the gods of the nations of the lands in any wise able to deliver their land out of my hand? 14 Who was there among all the gods of those nations which my fathers utterly destroyed, that could deliver his people out of my hand, that your God should be able to deliver you out of my hand? 15 Now therefore let not Hezekiah deceive you, nor persuade you after this manner, neither believe ye him; for no god of any nation or kingdom was able to deliver his people out of my hand, and out of the hand of my fathers; how much less shall your God deliver you out of my hand?

Sennacherib Exalted Himself Against God Almighty

Verses 16-19, And his servants spake yet more against Jehovah God, and against his servant Hezekiah. 17 He wrote also letters, to rail on Jehovah, the God of Israel, and to speak against him, saying, As the gods of the nations of the lands, which have not delivered their people out of my hand, so shall not the God of Hezekiah deliver his people out of my hand. 18 And they cried with a loud voice in the Jews' language unto the people of Jerusalem that were on the wall, to affright them, and to trouble them; that they might take the city. 19 And they spake of the God of Jerusalem, as of the gods of the earth, which are the work of men's hands.

The Chronicler in this brief paragraph has given the full and complete explanation of just ***why*** God put his hook in the nose of Sennacherib and removed him from the siege of Jerusalem.

Sennacherib's Army Slain by an Angel

Verses 20-23, ***And Hezekiah the king, and Isaiah the prophet the son of Amoz, prayed because of this, and cried to heaven. 21 And Jehovah sent an angel, who cut off all the mighty men of valor, and the leaders and the captains in the camp of the king of Assyria. So he returned with shame of face to his own land. And when he was come into the house of his god, they that came forth from his own bowels slew him with the sword. 22 Thus Jehovah saved Hezekiah and the inhabitants of Jerusalem from the hand of Sennacherib the king of Assyria, and from the hand of all others, and guided them on every side. 23 And many brought gifts unto Jehovah to Jerusalem, and precious things to Hezekiah king of Judah; so that he was exalted in the sight of all nations from thenceforth.***

The Near Fatal Illness of Hezekiah

Verses 24-26, ***In those days Hezekiah was sick even unto death: and he prayed unto Jehovah; and he spake unto him, and gave him a sign. 25 But Hezekiah rendered not again according to the benefit done unto him; for his heart was lifted up: therefore there was wrath upon him and Jerusalem. 26 Notwithstanding Hezekiah humbled***

himself for the pride of his heart, both he and the inhabitants of Jerusalem, so that the wrath of God came not upon them in the days of Hezekiah.

The Immense Wealth and Glory of Hezekiah

Verses 27-31, And Hezekiah had exceeding much riches and honor: and he provided him treasuries for silver, and for gold, and for precious stones, and for spices, and for shields, and for all manner of goodly vessels; 28 storehouses also for the increase of grain and new wine and oil; and stalls for all manner of beasts, and flocks in folds. 29 Moreover he provided him cities, and possessions of flocks and herds in abundance; for God had given him very much substance. 30 This same Hezekiah also stopped the upper spring of the waters of Gihon, and brought them straight down on the west side of the city of David. And Hezekiah prospered in all his works. 31 Howbeit in the business of the ambassadors of the princes of Babylon, who sent unto him to inquire of the wonder done in the land, God left him, to try him, that he might know all that was in his heart.

There can be no wonder that Hezekiah's wealth was so great, because the death of that immense army (185,000 men) of Sennacharib made all of their personal possessions the spoil for Hezekiah, as well as all of the vast treasures they had looted from Lachish and the other destroyed cities of Judah. History hardly affords another example of so great a windfall. No wonder he had to make a treasury for ***shields***, etc.

It is very evident here that the author of Chronicles was an inspired man, a magnificent refutation of any suggestion that this material is not historical. Only an inspired author would have catalogued the sins and pride of Hezekiah along with his marvelous achievements. That is not the manner in which uninspired men write the records of their heroes.

Conclusion of the Reign of Hezekiah

Verses 32-33, Now the rest of the acts of Hezekiah, and his good deeds, behold, they are written in the vision of Isaiah the prophet the son of Amoz, in the book of the kings of Judah and Israel. 33 And Hezekiah slept with his fathers, and they buried him in the ascent of the sepulchres of the sons of David: and all Judah and the inhabitants of Jerusalem did him honor at his death. And Manasseh his son reigned in his stead.

XXX

CHAPTER 33

The Wicked Reigns of Manasseh and Amon

XIII. MANASSEH (687-642 BC)

All of the material in this chapter is parallel with Second Kings 21, except verses 11-17 which relate the conversion of Manasseh. Our comments on this chapter are found in the parallel passages in our commentary on Second Kings. Here we shall focus attention upon the material peculiar to this chapter.

Summary of Manasseh's Evil Rule Over Judah

Verses 1-10, Manasseh was twelve years old when he began to reign; and he reigned fifty and five years in Jerusalem. 2 And he did that which was evil in the sight of Jehovah, after the abominations of the nations whom Jehovah cast out before the children of Israel. 3 For he built again the high places which Hezekiah his father had broken down; and he reared up altars for the Baalim, and made Asheroth, and worshipped all the host of heaven, and served them. 4 And he built altars in the house of Jehovah, whereof Jehovah said, In Jerusalem shall my name be for ever. 5 And he built altars for all the host of heaven in the two courts of the house of Jehovah. 6 He also made his children to pass through the fire in the valley of the son of Hinnom; and he practised augury, and used enchantments, and practised sorcery, and dealt with them that had familiar spirits, and with wizards: he wrought much evil in in the sight of Jehovah, to provoke him to anger. 7 And he set the graven image of the idol, which he had made, in the

house of God, of which God said to David and to Solomon his son, In this house, and in Jerusalem which I have chosen out of all the tribes of Israel, will I put my name for ever: 8 neither will I any more remove the foot of Israel from off the land which I have appointed for your fathers, if only they will observe to do all that I have commanded them, even all the law and the statutes and the ordinances given by Moses. 9 And Manasseh seduced Judah, and the inhabitants of Jerusalem, so that they did evil more than the nations whom Jehovah destroyed before the children of Israel. 10 And Jehovah spake to Manasseh, and to his people; but they gave no heed.

The date for Manasseh's reign given above indicates that a part of the fifty-five year reign mentioned in the text was probably as a co-regency under his father. We have often noted the difficulties in the chronology of Israel's kings.

The Captivity of Manasseh in Babylon by Assyrian Kings

Verses 11-13, Wherefore Jehovah brought upon them the captains of the host of the king of Assyria, who took Manasseh in chains, and bound him with fetters, and carried him to Babylon. 12 And when he was in distress he besought Jehovah his God, and humbled himself greatly before the God of his fathers. 13 And he prayed unto him; and he was entreated of him, and heard his supplication, and brought him again to Jerusalem, unto his kingdom. Then Manasseh knew that Jehovah he was God.

This, of course, is information found nowhere else in the Bible; and it was was once common among critics to reject this episode as unhistorical. Fortunately, wiser scholars now accept what is recorded here as authentic history. The Chronicler does not give us the date in Manasseh's reign when this happened; but Ellison placed the event very late in Manasseh's reign. "This explains why Manasseh's repentance and reformation (vv.12-17) are not mentioned in Kings, and why they left no lasting impression."[1] This also explains why the altars of the host of heaven were apparently not removed by Manasseh. He was a vassal of Assyria and would have been afraid to remove them. Such subservience of Manasseh to the Assyrian overlords has been proved by the Babylonian inscriptions.[2]

In the light of all the facts, there is no reason whatever to doubt a single word of what is recorded here. Jacob M. Myers also found nothing at all improbable about what is written here.[3] "It may be taken for granted that vassal kings were allowed to return to their countries after being put under the threat of divine retribution with its terrible consequences."[4]

J Barton Payne in ***Wycliffe Bible Commentary*** also dated this period of Manasseh's conversion during the last six years of his reign. "It was perhaps in 648 BC, when Ashurbanipal overcame a four-year revolt led by

---

[1] NBCR, p. 32.

[2] AAOT, p. 280

[3] AnBi, ***Chronicles***, p. 198.

[4] Ibid., p. 199.

his brother in Babylon. Egypt took that opportunity to throw off the Assyrian yoke, and Manasseh might have attempted the same thing with less success. It was in that affliction that Manasseh humbled himself. God sometimes has to drive men to their conversion."[5]

Manasseh's Ineffective Reforms

Verses 14-17, Now after this he built an outer wall to the city of David, on the west side of Gihon, in the valley, even to the entrance of the fish gate; and he compassed Ophel about with it, and raised it up to a very great height: and he put valiant captains in all the fortified cities of Judah. 15 And he took away the foreign gods, and the idol out of the house of Jehovah, and all the altars that he had built in the mount of the house of Jehovah, and in Jerusalem, and cast them out of the city. 16 And he built up the altar of Jehovah, and offered thereon sacrifices of peace-offerings and of thanksgiving, and commanded Judah to serve Jehovah, the God of Israel. 17 Nevertheless the people sacrificed still in the high places, but only unto Jehovah their God.

The people sacrificed in the high places, but only unto Jehovah their God (v. 17). "This was still contrary to the Mosaic Law and actually accomplished little more than apply a new name to the old Baal worship."[6]

---

[5] WYC, p. 417.
[6] Ibid.

These reforms in Manasseh's reign came far too late to have much effect; and besides that, his reign probably was concluded before he had finished all that he planned to do.

Conclusion of Manasseh's Reign

Verses 18-20, Now the rest of the acts of Manasseh, and his prayer unto his God, and the words of the seers that spake to him in the name of Jehovah, the God of Israel, behold, they are written among the acts of the kings of Israel. 19 His prayer also, and how God was entreated of him, and all his sin and his trespass, and the places where he built high places, and set up the Asherim and the graven images, before he humbled himself, behold, they are written in the history of Hozai. 20 So Manasseh slept with his fathers, and they buried him in his own house: And Amon his son reigned in his stead.

XIV. AMON (642-640 BC)

The Short and Evil Reign of Amon

Verses 21-25, Amon was twenty and two years old when he began to reign; and he reigned two years in Jerusalem. 22 And he did that which was evil in the sight of Jehovah, as did Manasseh his father; and Amon sacrificed unto all the graven images which Manasseh his father had made, and served them. 23 And he humbled not himself before Jehovah, as Manasseh his father had humbled himself; but this same Amon trespassed more and

more. 24 And his servants conspired against him and put him to death in his own house. 25 But the people of the land slew all them that had conspired against king Amon; and the people of the land made Josiah his son king in his stead.

As Ellison remarked, "There are only minor variations here from the parallel in Second Kings. No motivation for the assassination is given. Amon may have been the vicious son of a bad father, or it may have been out of disgust for his following a descredited policy."[7]

"Amon was the unhappy product of his father's pagan life, not of his pious death."[8]

XXX

---

[7] NBCR, p. 393.

[8] WYC, p. 417.

CHAPTER 34

The Discovery of the Book of Moses in the Temple

XV. JOSIAH (640-609 BC).

With the exception of verses 3-7 in this chapter and verses 22, 23 in chapter 36, all of the events in these three concluding chapters of Second Chronicles we have already discussed in the parallel accounts in Second Kings 22:1-25:12, where we have devoted pages 273 to 330 to our comments. We shall be content here, in the principal part, to refer the reader to our Commentary on Second Kings. There are variations, to be sure; but there are no irreconcilable differences.

The Reforms of Josiah

Verses 1-7, Josiah was eight years old when he began to reign; and he reigned thirty one years in Jerusalem. 2 And he did that which was right in the eyes of Jehovah, and walked in the ways of David his father, and turned not aside to the right hand or to the left. 3 For in the eighth year of his reign, while he was yet young, he began to seek after the God of David his father; and in the twelfth year he began to purge Judah and Jerusalem of the high places, and the Asherim, and the graven images, and the molten images. 4 And they brake down the altars of the Baalim in his presence; and the sun-images that were on high above them he hewed down; and the Asherim, and the graven images, and the molten images, he brake in pieces, and made dust of them, and strewed it upon the graves of them that had sacrificed unto them. 5 And he burnt the

bones of the priests upon their altars, and purged Judah and Jerusalem. 6 And so did he in the cities of Manasseh and Ephraim and Simeon, even unto Naphtali, in their ruins round about. 7 And he brake down the altars, and beat the Asherim and the graven images into powder, and hewed down all the sun-images throughout all the land of Israel, and returned to Jerusalem.

This paragraph, of course, contains material not mentioned in the parallel accounts; but all that is stated here is fully in keeping with the character and purpose of this zealous young king who was intent on turning Israel back to their true worship. All of those images, pillars, high places, Asherim, etc., were specifically condemned, not only in the Decalogue, but in the commandment of God through Moses that all such things were to be destroyed by the Israelites when they came into the land of Canaan. The shame of all Israel was that they not only disobeyed God's commandments in these particulars, but they adopted the licentious pagan worship of their predecessors in Canaan; and even sinned worse than the people whom God had driven out before Israel (33:9).

Josiah Orders the Repair of the Temple

Verses 8-13, Now in the eighteenth year of his reign, when he had purged the land and the house, he sent Shaphan the son of Azaliah, and Maaseiah the governor of the city, and Joah the son of Joahaz the recorder, to repair the house of Jehovah his God. 9 And they came to Hilkiah

*the high priest, and delivered the money that was brought
into the house of God, which the Levites, the keepers of the
threshold, had gathered of the hand of Manasseh and
Ephraim, and of all the remnant of Israel, and of all Judah
and Benjamin, and of the inhabitants of Jerusalem. 10
And they delivered it into the hand of the workmen that had
the oversight of the house of Jehovah; and the workmen
that wrought in the house of Jehovah gave it to mend and
repair the house: 11 even to the carpenters and the
builders gave they it, to buy stone, and couplings, and to
make beams for the houses which the kings of Judah had
destroyed. 12 And the men did the work faithfully: and the
overseers of them were Jahath and Obadiah, the Levites, of
the sons of Merari; and Zechariah and Meshullum, of the
sons of the Kohathites, to set it forward; and others of the
Levites, all that were skilful with instruments of music. 13
Also they were over the bearers of burdens, and set forward
all that did the work in every manner of service: and of the
Levites there were scribes, and officers, and porters.*

The Discovery of the Book of the Law of Jehovah Given By Moses

*Verses 14-21, And when they brought out the
money that was brought into the house of Jehovah, Hilkiah
the priest found the book of the law of Jehovah given by
Moses. 15 And Hilkiah answered and said to Shaphan the
scribe, I have found the book of the law in the house of
Jehovah. And Hilkiah delivered the book to Shaphan. 16
And Shaphan carried the book to the king, and moreover
brought back word to the king, saying, All that was*

committed to thy servants they are doing. 17 And they have emptied out the money that was found in the house of Jehovah, and have delivered into the hands of the overseers, and into the hand of the workmen. 18 And Shaphan the scribe told the king, saying, Hilkiah the priest hath delivered me a book. And Shaphan read therein before the king. 19 And it came to pass when the king heard the words of the law, that he rent his clothes. 20 And the king commanded Hilkiah, and Ahikam the son of Shaphan, and Abdon the son of Micah, and Shaphan the scribe, and Asaiah the king's servant, saying, 21 Go ye, inquire of Jehovah for me, and for them that are left in Israel and in Judah, concerning the words of the book that is found; for great is the wrath of Jehovah that is poured out upon us, because our fathers have not kept the word of Jehovah, to do according to all that is written in this book.

Once for all, this paragraph settles the matter of what that book was which was found in the temple. The title we have given this paragraph is from the sacred text itself; and a million unbelievers shouting that it was anything else cannot nullify what is written here.

The account here is brief. The critical allegation that Shaphan read "the whole book" before the king is ridiculous. The text says "he read therein," that is, he read certain portions of it, indicating that he had previously studied the book and chose certain passages to read before the king.

Of course, right here is the reason that the inventors of that ***Priestly Document*** fairy tale, and those who have swallowed such a falsehood, find the incontrovertible denial of their false theory; and all, repeat, ***all*** the objections which radical critics bring against Second Chronicles are for the purpose of defending their ridiculous theory against biblical truth.

Huldah the Prophetess of God Affirms the Discovery as Nothing Less than the Law of Jehovah given by Moses

Verses 21-28, So Hilkiah, and those whom the king commanded, went to Huldah the prophetess, the wife of Shallum the son of Tokhath, the son of Hasrah, keeper of the wardrobe (now she dwelt in Jerusalem in the second quarter); and they spake to her to that effect. 23 And she said unto them, Thus saith Jehovah, the God of Israel: Tell ye the man that sent you unto me, 24 Thus saith Jehovah, Behold, I will bring evil upon this place, and upon the inhabitants thereof, even all the curses that are written in the book which they have read before the king of Judah. 25 Because they have forsaken me, and have burned incense unto other gods, that they might provoke me to anger with all the works of their hands; therefore is my wrath poured out upon this place, and it shall not be quenched. 26 But unto the king of Judah, who sent you to inquire of Jehovah, thus shall ye say to him, Thus saith Jehovah, the God of Israel: As touching the words which thou hast heard, 27 because thy heart was tender, and thou didst humble thyself before God, when thou heardest his words against this place, and against the inhabitants thereof, and hast humbled thyself before me, and hast rent thy clothes, and wept before me; I also have heard thee, saith Jehovah. 28

Behold, I will gather thee to thy fathers, and thou shalt be gathered to thy grave in peace, neither shall thine eyes see all the evil that I will bring upon this place, and upon the inhabitants thereof.

Josiah Turns Israel to the Worship of Jehovah

Verses 29-33, Then the king sent and gathered together all the elders of Judah and Jerusalem. 30 And the king went up to the house of Jehovah, and all the men of Judah and the inhabitants of Jerusalem, and the priests, and the Levites, and all the people, both great and small: and he read in their ears all the words of the book of the covenant that was found in the house of Jehovah. 31 And the king stood in his place, and made a covenant before Jehovah, to walk after Jehovah, and to keep his commandments, and his testimonies, and his statutes, with all his heart, and with all his soul, to perform the words of the covenant that were written in this book. 32 And he caused all that were found in Jerusalem and Benjamin to stand to it. And the inhabitants of Jerusalem did according to the covenant of God, the God of their fathers. 33 And Josiah took away all the abominations out of all the countries that pertained to the children of Israel, and made all that were found in Israel to serve, even to serve Jehovah their God. All his days they departed not from following Jehovah, the God of their fathers.

The big thing here is the testimony of the prophetess Huldah. No believer in God and the inspiration of his holy prophets should allow any evil, unbelieving critic the privilege of imposing his godless opinion regarding what ***that book*** really was upon Christians in contradiction of the words of the prophetess Huldah. Of course, the evil critics make out the Chronicler in these chapters to have been an unqualified liar; but this writer insists that that allegation is itself the Big Lie and that it should be rejected by every thoughtful person.

Oh, but isn't it "uncharitable" to suggest that any alleged scholar is a liar? To which we reply, "***THEY ARE THE ONES WHO DECLARE THAT WE ARE HERE DEALING WITH A LIE,*** and this writer believes the liars are not the authors of the Bible but those who contradict it"! ***Our only difference with them is in identifying the liar!***

XXX

CHAPTER 35

Josiah Gives Order For Observance of the Passover According to the Word of Jehovah by Moses

This passover was utterly unlike the one kept in the reign of Hezekiah, in a number of important particulars. (1) It was kept at the prescribed time. (2) The ceremonial cleanness of participants was observed. (3) And all the particulars of the Mosaic instructions were strictly observed. (4) Although the singers were mentioned, the instruments of music were not mentioned, and apparently not used. These important distinctions fully justify the statement in verse 18 that, "From the days of Samuel the prophet, none of the kings of Israel keep such a passover as Josiah kept."

Verses 1-6, And Josiah kept a passover unto Jehovah in Jerusalem: and they killed the passover on the fourteenth day of the first month. 2 And he set the priests in their offices, and encouraged them to the service of the house of Jehovah. 3 And he said unto the Levites that taught all Israel, that were holy unto Jehovah, Put the holy ark in the house which Solomon the son of David king of Israel did build; there shall no more be a burden upon your shoulders. Now serve Jehovah your God, and his people Israel; 4 and prepare yourselves after your fathers' houses by your courses, according to the writing of David king of Israel, and according to the writing of Solomon his son. 5 And stand in the holy place according to the divisions of the fathers' houses of your brethren the children of the people, and let there be for each a portion of a fathers' house of the Levites. 6 And kill the passover, and sanctify yourselves,

and prepare for your brethren, according to the word of Jehovah by Moses.

Josiah and His Princes Provide Lambs and Kids For Passover and Small Cattle, and Bullocks for the Other Offerings

Verses 7-9, And Josiah gave to the children of the people, of the flock, lambs and kids, all of them for the passover-offerings, unto all that were present, to the number of thirty thousand, and three thousand bullocks that were of the king's substance. 8 And his princes gave for a freewill-offering unto the people, to the priests, and to the Levites. Hilkiah and Zechariah and Jehiel, the rulers of the house of God, gave unto the priests for the passover-offerings two thousand and six hundred small cattle, and three thousand oxen. 9 Conaniah also, and Shemaiah and Nethanel, his brethren, and Hashabiah and Jehiel and Jozabad, the chiefs of the Levites, gave unto the Levites, for the passover-offerings five thousand small cattle, and five hundred oxen.

Details of the Passover Observance

Verses 10-15, So the service was prepared, and the priests stood in their place, and the Levites by their courses, according to the king's commandment. 11 And they killed the passover, and the priests sprinkled the blood which they received of their hand, and the Levites flayed them. 12 And they removed the burnt-offerings, that they might give them according to the divisions of the fathers' houses of the

children of the people, to offer unto Jehovah, as it is written in the book of Moses. And so did they with the oxen. 13 And they roasted the passover with fire, according to the ordinance: and the holy offerings boiled they in pots, and in caldrons, and in pans, and carried them quickly to all the children of the people. 14 And afterward they prepared for themselves, and for the priests, because the priests the sons of Aaron were busied in offering the burnt-offerings and the fat until night: therefore the Levites prepared for themselves, and for the priests the sons of Aaron. 15 And the singers the sons of Asaph, according to the commandment of David, and Asaph, and Heman, and Jeduthun the king's seer; and the porters were at every gate: they needed not to depart from their service; for their brethren the Levites prepared for them.

Such a Passover Not Seen Since the Days of Samuel

This cannot mean that the passover was not observed in the days of David the king; so what is meant? We have found no help at all regarding this question in the commentaries; and the only thing which we can think of which made this passover different from those observed during the kingship of David is the conspicuous absence of the instruments of music, which were so dear to David's heart.

Verses 16-19, So all the service of Jehovah was prepared the same day, to keep the passover, and to offer burnt-offerings upon the altar of Jehovah, according to the commandment of king Josiah. 17 And the children of

Israel that were present kept the passover at that time, and the feast of unleavened bread seven days. 18 And there was no passover like to that kept in Israel from the days of Samuel the prophet; neither did any of the kings of Israel keep such a passover as Josiah kept, and the priests, and the Levites, and all Judah and Israel that were present, and the inhabitants of Jerusalem. 19 In the eighteenth year of the reign of Josiah was this passover kept.

Conclusion of the Reign of Good King Josiah

Verses 20-27, After all this, when Josiah had prepared the temple, Neco king of Egypt went up to fight against Carchemesh by the Euphrates: and Josiah went out against him. 21 But he sent ambassadors to him, saying, What have I to do with thee, thou king of Judah? I come not against thee this day, but against the house wherewith I have war; and God hath commanded me to make haste: forbear thee from meddling with God, who is with me, that he destroy thee not. 22 Nevertheless Josiah would not turn his face from him, but disguised himself, that he might fight with him, and hearkened not unto the words of Neco from the mouth of God, and came to fight in the valley of Megiddo. 23 And the archers shot at king Josiah; and the king said to his servants, Have me away; for I am sore wounded. 24 So his servants took him out of the chariot, and put him in the second chariot that he had, and brought him to Jerusalem; and he died, and was buried in the sepulchre of his fathers. And all Judah and Jerusalem mourned for Josiah. 25 And Jeremiah lamented for Josiah: and all the singing men and singing women spake

of Josiah in their lamentations unto this day; and they made them an ordinance in Israel: and, behold, they were written in the lamentations. 26 Now the rest of the acts of Josiah, and his good deeds, according to that which is written in the law of Jehovah, 27 and his acts, first and last, behold, they are written in the book of the kings of Israel and Judah.

The remarkable thing in this paragraph concerns the claim of Neco that the message he gave to Josiah came from the true God. Not for a moment, may we believe that Neco believed in Jehovah; but yet his claim here to have received a message from the true God is supported by a statement in the apocryphal book of I Esdras (1:27 f), which states that "The warning came from Jeremiah."[1] Meyers based this opinion on a reference he cited from the Apochrypha (1 Esdras 1:27 f), but we are not able to find any such reference in 1 Esdras.). Nevertheless our text here clearly indicates that it was indeed a true message from God that came to Josiah by the mouth of Neco (v. 22); where Neco received it, or how, we do not know.

Some have made a big point out of the fact that God's promise of a peaceful death for Josiah was not fulfilled; but all such objectors should read again Jeremiah 18:7-10. Josiah's disobedience here nullified the prophecy. Certainly we may reject the insistence of Curtis (Madsen), and their school of critics, that this

---

1 AnBi, ***Chronicles***, p. 216.

whole account is "probably fiction."[2] The reason for all such opinions is because Second Chronicles so effectively contradicts their darling theory of the ***D Document.***

At this junction in Israel's history, God did indeed speak to them, in some instances, through pagan kings, as witnessed also in the decree of Cyrus.

The historical situation at that time found Assyria a tottering, weakened empire, destined to fall within a couple of years to Babylon in the battle of Carchemish. Whether Josiah was acting as an ally of Assyria, or in hopes of establishing his independence is not clear; but neither the strengthening of Assyria nor the independence of Israel, doomed to fall to Babylon in the near future, was in line with God's will.

XXX

---

[2] ICC, *Chronicles*, p. 317.

CHAPTER 36

God Terminates Israel as a Kingdom

XVI. JEHOAHAZ (609 BC).

***Verses 1-4,** Then the people of the land took Jehoahaz the son of Josiah, and made him king in his father's stead in Jerusalem. 2 Jehoahaz was twenty and three years old when he began to reign; and he reigned three months in Jerusalem. 3 And the king of Egypt deposed him at Jerusalem, and fined the land a hundred talents of silver and a talent of gold. 4 And the king of Egypt make Eliakim his brother king over Judah and Jerusalem, and changed his name to Jehoiakim. And Neco took Joahaz his brother, and carried him to Egypt.*

Joahaz mentioned in v. 4 is only the abbreviated name of the deposed king Jehoahaz. At this point, Neco was master of Judah and Jerusalem, and God's people were merely vassals of Egypt.

XVII. JEHOIAKIM (609-598 BC).

The Eleven Year Reign of Jehoiakim

***Verses 5-8,** And Jehoiakim was twenty and five years old when he began to reign; and he reigned eleven years in Jerusalem: and he did that which was evil in the sight of Jehovah his God. 6 Against him came up Nebuchadnezzar king of Babylon, and bound him in fetters to carry him to Babylon. 7 Nebuchadnezzar also carried of the vessels of the house of Jehovah to Babylon, and put*

them in his temple at Babylon. 8 Now the rest of the acts of Jehoiakim, and his abominations which he did, and that which was found in (against) him, behold, they are written in the book of the kings of Israel and Judah: and Jehoiakin his son reigned in his stead.

See our comments in the parallel under Second Kings 23:34-24:7.

XVIII. JEHOIAKIN (CONIAH) (598 BC).

Verses 9-10, Jehoiachin was eight years old when he began to reign: and he reigned three months and ten days in Jerusalem: and he did that which was evil in the sight of Jehovah. 10 And at the turn of the year king Nebuchadnezzar sent, and brought him to Babylon, with the goodly vessels of the house of Jehovah, and made Zedekiah his brother king over Judah and Jerusalem.

XIX. ZEDEKIAH (598-587 BC).

Zedekiah's Wickedness Reaches a Point of No Return

Verses 11-16, Zedekiah was twenty and one years old when he began to reign; and he reigned eleven years in Jerusalem: 12 and he did that which was evil in the sight of Jehovah his God; he humbled not himself before Jeremiah the prophet speaking from the mouth of Jehovah. 13 And he also rebelled against king Nebuchadnezzar, who had made him swear by God: but he stiffened his neck, and hardened his heart, against turning unto Jehovah, the God

of Israel. 14 Moreover all the chiefs of the priests, and the people, trespassed very greatly after all the abominations of the nations; and they polluted the house of Jehovah which he had hallowed in Jerusalem. 15 And Jehovah, the God of their fathers, sent to them by his messengers, rising up early and sending, because he had compassion on his people, and on his dwelling place: 16 but they mocked the messengers of God, and despised his words, and scoffed at his prophets, until the wrath of Jehovah arose against his people, till there was no remedy.

This is only a tiny summary of the wickedness of Israel during the reign of Zedekiah. Jeremiah reveals much of that wickedness. See pp. 237, 381, 414, 423, 431, 432, 449, 553-559 in our Commentary on Jeremiah. Also, Ezekiel describes the pollution of the temple, discussed in pp. 87-97 of our Commentary on Ezekiel; also see p. 123 (in that commentary) for the "Contradiction" Zedekiah thought he found in the words of God's prophets. Also, Second Kings, chapter 25, gives additional details.

Jerusalem Destroyed by Nebuchadnezzar; the Temple Sacked and Burned; the People Deported

Verses 17-21, Therefore he brought upon them the king of the Chaldeans, who slew their young men with the sword in the house of their sanctuary, and had no compassion upon young man or virgin, old men or hoary-headed: he gave them all into his hand. 18 And all the vessels of the house of God, great and small, and the

treasures of the house of Jehovah, and the treasures of the king, and of his princes, all these he brought to Babylon. 19 And they burnt the house of God, and brake down the wall of Jerusalem, and burnt all the palaces thereof with fire, and destroyed all the goodly vessels thereof. 20 And them that had escaped from the sword carried he away to Babylon; and they were servants to him and his sons until the reign of the kingdom of Persia: 21 to fulfil the word of Jehovah by the mouth of Jeremiah, until the land had enjoyed its sabbaths: for as long as it lay desolate it kept sabbath, to fulfil threescore and ten years.

This was the second fall of Jerusalem to Babylon. There had also been the captivity of Daniel, Ezekiel and others at the beginning of the reign of Zedekiah. This second destruction of the city would probably never have happened if Zedekiah had honored his sacred oath of loyalty to the king of Babylon.

The Decree of Cyrus the King of Persia

Verses 22-23, ***Now in the first year of Cyrus king of Persia, that the word of Jehovah by the mouth of Jeremiah might be accomplished, Jehovah stirred up the spirit of Cyrus king of Persia, so that he made a proclamation throughout all his kingdom, and put it also in writing, saying, 23 Thus saith Cyrus king of Persia, All the kingdoms of the earth hath Jehovah, the God of heaven, given me; and he hath charged me to build him a house in Jerusalem, which is in Judah. Whoever there is among you***

of all his people, Jehovah his God be with him, and let him go up.

Through the two great prophets Isaiah and Jeremiah God had foretold and prophesied exactly what and when the captivity of the Children of Israel would be terminated. It was Jeremiah who prophesied the exact duration of the captivity in chapter 25 of his great prophecy. See our comments on that chapter in the commentary, beginning on page 279.

But another great prophet, namely Isaiah, had foretold and prophesied the nature and source of the very decree of Cyrus mentioned here even naming Cyrus generations before he was born. See our discussion of this phenomenal prophecy on pp. 8, 9, in our ***Commentary on Isaiah.*** The prophecy is recorded in Isaiah 45:1 f, which is also discussed on pages 467 and following pages of that commentary.

There is no logical doubt whatever of the validity and integrity of those prophecies. The Jewish historian Josephus verifies them; and the very fact of such a thing as a captive nation being given permission to return to their own land, and even to be encouraged to do so, and aided financially in the project, is so contrary to the inclinations of human nature, so unheard of in any other instance, that the only intelligent conclusion must allow God as the author of the prophecies.

xxx

BIBLIOGRAPHY

Bibliography for Commentary on First and Second Chronicles

VERSIONS OF THE BIBLE CONSULTED

American Standard Version, 1901 (Ft. Worth: Star Bible Publications, Inc.).

Authorized Version (King James Bible) (New York: Collins Clear Type Press).

Cross-Reference Bible with Various Readings (New York: Cross-Reference Bible Company, 1910).

Douay Version of the OT (New York: Catholic Book Publishing Company, 1948).

Good News Bible (New York: American Bible Society, 1974).

La Biblia, Dios Habla Hoy (Spanish Bible) (New York: American Bible Society 1979).

New International Version (Grand Rapids: Zondervan Publishing House, 1982).

New Standard Revised Version (Nashville: Holman Bible Publishers, 1989).

NIV Interlinear Hebrew-English OT (Grand Rapids: Zondervan Publishing House, 1979).

Revised Standard Version (New York: Thomas Nelson and Sons, 1946).

Bible in Modern English by James Moffatt, 1929.

DICTIONARIES AND ENCYCLOPEDIAS

Britannica World Language Dictionary (Chicago: William Benton, Publisher, 1961).

Encyclopaedia Britannica (Chicago: William Benton, Publisher, 1961).

Encyclopedia of Ancient Egypt (New York & Oxford: Facts on File, 1991).

International Standard Bible Encyclopedia (Chicago: Howard-Severance Company, 1915).

New Bible Dictionary (Grand Rapids: William B. Eerdmans Publishing Company, 1965).

Peloubet's Bible Dictionary (Chicago: The John C. Winston, 1926).

Webster Dictionary, Complete and Unabridged, International Edition (New York: J. J. Little and Ives, 1957).

Wycliffe's Bible Encyclopedia (Chicago: Moody Press, 1974).

AUTHORS QUOTED

Albright, W. F. ***On the Tel El Amarna Letters*** R. A. xix, Letter No. 6.

Albright, W. F. ***The OT and Archeology*** (Philadelphia, 1944).

Albright, W. F. ***The Date and Personality of the Chronicler*** in The Journal of Biblical Literature (XI, 1921).

Baker, William P., ***Everyone in the Bible*** (Westwood, N. J.: Fleming H. Revell, 1966).

Barker, P. C. in ***Pulpit Commentary Vol. 6*** (Grand Rapids: Wm. B. Eerdmans Publishing Company, 1950).

Breslich, A. L. in ***International Standard Bible Encyclopedia*** (Chicago: Howard-Serverance Co., 1915).

Bennett, T. Miles, ***Nahum and Zephaniah*** (Grand Rapids: Wm. B. Eerdmans Publishing Company, 1968).

Brown, W. Gordon, ***Article*** in WBE (Chicago: Moody Press, 1965).

Bunson, Margaret, in ***Encyclopedia of Ancient Egypt***, 1991.

Clarke, Adam, ***Commentary on Whole Bible, Vol. 2*** (London: T. Mason & G. Lane, 1837).

Clements, Ronald E., ***The Cambridge Bible Commentary*** (Cambridge: At the University Press, 1972).

Cohen, Simon in WBE.

Cook, F. C., ***The Bible Commentary, Kings and Chronicles*** (Grand Rapids: Baker Book House, 1953).

Curtis, Edward Lewis, in ***International Critical Commentary*** (Edinburgh: T. & T. Clark, 1910).

DeHoff, George W., ***DeHoff's Commentary, Vol. 2*** (Murfreesboro, TN: DeHoff Publications, 1977).

Delitzsch, F. in ***Keil-Delitzsch Old Testament Commentary*** (Grand Rapids: Wm. B. Eerdmans Publishing Company)

Dentan, Robert C., ***Kings and Chronicles***in LBC, Vol. 7 (Richmond, VA: John Knoz Press, 1964).

Deitz, Robert S. ***Maps and Drawings*** (Washington, D. C.: National Geographic and Atmospheric Administration).

Dummelow, J. R., ***Commentary on the Holy Bible*** (New York: The Macmillan Company, 1937).

Ellison, W. L., ***Second Chronicles*** in New Bible Commentary Revised (Grand Rapids: Wm. B. Eerdmans Co., 1970).

Elmslie, W. A. L., ***First and Second Chronicles*** in Interpreter's Bible (New York: Abingdon Press, 1954).

Francisco, Clyde T., ***First and Second Chronicles*** in Broadman BibleCommentary (Nashville: Broadman Press, 1970).

Genung, John Franklin in ISBE.

Goddard, Robert, ***Article*** in WBE (Chicago: Moody Press, 1965).

Goodman, D.W., in ***New Bible Dictionary*** (Grand Rapids: Wm. B. Eerdmans Publishing Company, 1970).

Gunner, R. A. H. in NBD (Grand Rapids: Wm. B. Eerdmans Publishing Company, 1971).

Haley, John W., ***Alleged Discrepancies in the Bible*** (Nashville, TN: B. C. Goodpasture, 1951).

Halley, Henry H., ***Bible Handbook*** (Grand Rapids: Zondervan Publishing House).

Holton, John C.. ***Maps and Drawings*** (Washington, D. C.: National Geographic and Atmospheric Administration).

Josephus, Flavius, ***Life and Works of***, translated by William Whiston (New York: Holt, Rinehart and Winston).

Keil. C. F., ***Commentary on the Old Testament, Vol. 3*** (Grand Rapids: WilliamB. Eerdmans Publishing Company).

Lockyer, Herbert, ***All the Men of the Bible*** (Grand Rapids: Zondervan Publishing House, 1938).

Masterman, E. W. G., in ***International Standard Bible Encyclopedia*** (Chicago: Howard-Severance Co., 1915).

Myers, Jacob M., in ***Anchor Bible, First and Second Chronicles,*** (Garden City, N Y: Doubleday and Co., 1973).

Norman, J. G. G. in NBD.

Oesterley, W. O. E., ***First and Second Chronicles*** in A . S. Peake' s Commentary (London: T. C. & E. C. Jack, Ltd., 1924).

Payne, J. Barton, in ***First and Second Chronicles***in Wycliffe Bible Commentary (Chicago: Moody Press, 1962).

Scott, Sir Walter, in ***Lady of the Lake.***

Simmons, Billy E. ***First and Second Chronicles*** in Teacher's Bible Commentary (Nashville: Broadman Press, 1972).

Thompson, J. A. , ***The Bible and Archaeology*** (Grand Rapids: Wm. B. Eerdmans Publishing Company, 1982).

Unger, Merrill F., ***Archeology and the Old Testament*** (Grand Rapids: Zondervan Publishing House, 1960).

Weir, Thomas H., in ***International Standard Bible Encyclopedia*** Chicago: Howard-Severance Company, 1915).

Whiston, William, ***Josephus, Life and Works of*** in JOSA (New York: Holt, Rinehart and Winston).Whitcomb, James C., Jr., ***Studies in Kings and Chronicles*** (Winona Lake, Indiana: BMH Books, 1971)

White, J. C. in NBD.

Willams, Larry, ***The Mountain of Moses*** (New York: Wynwood Press, 1990).
Wilson, William, ***Wilson's Old Testament Word Sturies*** (McLean, Virginia: Mac Donald Publishing Company).
Wiseman, D. J. in NBD.

Yamauchi, Edwin M., ***The Pagan Goddess Ashera*** in WBE.

xxx

INDEX

xxx